SPEAKING OF PIANISTS ...

SPEAKING

OF

PIANISTS...

BY

ABRAM CHASINS

NEW YORK   ALFRED A. KNOPF   1958

L.C. catalog card number: 57–12173
© *Abram Chasins, 1957*

THIS IS A BORZOI BOOK,
PUBLISHED BY ALFRED A. KNOPF, INC.

Published October 14, 1957
Second printing, January 1958

To my teachers and my pupils,

WHO MADE ME AWARE OF EVERYTHING I HOLD MOST DEAR

Acknowledgments

F<small>IRST</small>, my profound though not unmixed thanks go to Irving Kolodin of the *Saturday Review,* whose encouraging editorial invitations plunged me into the swirling waters of criticism. I am indebted to that magazine for permission to draw upon material first published in its pages; to Columbia Records and RCA Victor for similar generosity; and to Elliott M. Sanger of WQXR for his kindly patience with a music director who *would* write a book.

To Dorée Smedley I am grateful for arming me with the sober facts of a book-writer's life, and for showing me trade tricks with manila envelopes, scissors, and paste; to Thomas Lask of *The New York Times* and to Wills Hollingsworth of WQXR for their unflinching hospitality whenever I charged their desks with questions regarding what may humorously be called my syntax; to Miriam Molin for painstaking preparation of the Index; to Paul Hirschman for proffering helpful advice and for reading proofs; and to my editor, Herbert Weinstock, whose adamant demands somehow always managed to sound like friendly, casual suggestions.

My deepest thanks I owe to my wife, whose forbearance and helpfulness prevailed throughout writing periods that often uprooted her professional and personal life.

A<small>BRAM</small> C<small>HASINS</small>

Contents

x *Contents*

IV THEME AND VARIATIONS

Also With Us   161
The Expendables   171
The Chains of Management   177
High Fidelity—High Fatality   187
State and Art   193

Mozart's "Clavierland"   205
Beethoven's Five   214
Chopin   220
Schumann   227
Liszt   234
Brahms in D minor and B flat   240
Tchaikovsky's Human Documents   246
The Rachmaninoff Concertos   254
Gershwin—Paradox in Blue   259
And Others   267

VI RECAPITULATION AND CODA

Recapitulation and Coda   287
Closing Phrases: In Lieu of a Discography 291

Index   *follows page* 291

SPEAKING OF PIANISTS . . .

Introduction

IN THIS BOOK I have set down a variety of recollections and impressions related to a part of my pianistic life, that part which I lived as a student, listener, and observer rather than as a concert pianist. I invite the reader to share with me some of the experiences, some of the sounds and ideas gathered during fifty years of association with the piano, much of its literature, and many of its players.

I do not promise that other matters will not creep into these pages. The piano is a rich subject for illustrating many elements of music, even of life itself, and I have often been unable to resist its suggestiveness. Yet, essentially, this is a series of reminiscences relevant to piano-playing and piano music—reactions stimulated by personal associations, by performances on and off the platform, and by recordings.

Although the history of music exists in composition, the life of music exists in performance, actual or recorded, constructed as in score-reading, or reconstructed in the mind. From time to time I shall pause to comment on things heard and heard about, on past and present ideals and practices, on things I love and loathe. The reader and I may not always agree. Happily, that is our aesthetic as well as our democratic right. Should this book prove at all provocative to those whose lives are enriched by music, it will modify some of the misgivings I hold about my ability to put into words anything so intangible and intricate as musical reaction, not to mention the electrifying fusion of genius and knowledge.

My own taste and opinions stem from standards and principles learned from artists I had the privilege of calling master and friend. They, who personified artistic standards so convincingly, should actually have written this book. Of course, in many ways they have—a good deal of it. But perhaps they would have needed another lifetime to formulate and set down what it took each of them one lifetime to achieve.

It was they who persuaded me and substantiated in their art that the laws of beauty have an inexorable logic. Their precepts and practices are the main sources of my feeling about the piano and its literature, inescapably woven into the texture and fabric of my entire musical outlook.

In the hope that the reader will care to come along with me and to hear for himself some of the things I heard, I should like to begin by having him meet Josef Hofmann.

Exposition

Josef Hofmann

It was an abnormally hot afternoon in the spring of 1926 when I found myself at the door of Josef Hofmann's suite at the Great Northern Hotel in Manhattan. I waited for quite a few minutes before knocking, hoping that my heart would stop pounding. Hofmann had been my pianistic idol for many of my twenty-two years, but I had never come closer to him than the distance between the top balcony and the stage of Carnegie Hall.

And here I was, paying him a visit at his invitation. It had all come about two weeks before, when I had met Mrs. Hofmann and had been astonished to hear her say: "Josef's been told about your Chinese pieces. He'd like to hear them and anything else you'd like to play for him. We're coming in from Philadelphia for a few days before we sail for Europe. We'll be at the Great Northern. Will you come?"

Would I?

My first jolt that afternoon came when Hofmann himself answered my knock and I—all five-foot-six of me—had to lower my gaze several inches to meet his squarely. The contrast between the mild-mannered little man who greeted me and the mental image I had held of him was startling. It was hard to reconcile the soft voice, delicate features, small hands, and meticulously debonair dress with the relentless Titan of the keyboard. The only physical sign of his power was in his massive back and shoulders. He looked like a chunky quarterback who moved with the litheness of a dancer.

At that time Hofmann had just turned fifty, but looked ageless. He could just as well have been forty or sixty.

While we talked I observed the impeccable neatness of the man and the orderliness of his simple hotel parlor. An immaculately dusted Steinway grand stood in the corner, its keys gleaming, but with not a single piece of music on it—just a lone and shining metronome. Hofmann asked me about my piano studies, theoretical training, and compositional work. His questions were pointed and precise. He never wasted a syllable. He spoke flawless English with a slight accent, origin untraceable. I later learned that he was equally at home in German, French, and, naturally, his native Polish.

In the first few minutes of conversation he revealed a rigidly disciplined mind, an intense concentration, and a fierce passion for separating opinion from fact, truth from half-truth. He also had a quick sense of humor. Finally, gesturing with an economical wave toward the piano, he said: "Please."

First I played my *Three Chinese Pieces.*

"Very effective. I'll play them," he said.

Then I played Chopin's F sharp minor **Nocturne.**

"Ahem," he said, "and now?"

A group of Chopin's preludes.

"Ahem, and now?"

The first movement of Beethoven's "Waldstein" Sonata.

"Mmm, something else?"

"Mr. Hofmann," I said. "I know your time is limited. Would you please tell me what you think?"

Everything about that afternoon remains indelibly in my memory, but most of all I remember the things that Hofmann said at that point. He still spoke very quietly, but grew unexpectedly tense and voluble. Drawing his head back and tilting it to one side as his penetrating gray eyes appraised me, he said:

"You see, there is no question of your talent. The question is what has been done with your talent. For example, you have feeling, but it does not emerge fully. You have a sensitive ear, but it is an inner ear which hears more what you want to produce than what you are actually producing. You have mechanical facility which is not yet elevated into an integrated and expressive technique, a warm tonal equipment which is not emotionally signif- icant, a rhythm basically good but one which does not set nor sustain a basic pulsation, and so on. What you do not have is the knowledge, even an awareness, of vital principles of music and pianism. You do not have the standards with which to judge, to refine, to correct your playing.

"Now, let's go back to the music. Start the Nocturne again, and I'll try to be more specific, all right?"

After eight bars he stopped me.

"I'm sure," he said, "you don't realize that you have not yet established any fundamental rhythmic premise."

"Isn't the tempo right?"

"I'm not talking about tempo, but about basic pace," he answered. "First, I don't know what your tempo is be- cause no two bars are alike. Second, there is no such absolute as 'the right tempo.' We ourselves set a tempo as we start to play; if it destroys the general spirit or mood, it is a 'wrong' tempo. If it enables us to realize the mood we want to express, it is a 'right' tempo—not *the* right one —and we can work within it. From then on, the emotional, harmonic, and dramatic development of the composition leads us to vary our pace. But first we must establish a 'norm' from which we can depart and to which we can return.

"Rhythm is order," he continued, adjusting the metro- nome slightly, "not the order that moves with cosmic pre- cision, but that of humanity with all its mercurial emo- tions. Within us is a flexible human metronome—the heart. It is regulated by an educated taste." He paused for breath. "Now try to get a 'presiding pace' and let's go on."

He did not stop me again. When I finished he said:

"You have learned something. This time you established a recognizable tempo and generally maintained its basic momentum within freedoms. But you cannot imagine how much your 'freedoms' distort the music you play. Let's take only one aspect of your playing: you constantly violate the principle of motion and rest. When the melodic line reaches a point of rest, you always rush the accompaniment to 'fill the vacuum' until the melody again moves, utterly destroying its repose and design. Also, every new theme, every alteration of dynamics takes some toll in a departure from your previous tempo. Further, in an effort to become expressive you employ sentimental delays or crude picture-postcard coloration completely out of the scheme you yourself devised. Your 'freedom' is license, not liberty. Real freedom comes from discipline, from feeling that has been cultivated by knowledge.

"The validity of interpretation depends on inexorably logical relationships. At this moment you do not have an apparatus for solving your problems. It is not that you lack either the talent or the skill to master, for instance, rhythmic liberty within a sustained momentum. It is merely that you do not demand it of yourself because it is not part of your ideology; nor will it be until you acquire the refinement to make such subtle precision an ideal."

That is what Hofmann said and the way he said it. I typed it word for word as soon as I got home. The meticulously chosen vocabulary, the balanced phrases fascinated me almost as much as what he said.

"Oh, one more thing I'd like you to think about," he continued. "Constantly, your attempts to attain an expressive serenity are defeated. I'll tell you why. You establish a calm, then you begin to hear that your playing is growing colorless and dull. Something's wrong, but you don't know what it is or what's causing it. So you try for expressivity by turning pulsation and coloration on and off like a faucet. Your 'expression' now consists of a series of restless and unexpected little fits and starts. Good-by to all repose."

Two hours earlier I had walked into this room as a

young pianist on the brink of a career, one who had been encouraged by many eminent musicians to make a New York debut long before this day. Now I felt that I knew nothing about piano-playing. I had finally encountered standards, Olympian standards, and a conception of music and performance which had never before touched me at all.

How was this possible? Had I not heard Hofmann and other giants countless times and recognized in their art the embodiment of all my ideals? It gradually dawned on me that I had not heard them at all, that I had been luxuriating in a formless sea of sound in a semi-hypnotic state. I did not know what I was hearing. I had no idea what, besides genius, produced great interpretation. Never had it occurred to me that there were basic principles behind such an art or that they could be formulated and analyzed and understood. My head swam.

In a voice that was sympathetic but icily objective, Hofmann brought me back with a characteristic "Ahem."

"There are a few things you have to learn, quite a few things, and they would make a vast difference to your playing, to your entire life in music. I think I might be able to help you with some of them. Betty and I are sailing next week to Europe for three or four months. If you would like to go abroad and do some work with me, I shall arrange it."

Would I?

That is when and how a thirty-year association began with a master and a friend who will live within me until I no longer draw breath.

2

IT WOULD be difficult to exaggerate the benevolence and integrity of my first piano teachers, Bertha Feiring Tapper, Richard Epstein, and Ernest Hutcheson. I owe them all incalculable gratitude. They led me, in a succession of valuable lessons, to control my fingers, to acquire a large and significant repertoire, and to hold a serious attitude toward a musician's obligations. I had further opportunities to be helped and inspired through association with many other remarkable musicians who were not my teachers but nonetheless showed generous interest in my studies.

Yet, from my first two-hour lesson with Hofmann in London I learned more than during my entire previous experience. Each comment let in a new flood of light. His method was the sustained attempt to show each work as an entity, a coherent consistency, and to observe its connections and relationships. He would exemplify the fluidity and flexibility of interpretation by demonstrating several different conceptions deriving from contrasting premises and make each one valid and convincing.

He compelled me to know at every moment where I was, where I had come from, and where I was going, and to articulate my intentions. I was always in the midst of an exciting search for melodic, harmonic, and structural significance. I came to feel as though I had been living my musical life under a perpetually gray sky. With every word or gesture, every literary or human or pianistic illustration, Hofmann dispersed another cluster of clouds. The sky gradually cleared. On occasion the sun even burst forth when I did well and he would smile.

Plowing right through my rock-ribbed habits, he would stop me to ask: "What elements go into differentiating one compositional style from another? What can make one passage played slower than another sound actually faster? What factors make a tone or chord sound 'ugly' or 'beautiful' played at the identical intensity?"

As soon as one answered, he would say: "Demonstrate it."

Mechanical difficulties were *your* problems, not his. But he helped greatly by illustration, by revealing an idealized aural image of a passage or a piece. There it was, in all its perfection. Somehow it released you from minor tensions and muscular preoccupations. You had the sound, the objective, before you. Hearing the total effect, you found it more easily accomplishable. It was as though he had waved a magic wand that enabled you to do more than you could do.

At other times he hammered away by applying principles to ordinary experience. For example, discussing the problem of projection, he once said:

"If someone entered this room and you spoke to him in a normal conversational tone, he would hear you easily. If you used the same tone from the stage of a theater, the people in the fourth row would ask: 'What's that? What's he saying?' Public communication necessitates heightened projection; otherwise we are talking or playing to ourselves. And it is a far larger problem than one of amplified volume. It embraces our choice of tempi, textures, and architectures; the degree and kinds of accentuation and pedaling we can use; the variety and proportion of agogic and dynamic effects we make, and much more. Remember, we are playing to express ourselves through the music we play, but we are expressing ourselves to *others*."

Hofmann was entirely persuasive, especially because he was as inflexible about primary principles as he was elastic in their application. He was untiring in pointing out the many roads that lead to Rome. "A work of art is large enough," he said, "to hold innumerable and contrasting interpretations without losing an iota of its inherent truth."

The exciting lessons continued for four months in Berlin, in Paris, and back again in London. Despite the newness of my surroundings and the difficulty of wrestling with strange languages, I worked hard and began to gain feelings of purpose and possibility, of confidence based upon conviction.

During this period Hofmann also revealed many of his human traits. Once, while on a train to Berlin, I turned to say something to him. But he put up a restraining hand and shook his head from side to side. "Excuse me," he said, with eyes closed, "I'm practicing." Through the years I saw him hundreds of times in the midst of mental practice, which he held to be invaluable because it freed the performer from instrumental considerations. He rarely stopped thinking or hearing music except when he played tennis or poker or chess. His surest escape was an all-night session in his tool shop, surrounded by his beloved precision instruments and implements.

Hofmann had a penchant for Abdulla cigarettes, an expensive, pungent Turkish blend, which he always smoked through a long thin holder. When he opened a new box, he would meticulously cut each cigarette in half with a small scissors, loftily proclaiming that nobody ever smoked a whole cigarette anyway. He adored fine food, and I was a frequent and appreciative guest as the Hofmanns and their friends sampled the great restaurants of the cities we visited. With a good wine within reach and a gourmet's repast under his belt, Hofmann grew warm and expansive. He told marvelous stories and was an excellent listener to the stories of others, which he carefully preserved in a little black book used for nothing else.

Amid the delightful interludes, slavish work went on. Hofmann practiced, performed, and allotted a generous portion of his free time to teaching me. I was driven by his urgency for precision and coherence, his ceaseless quest to investigate and to solve artistic problems whole, to radiate every solution outward toward a more vital realization of music and even toward a greater understanding of life itself.

As for pianism, the model was before me daily. In full view was a master who conceived ideals of harmonious magnificence, who molded and fashioned them and set them forth in beauty and perfection.

3

ALTHOUGH THE mass public took its sweet time in granting sovereignty to the Hofmann who was no longer a *Wunderkind,* there was evidently no time when he was not the pianist's pianist.

During my first visit to London the ever gracious William Steinway was showing me various concert pianos at his company's headquarters. He mentioned that "the young Russian wizard" Vladimir Horowitz had been there the day before, picking out a piano for his forthcoming appearance.

"And what is that piano in the corner?" Horowitz asked.

"That's Hofmann's piano," Steinway answered.

"Josef Hofmann's *own* piano?" asked Horowitz in an awed voice. He hesitated, and then said: "Please . . . may I just touch it?"

Long before we met and became friends, that incident endeared Horowitz to me.

Some years later, at one of Hofmann's memorable recitals in New York's Carnegie Hall, following a truly bedazzling performance of Chopin's B minor Sonata, Sergei Rachmaninoff sat silent for a few moments and then said: "Well, there goes one more composition out of my repertoire. Not since Anton Rubinstein have I heard anything like this. There's no use. It is the music itself and the only way to play it, and nobody else can do it."

Another vivid recollection is a story Leopold Godowsky told me. Every pianist knows Godowsky's fanciful and formidable transcription of Johann Strauss's *Künstlerle-*

ben. Few have ever conquered its terrifying complexities. Godowsky related that when the piece had just been completed and was still in manuscript, he played it to Hofmann, who seemed delighted by it. Hofmann asked to hear it again immediately. After dinner he again requested Godowsky to play the fascinating piece. A few days later Hofmann returned. "He sat down," reported Godowsky, "and played my piece through with such unbelievable infallibility that I ran to see if my manuscript was still in the house. It was, of course. Josef had actually memorized it after hearing it only three times. After that I just listened, forgetting the fantastic feat in the intoxication of his playing."

From the time when he was six, when he electrified an audience at a recital in his native Poland, Hofmann was one of the wonders of the musical world. At ten he astounded Berlin, playing the Beethoven First Concerto under Hans von Bülow. Following a sensational tour of Europe, Hofmann's father brought the eleven-year-old prodigy to the United States. His debut here took place in November 1887, and many who were present have reported that no subsequent event in their musical experience ever matched the thrill of seeing the diminutive figure in a white sailor suit come out on the huge stage of the Metropolitan Opera House and proceed to play like an angel pursued by the devil. When he finished playing, the audience broke into a wild demonstration—screaming, applauding, dabbing at tear-filled eyes. W. J. Henderson, the most distinguished critic of the day, called the boy "a miracle."

A triumphal tour of over fifty concerts followed. The itinerary came to an abrupt end when the Society for the Prevention of Cruelty to Children stepped in to halt what they termed "exploitation." At this point the American millionaire Alfred C. Clark offered Hofmann's father fifty thousand dollars, a far greater sum then than now, to further the boy's education on condition that he be withdrawn from the platform until he reached eighteen. The offer was accepted, and Hofmann went back to Europe to study first under Moritz Moszkowski, and then for two years with Anton Rubinstein.

Rubinstein's playing and tutelage made a monumental impression on Hofmann. Once when I tried to express to Hofmann the overpowering drama and vastness of his playing of Beethoven's opus 111, he looked at me pityingly and said: "I'm very sorry for you that you never heard my master. Why . . . I'm a child—all of us put together are infants—compared to his titanic force."

On one occasion I attended a Hofmann recital with Mischa Levitzki. Both of us were stunned by his reading of Schumann's C major Fantasy. Knowing that Hofmann shared my admiration for Levitzki's beautiful pianism, I ventured to tell Hofmann how we felt. Hofmann looked at us and said: "You know, I played that work for Anton Rubinstein when I was sixteen or seventeen. When my lesson was over, Rubinstein said to me: 'My boy, you play this work quite perfectly, but you won't know much about it for twenty years.'" Hofmann stopped a moment and then said: "It's now over thirty years, and I know that there are worlds in it I haven't begun to explore."

It is only from Hofmann himself that we have learned how much Rubinstein contributed toward bringing his gifts to their fullest fruition, for to the world Rubinstein declared that music had never seen the equal of this boy's genius. At eighteen, with his master's approval, Hofmann set out to tour again, throughout Europe and America. In Russia, particularly, he was very shortly an object of worship. St. Petersburg witnessed nineteen of his appearances during one season, appearances for which every seat was sold before the first note of the first concert had been played. Through the long, bitter nights preceding each event, lines of students waited in the cold to buy standing room. Many of them were undoubtedly among the frenzied enthusiasts who later carried their idol on their shoulders after the performances.

Recognition came less swiftly in America. The cognoscenti knew Hofmann's greatness. The public took longer to recognize it. Hofmann once mentioned that his withdrawal from the stage had some very costly aspects. Not only had he to re-acquire the platform ease that had been natural to his childhood, but also he found that it was not easy to re-interest our general public in the solid achievements of a mature artist who had once been a sensational prodigy.

Eventually, of course, and without the ballyhoo of publicity (which Hofmann always abhorred), genius triumphed. Critics strained at their adjectives and the public battled for admission to performances that provided never-to-be-forgotten interpretations. Those who heard Hofmann in the Chopin concertos, the Schumann Concerto, the Beethoven Third, Fourth, and Fifth, and the Rubinstein concertos will carry uniquely inspiring remembrances with them forever. So will those who heard from him the Chopin and Schumann sonatas, the Beethoven *"Pathétique," "Moonlight," "Waldstein," "Appassionata,"* and opus 111, the Handel-Brahms Variations, Schumann's *Carnaval* and *Symphonic Etudes,* and countless other works large and small.

I always considered myself fortunate that I heard Hofmann for the first time when I was already in my early teens, just old enough to have studied some of the works he played, to have heard many compositions on his programs performed by others, and to have acquired a certain basis for evaluation. Standards in those days were of no mean order, for it was an opulent period of great pianists. Once having heard Hofmann, however, I felt about him as he felt about Anton Rubinstein. By the time I came to that realization, he was already conceded all over the world to be a pianist in that royal line tracing from Liszt.

The public always has cause to be grateful to artists of special distinction and integrity. To some we are indebted for stylistic perfection or technical virtuosity of a musicianly order; to others for nobility of melodic expression or imaginative coloring. In Hofmann every quality was blended. He had superlative restraint and also unconstrained impetuosity; a touch that ranged from icy cold to burning hot; unlimited shades of color that came from changes of tone quality or alterations of balance rather than from an increase or decrease of volume; a rhythm that varied from metronomic to rhapsodic without any loss of the basic pulsation. He was the dramatic orchestrator of the piano whose playing evoked the forces of nature and of humanity.

Hofmann had practically no mannerisms of facial expression or physical motion. It was not that he was unaware of their effects. He was merely sparing in their use. When he deviated from his usual composure, it was most often to create an optical impression calculated to enhance some breathtaking aural surprise that he had in store for us. I have never seen him indulge in theatrics that did not have the specific purpose of intensifying some dramatic musical idea. Otherwise his face and body remained almost motionless. He used to say:

"Create excitement in others through your understanding and memory of excitement. If you yourself become agitated, you become less able to communicate excitement."

Hofmann rarely demanded of the instrument more than it had to give, but occasionally in an emotional outburst at a climactic point he would forget his own precepts, lift his left hand high, then slam it down to smite the bass a mighty blow with his open palm. At times like that a sound not unlike the roar of an enraged lion would emerge from the piano.

Hofmann played like one who himself is creating right there at that very moment. Actually he was, for he never

played any work the same way twice. The music poured
out as an improvisation that gushed from his inner being.
When he played familiar works, he lavished upon them
so rich an imagination, so original a conception, that
one had the impression of hearing the music for the very
first time. His greatest colleagues (even Rachmaninoff,
who had his own magic power to take us to the mountain-
tops, to imbue us with a sense of prophecy and fulfillment) placed Hofmann alone on the highest peak, the
absolute monarch of the pianistic realm.

It is less generally known that Hofmann composed a
symphony and several piano concertos and solos under
the *nom de plume* of Dvorsky. Perhaps it is even less
known that he invented shock-absorbers, air springs, and
other automobile appliances used on standard cars.

The same brain applied itself to the pursuit of beauty
through observation and codification of aesthetic and
physical principles. He then related and applied his find-
ings, seeking every conceivable possibility of utilizing
them to attain clearer communication, greater expressivity in his playing. He used his understanding of acoustical phenomena to play a passage more slowly than anyone else and make it sound much faster; to play a chord
with half the force of another and have it emerge with
twice the sonority. Each pedal was used in a dozen posi-
tions between the down or up employed by most pianists.
He demonstrated time and time again that in the art of
interpretation there are no absolutes. He would enunciate
a theory and then sit down at the piano to illustrate it.
The sounds themselves were unforgettable inspirations,
and just as one had concluded that this was the way, the
only way, he would turn everything upside down and
prove that way equally valid.

In the realm of his art, imagination had full sway. In
the realm of facts, he was a precisionist. The scientist in
him sought to remove all discrepancies; the artist in him
capitalized on them. His unlimited resources included the

constant demonstration that brilliance results from clarity, not from speed; that virtuosity, when it does not abuse its function, is actually the dramatization of velocity through rhythmic accentuation and variety of color. His knowledge of muscular activity was of medical caliber, and he knew the mechanism of the piano more precisely than most professional regulators.

One of the most revealing lessons with my master took place a few days after a recital in which he played the *"Appassionata."* Never had I heard, even from him, such controlled accuracy maintained through a spirit of seemingly heedless recklessness. It was as though a storm was driving straight through the heavens. Arriving for my next lesson, I asked Hofmann to admit that this was an inspirational achievement arising from subconscious and autonomous sources, and that it defied analysis. Without answering, he went to the piano. Illustrating with snatches from the sonata, he showed me the "premises" of his architecture, demonstrating how the minutest deviation from the established tempos, dynamics, and moods could have ruined the scheme. He had known exactly what he was doing.

He talked in terms of the degree of arm and finger weight used to attain desired textures, the speed of rebound of key and hammer, the modification of tone colors by judicious use of the pedals, the essential elements of Beethoven's dramatic style. Suddenly he stopped and rose from the instrument. "As for the rest," he said, "some of it may be impossible to teach, but lots of it can be learned if the imagination is properly educated and stimulated."

Somehow, that afternoon, something I had always felt was suddenly clarified: that genius starts out with a vision of remote beauty, which is then subject to refinement, just as refinement can be brought to a lower order of talent which occasionally may yield superior accomplishment but inescapably falls short of genius. In Josef Hofmann, instrumental virtuosity, artistic vision, and scientific pursuit combined to draw from the piano a particular magic no other artist could summon.

It was in tribute to this artist that a brilliant audience at the Metropolitan Opera House on November 28, 1937, rose to its feet as he reappeared on the very stage where he had made his historic debut fifty years before. The nature of the occasion virtually dictated the program. It was eminently right for Hofmann to play the concerto of his master, Rubinstein, a composition of his own (*Chromaticon,* for piano and orchestra), a group of Chopin solos long identified with his career, and encores of audience favorites.

Nevertheless, this was no concert redolent of lavender and old lace. The mood had been set by a vital performance of Brahms's *Academic Festival Overture* by the Curtis Institute Symphony Orchestra conducted by Fritz Reiner. Thus Hofmann shared the memorable evening with students of the famous school he directed and with a fellow member of the Institute's faculty. The event was electric with the blithe spirit of youth and the golden glow of tradition.

It was a matter of chance that records came to be made of the concert. Mrs. Hofmann thought that some memento should be made of this touching occasion in Josef's life. She asked a friend, as a personal favor, to bring some recording equipment to the opera house. Tape machines and LP techniques were not in existence in those days. The friend brought one of those portable sets ordinarily used to make records of family celebrations and other such informal affairs in the home. A microphone was placed on the huge Metropolitan Opera House stage at a convenient though not particularly advantageous spot. Mrs. Hofmann had no idea of making the records available except for Josef's personal use. The discs themselves were used and abused for a decade and lent to friends, some of whom carelessly used dull needles or played the records on machines out of repair.

Almost twenty years passed before officials of Columbia Records learned of the existence of these records. They diligently tracked down each record and then used all of their persuasive powers to gain Hofmann's permission to issue them. It was a long struggle. Finally he agreed. They salvaged the most usable of the collection, and with unusual skill transferred them to an LP record. The disc contains ten of the solos performed at that historic concert. The piano-with-orchestra works were evidently too far gone or unobtainable. Therefore, with the exceptions of Chopin's first ballade and the Andante Spianato and Grand Polonaise, it is the exquisitely wrought art of Hofmann in the smaller frames which we have here. It is the art of variety within unity, of subtle and disciplined gradation, of imagination overflowing with invention, of freedom guided by precision.

Still, it is no document of Hofmann at his greatest, and the admission only underlines the extent of his art at its height and fully explains his reluctance to permit its publication. Shortly after Hofmann's death, an outfit called Allegro issued a disc compiled from Hofmann's 1939-40 radio appearances. It stands as an earwitness to the last tragic years, as a tasteless disservice to the memory of a master whose mastery had turned to ashes.

Perhaps some isolated, more worthily representative recordings may crop out here or there, but at the moment the Hofmann discography consists of the Jubilee disc. The absence of others has been properly lamented, but explained as largely Hofmann's fault. I do not think so. At any rate, it is at least a moot point. Here are the ramifications as I know them, and the reader may judge for himself.

During most of the years of Hofmann's greatest period (*circa* 1905-32) Europe was the origin of the significant piano recordings of the large-form works, and such European favorites as Backhaus, Schnabel, and Rubinstein supplied the bulk of the playing. Hofmann's career had firmly become all-American, and our recording companies were concentrating on small works that could be heard in their entirety on one side of a 78-rpm disc. Evidently they had gauged the public taste perfectly, for they made fortunes on a literature of encore-size pieces, and so did the artists who performed them: Caruso, Kreisler, Elman, Heifetz, Alma Gluck, McCormack, and Paderewski.

Hofmann told me that he was reluctant to be represented only by small works. His suggestions that he record larger works were unenthusiastically received. He was also naïvely surprised to "sense some resistance" to his demand for "absolute veto." Everyone knew of Hofmann's dedication to artistic and technical perfection. The recording executives were undeniably right to envision the possibility of a week of solid work and costs to obtain one Chopin ballade that Hofmann might grudgingly admit was "not too terrible."

He also held stubbornly to the conviction that recordings adversely affected box-office, and therefore he insisted on royalties that were higher than usual. This undoubtedly posed grave problems to a company faced with an artist who not only demanded more money but also insisted on performing a repertoire that was expensive to produce and promised small sales.

Hofmann never told me what he actually asked. I therefore cannot judge whether or not his terms were exorbitant. But I do know from his personal disappointment and his bitterness on the subject that persuading Hofmann to record was not impossible. It seems to me that had the guiding lights of the recording companies of those days fully understood what Hofmann represented to the history of piano-playing, nothing would have stood in the way of perpetuating his playing; that had he asked for the moon, they would have made every effort to get it for him. It is tragic that they did not weigh the consequences, weigh small financial returns or no returns against the artistic returns, in order not to leave posterity almost bereft of examples of his unique art.

While probing the possibilities of working out some long-term project, Hofmann did make several experimental discs. The playing reflected his apprehensions. The acoustic shellacs caught very little of his inimitably subtle and colorful art. That was another reason why he became difficult.

Examples of Hofmann's playing in large-form works are therefore unavailable except to those who carry them as ineradicable memories, and so the Golden Jubilee disc must serve to fill a gaping void in the consecutive history of piano-playing. It features six Chopin solos, Rachmaninoff's G minor Prelude, Moszkowski's "Spanish Caprice," Mendelssohn's "Spinning Song," and Beethoven's "Turkish March."

Hofmann's art was the adventure of technical perfection and imaginative insight among the emotions. It recalls the truth that art begins where technique ends: this has never meant that an expressive art ignores technique, but rather that it experiences and then transcends all the disciplines of technique to attain complete emotional freedom and communicative power. Every Hofmann performance furnishes ample material for a treatise on the art of pianism and interpretation.

The sensitive listener will relish finger passages that emerge as perfectly graded necklaces of jewels, as in the Chopin Berceuse and D flat Waltz, and in the "Spinning Song"; the rhetorical eloquence of the Chopin nocturne and Andante Spianato, and the improvisational opening of the ballade, before the legend begins; the matchless elegance of the embellishments in the berceuse and the polonaise, and the nobility of the latter. Hofmann's art utilized every element, alchemized into pure emotion, and amalgamated by a regal rhythm. (He used to say: "An aristocrat never hurries.")

Obviously the discs themselves cannot claim the characteristics of modern recordings. If that matters importantly to anyone, he certainly will not know what I have been talking about. All others will lend appreciative ears to the unique sounds, recognizing them as treasures from a virtually extinct art which enable the living present to observe a mighty past.

Hofmann was my primary link to that past, and my association with him continued fairly steadily until 1942. After that he became a confirmed Californian and a virtual recluse. The last time I heard him was in 1939 on a broadcast. It brought me such anguish that I resolved never to hear him again. But we corresponded up to the last. His carefully handwritten letters were full of ironic humor, full of violent and unprintable comments on piano performances and recordings he was hearing over the radio. Almost every sentence had the bittersweet flavor of the past in a direct or oblique reference to the present.

"I heard," he once wrote, "your friend (no longer mine) 'interpret' the 'Choppin' E minor Concerto over the radio recently. Later your friend (and always mine), Sascha Greiner of Steinway, informed me that a beautiful new three-year-old piano had been used (abused). Were a certain Society tuned in, the alleged artist would surely be imprisoned for cruelty to children!"

On another occasion Hofmann wrote: "I have a new little sixteen-foot boat. It is a peach! I gave her the very modest name of 'Majestic.' From this, you will gather that by now I am fully articalized, modern style."

Whatever documentation and remembrances remain of Hofmann's "unmodern artistry" lead to the realization that when Josef Hofmann died, an era died.

Leopold Godowsky

THE SIGNIFICANT artists of the day assembled at Godowsky's home with the regularity of homing pigeons. Wherever he hung his hat, whether in Europe, Asia, or the Americas, there arose a salon, a salon in the tradition of the romantic era which attracted every intellectual within range. No musician was more capable of constantly gathering around him creative companions in so many fields of artistic work.

Abroad, Diaghilev, Nijinsky, Gide, Matisse, and Derain were as much a part of the Godowsky circle as Ravel and Respighi. In New York you would find most frequently, among musicians, Rachmaninoff, Stravinsky, and Gershwin, Hofmann, Pachmann, Lhevinne, and Rubinstein, Casals, Kreisler, Elman, and Heifetz. Once anyone entered Godowsky's door, he became a disciple.

Short and round, Godowsky suggested a Slavic Buddha, but with none of the timeless, resolved placidity of a saint. He had an encyclopedic knowledge and a jolly, insatiably curious mind. He loved mental fireworks, and his beaming blue eyes sparkled, his pot belly quivered through the smoke of verbal battle. Pouring out his musical wealth generously and excitedly, he had the rarest capacity to stimulate whoever came, to prod him to sharper insight and searching self-examination. He was the merciless mentor of every artist who played for him; his compositional style of piano writing influenced nearly every contemporary who wrote for the instrument, and especially Medtner, Prokofiev, Rachmaninoff, and Ravel.

It was through Hofmann that I became close to Godowsky. Before then I had heard him many times and had slaved over his knottiest transcriptions. I had even met him several times at the home of my uncle and aunt, Mark and Vera Fonaroff, when I was in my teens. He was always extremely courteous, but I realized that I did not really exist for him. Some years later our paths crossed again. It was in 1925, and I had committed the offense of writing a piano piece that had become a "best-seller." I immediately fell victim to Godowsky's famed wit.

"Is it true," asked Godowsky, "that your *Rush Hour in Hongkong* has been published only six months and is already in its sixteenth edition?"

"Why, yes, Mr. Godowsky," I answered, with the dumb aplomb of youth, unaware of the deadly missile hurtling in my direction.

"You know," Godowsky said, "I was never *crazy* about that piece, but *so* bad I didn't think it was!"

That was my first "lesson" from Godowsky, my introduction to his famed characteristic of masking meaningful comment with wit. I remember laughing heartily. There was no room for wounded vanity around Godowsky. Perhaps it was the twinkle in his eyes which enabled him to indulge his lethal humor unscathed, the twinkle that led so many of us to call him "Popsy." Notwithstanding his caustic tongue, he radiated paternal kindliness. One felt warm and proud to have Popsy bestow a *bon mot* on him. A few years after his first quip at my expense, he visited my New York studio when I was preparing to leave for a concert trip. The piano was strewn with volumes of Bach, Beethoven, Chopin, Schubert, Ravel, Godowsky, and Prokofiev.

"You know, Abe, you surprise me," Popsy said. "I was always under the impression that you composed by heart."

Godowsky's home made Sanger's Circus seem like a rest home. Hubbub and commotion reigned day and night in four languages. Everyone and anyone was welcome. There seemed to be a perpetual party going on. The table was always set and loaded with food and drink. Godowsky was a born host. His sons and daughters came naturally by their linguistic virtuosity and easy sociability. Popsy loved people and loved to be surrounded by them. If he invited you to come over "just for a little quiet talk and music," you might arrive to find twenty people who had just dropped in, among them not only some of the musicians I have mentioned but also, likely as not, Popsy's music-loving tailor or butcher, a man he had met the day before who said he liked music, Albert Einstein, or Edward G. Robinson. Everyone was treated with equal informality and graciousness. Popsy's old-world courtesy and sparkling humor pervaded every word and action as he waddled between the living-room and adjacent dining-room filling plates and glasses, emptying ashtrays, scattering wry remarks and vicious gibes—as on the day when a rather pompous pianist rose to leave, saying: "I have to teach." Godowsky interpolated: "He means that he has to give a lesson." Or the time he set Harold Samuel back on his heels with: "Your last recital shows you've been working very hard. I noticed particularly much more feeling in your right elbow."

Levity was not always Godowsky's vehicle; sometimes it was brutality. He had a special detestation of superficiality and negligence. If you played for him and disregarded a phrase mark or treated an eighth rest as a sixteenth, your life was not safe. Once you knew what was in a score, however, he would delight in showing you dozens of places where changes would make the piece "sound better"—altering harmonizations and the disposition of voices, removing parallel fifths or octaves, or especially completing some contrapuntal line that the composer had abandoned. This delighted him. In his philosophy, rewriting was really a service to the composer—who might not have thought of such a good idea—but inattention was ignorance and disrespect. "Few artists," Godowsky claimed, "could sit down and notate with any degree of accuracy one tenth of the music they dare to perform."

Godowsky himself actually knew every note, every sign on every page of virtually every edition of the standard piano literature. The slightest evidence of an incurious or slipshod attitude provoked him to a savage sadism. He gave no quarter, no matter who displayed such evidence or who was present. Purple with rage, he would push your nose into the music as his trembling lips screamed devastating insults. "Only the stupidity of critics and idiocy of the public," he shouted at a well-known pianist, "could enable such a careless and unmusical fool like you to continue to play masterpieces you don't understand, don't even know!" He shouted it with a half-dozen people in the room and three days before the demoralized man's next New York recital. The look of dismayed resentment which spread over his victim's beet-red face only goaded Popsy on. "A pianist with your reputation," he continued bitterly, "should be able to hear yourself and know yourself so that no one could ever criticize you or evaluate what you do so severely or accurately as you yourself."

No afternoon or evening was complete at Godowsky's until it finally blazed with some display of fireworks. It was just as likely to occur in open conflict with Godowsky's most admired and admiring peers. Naturally, one waited to see who would draw blood first. Discussions (hostilities is actually a better word) would always begin on a very high-minded plane, very amicable and respectful, very objective and detached, the amenities being gracefully observed. Then Popsy would go too far, usually with a crack that would soon be heard round the world, and the walls would cave in.

I vividly recall one visit to Godowsky which began at luncheon and ended at three the next morning, and will give the reader a characteristic picture of the man against the background of his eventful home life. When I got to the house, I found Josef Hofmann waiting for the elevator to Godowsky's apartment. It was a huge but "homey" place, the rooms built for large gatherings and crowded with comfortable sofas and ornate furniture. The tall street windows were hung with brilliant scarlet drapes with gold rope tie-backs. There was an element of incongruity between the upholstered opulence of the crystal-chandeliered living-room and the Bohemian untidiness of the books, music, manuscript paper, and pencils strewn helter-skelter on every flat surface but one. The top of one of the two grand pianos had nothing but one lone sheet of manuscript on it. That, I discovered later, was Popsy's work table.

The love and respect that Godowsky and Hofmann held for each other was apparent in their fervent hand-clasp and in the cool voices used to conceal the depth of their pleasure at being together. It was miraculously quiet that day; just the three of us sat down to lunch. No sooner were we seated than Popsy led off with: "Did you ever see the Schnabel edition of the Beethoven sonatas?" Without waiting for an answer he continued: "It was designed neither for the music nor for the human hand. No wonder. He studied with Leschetizky, who retarded piano progress by a full century, don't you think so, Josef?"

Hofmann remained eloquently silent. This did not please Popsy. "Schnabel advises his pupils to practice mechanical work only within the music they play, do you know that, Josef?" Again Hofmann was silent. I began to smell gunpowder. There was something on Popsy's mind, evidently, and he was leading up to it. Fortunately, the bell rang at that moment. Popsy answered, and returned with Josef Lhevinne and Mischa Levitzki. Two more places were set. The conversation grew gay and gossipy. The name of an eminent Jewish artist came up, one who had many times denied his racial origin. Levitzki reported that a few days earlier the artist had been asked point-blank whether or not he was Jewish, and had replied: "I haven't one drop of Jewish blood in my veins."

"My God!" said Popsy. "That poor fellow must be terribly anemic."

After a lot of lunch and more laughter, we went into the living-room. Hofmann turned to me and asked me to play Chopin's A flat Ballade, which I had brought to a lesson earlier that week. It had been an especially fascinating session during which Hofmann had supplied dozens of wonderful ideas, had actually awakened me to the full beauty of that piece. Although I was as full of undigested food as I was of undigested suggestions, I sat down immediately. This was no opportunity for a young pianist to miss.

Everything was going along pretty well until I came to the C sharp minor section, where Hofmann had pointed out particularly beautiful possibilities. In trying to realize them, I undoubtedly exaggerated them. Godowsky jumped up and yelled:

"No, Abe. Please. There's too much underlining, too much emphasis, too much rubato."

Hofmann then got up, walked to the other piano, and took over. "Chasins hasn't yet made it his own; I agree there is distortion, but this is what we were working for," he said, and proceeded to illustrate the section. He played the left-hand figuration not like filigree, but like a melodic countertheme to the right-hand motive, molding everything with captivating rhythmic subtlety and gradations of color. Lhevinne, Levitzki, and I were all hanging on every note when Popsy broke in:

"No, no, Josef. That's too much, really."

Hofmann stopped, looked around, and asked: "Isn't it convincing? Isn't there enough going on—with such contrapuntal figuration, harmonic tensions, rhythmic syncopation—to substantiate such a rubato?"

"Perhaps," Popsy answered. "It's convincing the way you do it, but it would gain in continuity and cumulative excitement if it moved straight ahead."

"I'm sorry. There's too much of importance and beauty that would be missed were it not underlined. Moving straight along would make it sound aggressive rather than intense. If I lose too much momentum, that's bad, but I don't think I do."

They glared at each other. Hofmann returned to the sofa, and I started to play from where I had left off. The bell rang. It was the postman with a special-delivery letter. As Popsy was signing for it, he noticed the postman peering into the living-room with interest.

"You like music? Come in, come in," Popsy said as he literally pushed the bewildered man into a comfortable chair, bag and all. He sat transfixed through the rest of the ballade and through a fifteen-minute post-mortem. The mail on that route was late that day.

After the postman left, Hofmann rose to go, promising to return in the evening to hear Popsy play his newly finished Passacaglia on the opening theme of Schubert's "Unfinished" Symphony. After Hofmann left, several other guests arrived, none of whom I knew.

Popsy left the room for a few moments. He came back in a state of amused agitation, waving an old copy of the *Ladies Home Journal* at me. "Look at this. Look at what somebody sent me," he cried peevishly.

I looked. Many years before, Hofmann had written an article. One sentence was underlined in red: "I do no technical work outside of the composition." So *that* was what Popsy had been leading up to at lunch.

"Josef shouldn't tell that to young people," Popsy said. "If he does, he should explain that the compositions he plays have been in his repertory for almost fifty years; that most of them were learned after he developed mechanical perfection through long years of attention to every conceivable muscular aspect of technique."

When Levitzki asked: "Is it always wrong to advise students to practice mechanical difficulties within their repertoires?" Popsy said: "The correction of muscular faults is a mechanical problem. When it is complicated by a musical problem, both must suffer. When a Bach prelude is used to strengthen weak fingers, or a Beethoven sonata to develop evenness in scale passages, the artistic significance of the music can never again be dissociated from the mechanical struggle."

I was surprised. Although Godowsky spent no end of time at mechanical work, he also utilized sections of compositions for muscular development. His unequivocal opinion must have been a new and final conclusion.

More guests began to arrive: Pachmann, Mischa Elman, and José Capablanca, who had been playing chess. When dinnertime came, we all fell to. Conversation was lively, a good part of it intramusical and malicious. It was better for a musician to be present that night. An absent colleague's name arose, a pianist who had suffered many painful lapses of memory throughout his recital the week before, which had been attended by Godowsky and several others present.

"Isn't it frightful, this forgetting?" exclaimed Capablanca, who was a real pianophile and had heard the debacle.

"It isn't what he forgot," said Popsy, "it's what he remembered that was so frightful!"

After dinner he showed us an indignant letter from a former pupil of Godard who had seen Godowsky's transcription of the *Canzonetta* and called it "vandalism!" The transcription happens to be one of Godowsky's happiest inspirations, the conversion of a gracious but superficial violin piece into a gem of a piano piece.

"Vandalism!" Popsy shrieked, his voice an octave higher than usual. "Nonsense! Transcription is not a process like retouching a painting. In music the original remains for anyone who wants it. For example," he added slyly, "anyone who wants to play Dvořák's *Humoreske* in its original piano version rather than in Kreisler's arrangement for violin is as welcome to that as he is to his ignorant reverence."

Later in the evening Ossip and Clara Gabrilowitsch walked in, then the Ernest Hutchesons and Rubin Goldmark. Finally, when Hofmann returned, Godowsky sat down at a piano to give us the promised treat. He played his new Passacaglia, reading it from green-colored proof sheets stacked on the piano rack.

And how he played! This was sheer enchantment, both the work itself and Godowsky's pianism. It had the cool, colorful clarity of a stained-glass window. Although I was greatly moved and impressed by what I heard, Godowsky's effortless mastery made me unaware of the vastness of his pianistic feat that night. Years later I realized it when one of the greatest virtuosos told me that he had worked on the "fiendish piece" for a year, several hours each day, and had finally had to give up the unequal struggle. "It is impossible to master," he said. I felt tactful that day and refrained from telling him with what devastating ease Godowsky had disposed of it, making it seem like nothing at all.

During that *première* performance at Godowsky's home, Popsy lingered over every particularly ingenuous or eloquent spot, over an expressive counterpoint or an unexpected modulation, his brilliant little eyes stealing a furtive look to see if we "got" the subtlety. When he had finished and everyone had showered him with heartfelt praise, Hofmann took him aside, signaling me to join them.

"Fabulous, Popsy. Marvelous," said Hofmann, "but, you know, you did exactly what I did in the ballade this afternoon, just what you argued about. And you did it for the same reasons—to give us a chance to hear the music, to grasp it, to appreciate its finest moments."

"Ah," said Godowsky, "but you don't know this music, and I want you to understand it, to know what is in it."

"Exactly," cried Hofmann, "and that's what I always

want my audience to know about Chopin or Schumann. We musicians come to your music tonight the way the public comes to the standard literature. We must tell our public what the composer entrusts to us to tell them. We speak for the composer, and we must speak clearly, very clearly."

"Exaggeration is nevertheless distortion. Gilding the lily is always bad."

"And worst of all is smallness," answered Hofmann acidly, "smallness of utterance, smallness of heart and manner. For those whose business it is to project, to communicate, it is rudeness, just like whispering secrets in public."

That is the way they would occasionally hack at each other. It often hurt, but I learned a lot. That particular exchange highlighted their essential difference as performers. The crux of Hofmann's public success was the projective clarity and eloquence with which he unfolded music before his audience. On the platform Godowsky was never less than the precise scholar and technical magician. But the dramatist and colorist remained at home, to emerge fully only when Godowsky was serene in his environment, as he was on the night I am describing.

Came midnight. At the Godowsky house, midnight meant supper. We walked into the dining-room. The table was laden with cold meat, chicken, salads, and mountains of bread and butter. On the sideboard was a huge samovar of tea surrounded by cups and saucers, sweets, and plates of sliced lemon. For a while the dining-room was a gay mob scene. Gradually some of the guests strayed back into the living-room. Others remained around the big table. Still others went home. A half-dozen of us sat at small tables chatting and hovering over food and drink.

Suddenly the twinkle went out of Popsy's eyes. He stood up with an air of having just remembered something. Slowly he made his way to the corner of the room, leaned against the grand piano, reached for pencil and manuscript paper, and began to write quickly. As we quieted down, the sudden silence seemed to distract him. Lifting his baby face and waving his left arm while he continued to make notes with his right, he said: "Go on. Go on, I'll be finished soon. Please talk, play, eat something, drink something. Don't let me disturb you."

He worked steadily and intensely for a long time, never taking his eyes off his work. Eventually everyone but Levitzki and I stole out. At last Popsy put his pencil down with an air of finality and looked around. In a surprised voice he asked: "Where's everybody? Where did everybody go?" He seemed disturbed and hurt that they had left.

"They should know," he said, "that it doesn't bother me to have people. I've never had privacy. I never needed it. I always work with people around. A roomful of friends is the best condition for my work. All my life it has been so."

It is hard to believe that such fervid concentration exists unless you witness it, but this is evidently the way Godowsky composed more than four hundred works enchantingly wrought for the piano—works of such complexity and difficulty that they demand more from ten fingers than the virtuosic works of Chopin, Liszt, or Brahms.

Godowsky continued to write until the very last, but his concertizing days came to a sudden end in 1930 when an exhausting recording session left him unable to raise his arms. The shocking experience merely intensified his analytical powers and pursuits. An association with Albert Einstein which ripened at this time into deep mutual affection and admiration undoubtedly stimulated Godowsky's faculties of observation and codification. He lavished all he knew and all he had on all who came to him, professionally and socially, at any and all times of the day and night.

Despite an eager receptivity to fresh ideas, Godowsky

held certain beliefs from which he could not be budged. He held that intellectual and organizational power was a more impregnable base for creativity than genius. Regarding performers, he insisted that talent was insignificant unless it was developed through accurate knowledge of the "organic laws" of music and of interpretation. His contempt for undeveloped talent as "the worst sin of human indulgence" was evidenced in his cynical definition of a "wonder child" as one in whom "the wonder usually disappears and the child remains." He contended that the fruits of the imagination can be ripened only through nourishment on fact. He taught—and Tobias Matthay later extended these ideas into publication and rendered determinative more than a few—that poor playing results less from inferior musical talent than from incorrect mental and muscular practice habits.

During vacations in Maine, I heard Godowsky and Hofmann discuss these matters by the hour. Although Hofmann's emphasis was on emotional relationships and Godowsky's on intellectual and physical mastery, a good part of their conversation was spent on that terrain where art meets science. Neither confused the methods or objectives of art with those of science, but both viewed logic as the quality common to art and science. In an attempt to find their differences, I might risk the generalization that Hofmann considered knowledge as the servant of art; Godowsky regarded it as the master.

When James G. Huncker called Godowsky "the superman of the piano" during the early nineteen hundreds, he reflected the opinion of the musical world's inner circle. However, when he described the pianistic superman's fifty-three unique compositions based on the Chopin études, and wrote: "Godowsky is writing for the next generation," Huneker suffered from overprediction. I read his prophecy twenty-five years after it was made, and at that time only one pianist—David Saperton, Godowsky's son-in-law—represented Huneker's mythical generation. Saperton alone had both the will and the skill to play and record a sizable number of Godowsky's compositions and transcriptions.

Regardless of the aesthetic value of Godowsky's works, they reveal a new world of possibilities in piano writing and piano sonority. They show a chaste love for the beautiful, the balanced, and the logical in their strictest forms. Their creator worked on, oblivious to the styles of the hour, aloof from the musical revolution raging around him. His music exacts a master's command and a master's painstaking procedure. Only pianists know this, for none of it sounds remotely as difficult as it is.

These facts, together with Godowsky's poetic and conservative idiom, made his oblivion as a composer almost a certainty. It is now unhappily almost complete.

Sergei Rachmaninoff

THE EXTRAORDINARY Sergei Rachmanioff had one ordinary characteristic—ordinary, that is, for the true artist.
In common with all visionaries, he was an anguished soul
because his achievements, despite their worldly success,
never quite matched his dreams. He pursued that ever
retreating vista which drives every poet on and on until
death frees him at last from the pain of the unattainable.

Yet, professional recognition was comparatively easy for
Rachmaninoff, first in Europe and later in the United
States. His natural melodic opulence and communicative
power as a composer brought him frequent and important
representation on orchestral, instrumental, and vocal programs. His position as a conductor was so firmly established that in 1917 he was offered no less than the permanent leadership of the Boston Symphony Orchestra.

He declined it, incidentally, on the advice of Josef Hofmann. Faced with a decision as to what specific direction
his career should take here, Rachmaninoff sought Hofmann's opinion by transatlantic correspondence. Hofmann warned Rachmaninoff that "the power politics of an
orchestral organization" would plague his life, and urged
him to seek a pianistic future in the United States. In that
realm, in fairly short order, and in every country where
Rachmaninoff chose to play, there were no engagements
he could not command.

Personally, Rachmaninoff was a greatly misunderstood
man. It was bound to happen, and the world cannot be
blamed for not knowing what it is not permitted to know.
Rachmaninoff's forbidding manner and gaunt face, with
the stern sorrows of the ages engraved upon it, created the

impression of a creature not of our time or kind but rather one from some historical era of past glories that he alone seemed to remember. He was far from unconscious of the muck of the world. He simply chose to remain aloof from it.

The bored exterior of the man and his remoteness were façades for an enormous sense of excitement and wonder about everything he loved, music above all. This capacity to react intensely is the artist's edge over other men, the quality most people lose after childhood. In Rachmaninoff's youth, his compositional ambitions and the conviction that he could not reach them drove him to paralyzing depression. The pianistic goals of his maturity were more attainable, and they drove him to relentless drudgery. I never encountered a higher artistic morality in any musician or a deeper sense of obligation maintained to the very last. His pianistic gifts were so stupendous that he could easily, with much less consecration and slavery, have sustained his monumental mastery. But that was not his way.

"The artist tries, and tries again to achieve the impossible," he said. "Sometimes he is lucky and gets a little nearer to his goal. But all of the time he is forced way out someplace, way out where no one can comfort him, nothing can help him."

Warmth, concern, and consideration for others may appear incongruous to the character of Rachmaninoff in the opinion of all who knew him only superficially. But members of his family and old friends knew better. On them he lavished all these qualities, and to a sentimental degree.

Even some new friends came to know him as he really was. Over several years I had corresponded with him, had spoken perhaps a dozen times to him on the telephone, and had visited him in his New York apartment. Although I had suspected that his gloomy countenance and misanthropic behavior were protective devices, our relations remained professional and formal until I met him again at a Christmas gathering at Steinway's in 1937. The press had just published an announcement of my forthcoming appearances with the New York Philharmonic under Barbirolli as soloist in my Second Piano Concerto. I had not played the work since its *première* in 1932 with the Philadelphia Orchestra under Stokowski.

"Who practices with you your concerto?" asked Rachmaninoff.

When I answered that the orchestral parts had not yet been reduced to a second-piano version and that therefore I was practicing alone, he said quickly: "But that is impossible. Send me the score. I will look it over and practice with you."

Sure enough, two weeks later he came to my studio, sat down at the second piano, and worked with me for some four hours. I really came to know him that day. His meticulous workmanship was again demonstrated in the perfection with which he knew and played the orchestral part. He exacted the utmost precision from himself and from me. Over and over and over again we practiced some thorny passage, crawling along at a painfully slow pace. He was unsparingly generous with suggestions both compositional and pianistic, all made with supreme tact and gentle humor.

Oh, yes, Rachmaninoff had a sense of humor. Fritz Kreisler told a story that emanated from one of their joint recitals in New York. It seems that Kreisler had a momentary lapse of memory during the concert. He edged over toward the piano and whispered to Rachmaninoff: "Where are we?" Rachmaninoff never skipped a note as he answered: "In Carnegie Hall!"

English speech was not too easy for him generally, but he understood our language surprisingly well and would guffaw gleefully at jokes told in dialect. He enjoyed our radio comedians, and was a devoted fan of Jack Benny. Rachmaninoff spoke enthusiastically and knowingly of our musical comedies, but our drama was not for him. He remembered another kind of theater.

He was as thrilled as a child at the circus when the Moscow Art Theater came to New York in 1923. Each performance found Rachmaninoff there, tears of happiness streaming from his eyes while those gigantic hands wiped them from his face. Every spare moment was spent at informal gatherings with the superb artists of the cast who were his old friends: Stanislavsky, who headed the company, actors Kachalov and Moskvin, and the actress Knipper-Chekhova, widow of Chekhov, Rachmaninoff's favorite dramatist. Also present at those sessions, which lasted until the small hours, were Rachmaninoff's cousin Alexander Siloti and their intimate friend Chaliapin.

In this atmosphere Rachmaninoff was the man the world did not know. Carefree and gay, he would roar at stories, tell some himself, and then go to the piano to accompany Chaliapin in Russian folk songs by the hour. His voluntary exile from Bolshevik Russia continued to the end. Although he came to love our country, he was always homesick. Occasions like these took him back to his heart's home.

Otherwise, Rachmaninoff's life was one of sporadic composition and constant concertizing in a succession of triumphs. No life flows without difficulties, of course, but, apart from the artist's inner despair over unrealized ideals, Rachmaninoff appears to have emerged victorious from his artistic and personal battles. He was spared most of the minor irritations of daily living by the devotion of his remarkable wife.

The tumultuous circumstances surrounding Rachmaninoff's marriage to his first cousin, Natalie Satin, gave no hint of the eventual stability of their domestic life. The mere engagement announcement shattered family, friends, and civic and religious authorities alike. One barrier after another had to be removed before final permission from "high moguls" of church and state enabled the pair to consummate their marriage in 1902. Mrs. Rachmaninoff's strength of character, fine judgment of people, and solid intelligence were all used to serve her husband with rare self-effacement. She created for him the conditions of equilibrium which are theoretically regarded as destructive to the creative powers.

Whatever comforts were provided for the man, however, were sufficiently counterbalanced by the artist's essential dissatisfaction with his work. Rachmaninoff was a dedicated and driven perfectionist. He worked incessantly, with infinite patience. Once I had an appointment to spend an afternoon with him in Hollywood. Arriving at the designated hour of twelve, I heard an occasional piano sound as I approached the cottage. I stood outside the door, unable to believe my ears. Rachmaninoff was practicing Chopin's étude in thirds, but at such a snail's pace that it took me a while to recognize it because so much time elapsed between each finger stroke and the next. Fascinated, I clocked this remarkable exhibition; twenty seconds per bar was his pace for almost an hour while I waited riveted to the spot, quite unable to ring the bell. Perhaps this way of developing and maintaining an unerring mechanism accounted for his bitter sarcasm toward colleagues who practiced their programs "once over lightly" between concerts.

At luncheon that day Rachmaninoff surprised me by his lively curiosity about composers and orchestrators of popular music, radio personalities, and movie stars. The only name he mentioned in the field of serious music was that of his favorite pianist among his contemporaries, Josef Hofmann, about whom he inquired very specifically and solicitously. I found this strange, for Hofmann's Los Angeles home was not more than a ten-minute drive from Rachmaninoff's quarters at the Garden of Allah. His conversational reference to his manager, Charles Foley, showed an unexpected tenderness. His eyes actually filled as he described the man who had guided his career since

1918 and who had become his closest and most trusted friend.

Knowing Rachmaninoff's enthusiasm for motoring, I suggested late that afternoon an automobile drive in an Isotta-Fraschini—one of those fantastic Italian cars had been lent to me by my California host for this auspicious pilgrimage. He accepted eagerly and kept exclaiming excitedly over the car's performance. When we got to Santa Monica, he could not hold out any longer and asked if he might drive it. At the wheel, he performed with the same precisional co-ordination, the same sense of perfectly graduated acceleration, momentum, and retardation, that he displayed in his playing.

At the keyboard, this flawless mastery was placed entirely at the service of Rachmaninoff's scrupulous sense of design and meaning. One no sooner reflects that perhaps the most fabulous aspects of his playing were his melodic eloquence and dramatic virtuosity than one remembers the unique rhythmic bite in sustained, short, or syncopated accentuation, or his way of orchestrating chords with special beauty through individual distributions of balances and blendings. Rachmaninoff brought as much art to the performance of his own works and devotion to those of others as was brought to their creation.

Rachmaninoff the composer never sought that easy kind of originality which stems from an avoidance of the natural. He understood the paradox of art through which the creator communicates basic generic truths in a highly personal way. Even those committed to "modernism" as a faith in itself have not failed to become enticed and impressed by the lyric and dramatic qualities of his work. It is supposed to be very clever these days to cast doubts upon the integrity of a composer whose language is romanticism. Integrity by itself is not the full measure of the value of an artist's work, but the integrity of a man whose music speaks the very soul of rapture and in his own way is not to be questioned.

The point is that Rachmaninoff was no iconoclast. When his critics accuse him of not expressing the world in the way of his contemporaries, they are right. But Rachmaninoff's world was his own, like that of every true artist; his work was an expression of himself, and that self was a product of his times on his terms. Compositionally, his idiom was certainly not stylish. Neither was J. S. Bach's, for that matter. There is no greater test of a composer's craft and imagination than his ability to take ideas that are not by themselves startlingly new and to make them his own. Very few of the classic composers could stand up against the critical norm used for measuring newer music. Every piece by Schumann is not a masterpiece or entirely his own creation. We remember this apologetically, as though we were committing a crime in recognizing the fact that Schumann was sometimes a dependent man as well as a visionary genius. We should feel it stupid to spend time on pointing out a classic's lapses when we could be listening to his inspirations. Let us feel the same about our contemporaries.

Rachmaninoff's music has spoken and continues to speak to an enormous audience. The public and performing musicians alike adore his compositions. Little information is to be gained from ignoring or disdaining the fact. Rachmaninoff may descend to banality, but never to obscurity. He is never less than the communicable and sumptuous melodist, harmonist, and orchestrator. He has won his place and his public, a public tired to death of professional matters, of experimental materials made public, of the paraphernalia of "modernism," of the uncharted seas of atonality. It is not an unsophisticated public. It is an emotionally starved public that has also selected and adopted contemporary masterpieces of the most advanced techniques, the same public that accorded Stravinsky, Ravel, Prokofiev, Vaughan Williams, and Hindemith the status of classics in their own time. And Rachmaninoff too, even when he triumphs by default.

Only the avant-garde among professionals view him with a jaundiced eye. Personally, I have what these colleagues consider a sinful affinity for Rachmaninoff's thematic ideas and a shameful admiration for his capacity to develop them so luxuriantly.

Prophecy being vain, the fact remains that the long view of posterity is not concerned with the degree to which this or that work was abreast of its time. Whatever is important to its own time need not worry about being important for all time, for in the light of history there is a strong likelihood that it will be. Rachmaninoff's work is a telling part of musical evolution. It is wonderful to have so much of it recorded for posterity as performed by its composer. The perpetuation of his unique pianistic art in the music of others is another potent contribution to musical advancement.

In all phases of his artistic activities Rachmaninoff made a genuine contribution to twentieth-century music. The composer was always popular, but never *à la mode*. No better indication exists that he will not grow outmoded.

Artur Schnabel

Now THAT I think of it, although I heard and met Artur Schnabel dozens of times and felt that I knew him well, we never spent more than three or four evenings by ourselves. But Schnabel was not hard to know. He was engagingly frank. He was articulate even throughout the most passionate outbursts. He had a genius for using himself completely at the piano or away from it.

His physical appearance—the piercing eyes, broad, high forehead, stubborn chin, stocky frame, bristling mustache, and unruly hair untamed by close cropping—all lent authority to his presence. The years did not alter him materially.

An evening with him was more certain than any chemical experiment to produce spontaneous combustion. A room with a piano, a good cigar, and a few kindred spirits provided the ideal incentives for Schnabel to express himself and his ideas with atomic vigor.

Schnabel had a definite goal—to attain expressive communication on behalf of the music he revered. He reached it an uncommon number of times. His art was a fighting faith. He was perpetually vigilant against attempts to serve expediency or compromise. He was often driven to frenzies of artistic temperament and to academic ponderosity over issues, from the pettiest to the loftiest. Yet it was impossible to resent even his most torrential statements because of the man's underlying sincerity. Schnabel had a love for music which made anything short of dedication seem like indifference. It lent intensity and importance to everything he ever did or said. His editions, his doctrines, his recordings, and the memory of his eloquent playing are a significant part of our heritage as musicians.

The significance of his life does not rest wholly in his musical achievements. His creativity functioned beyond art into life itself. He lived the classic tradition of learning and teaching. A pupil of his once told me: "Schnabel taught me much more about life than about the piano."

Like Liszt, Schnabel never gave lessons in the pedagogical sense. "Liszt," wrote Amy Fay in her illuminating book, *Music Study in Germany*, "doesn't tell you anything about technique. That you must work out for yourself." Schnabel not only did not teach the mechanical part of technique—he had a noticeable distrust of it. He was aware, without Freudian fanfare, that art derives from the emotions of the unconscious. He mistrusted the ability of our age—and he could not have been more right—to put technique at the service of emotion and ideas.

There are those who say that Schnabel was antagonistic to mechanical mastery because he himself never possessed it. They are undoubtedly influenced by his public performances during his last years when he freely admitted that pure mechanical work seemed to him a tragic waste of precious time that should be spent on interpretative pursuits. It is perfectly true that Schnabel never had a virtuoso technique. He never wanted it. Nor did he need it, for at his prime there was little he wanted to do that he could not do. But no pupil who studied with Leschetizky from the age of ten to fifteen could possibly have escaped a severe technical discipline. What Schnabel inveighed heavily against was that facility which not only became the end rather than the means, but also progressed through exhibitionism to vulgarity and compromise. Schnabel was always the huckster's natural enemy, and he was a militant foe.

Such a personality—one whose very presence affirmed irresilient idealism—was bound to oppress some, just as it inspired many. Schnabel had his share of hostile colleagues. But enemies are philosophically accepted and relegated to a fast-fading oblivion by a vigorous man who sees life fully. Occasionally Schnabel earned the displeasure of those whose zeal was no less than his own. He was once rehearsing a Brahms concerto with the New York Philharmonic under John Barbirolli. The conductor was having a difficult time with the orchestral tuttis. During a particularly exasperating moment when the ensemble was at sixes and sevens, Barbirolli happened to glance left to find Schnabel waving his arms toward the orchestra with compelling gestures and superb indifference to Barbirolli's conductorial responsibility or authority. Barbirolli stopped the music, turned to Schnabel, and said: "Mr. Schnabel, you have no more right to conduct my orchestra than I would have to play your solo."

Schnabel gave me some stormy sessions, too. I once asked him if a frequently repeated story was true. It told of his playing a flashy passage by Liszt and saying to a pupil: "That is easy," then following it with the playing of a lyrical phrase by Beethoven, saying: "That is hard." He affirmed it. I then asked whether he did not think that this was an oversimplification of the problem and that the words "easy" and "hard" could be misleading.

"Why?" he asked.

"Because," I answered, "from another standpoint it is harder to endow Liszt's music with significance than Beethoven's."

"Ah," he exclaimed, "then you admit that Liszt is popular rubbish!"

I said I admitted nothing of the kind. It was a long, bitter argument. I was never able to get him to admit that he knew what I was driving at. I explained that I thought the important thing was to get people to play and to listen to both Liszt and Beethoven, and not to kick out one as unworthy to enter "the sacred groves of Arcady." Partially, I was to blame for his refusal to concede the point, for I followed the last remark with "I think it's Arcady

—it has been so long since I was there." Sarcasm was strictly his territory, and I had trespassed.

Anyway, he got me to agree that Beethoven's opus 111 is greater music than Liszt's *Liebestraum*. When I asked: "But who am I to tell anyone who loves Liszt's music that he is settling for an inferior experience?" he said: "You are a musician in a position of trust, and it is your mandatory duty!"

Imagine my astonishment a few months later, when the identical subject arose, to hear Schnabel proclaim to a gathering: "It does not matter one iota what kind of music people like, just so long as some type is liked by somebody." I was flattered—naïvely convinced that I had accomplished a conversion—until a mutual friend jolted me rudely with the comment: "Oh, give Artur time, and you will hear him condemn and champion the very same things ad libitum."

It was quite impossible to be complacent about Schnabel. His admirers frankly worshipped him. To them he was a cult. It was easy to succumb to this man. He could be irresistible. One night when he was in one of his most genial moods, he grew philosophical and serious. He was so compelling, he removed one so far from the material world, that one noted with surprise upon stepping out into the street that the taxis and buses were still running and that people still walked about and talked. One had the feeling somehow when Schnabel held forth like this that the world ought to be observing a period of silence.

I felt most tenderly toward him on another occasion. During an otherwise pleasant evening at the home of common friends, one of Schnabel's less talented and more hysterical pupils cornered me, attacking with: "I heard your all-Chopin program last week. A musician like you shouldn't set such an example. Chopin is just a salon composer."

"Where," I asked quietly, "and from what evil source did you ever learn such blasphemies?"

"Master," she shrieked across the room to Schnabel, "didn't you say that Chopin was just a salon composer?"

Schnabel turned his head slowly. He suddenly looked very old and very tired. My heart went out to him. Sighing deeply, he answered evenly: "Only at times." Later, as we stood together at the buffet table getting some food, he said to me under his breath: "May God save us from disciples! Like the Greek philosophers, I have been cursed by my pupils."

He did not really believe that. He took great pride in many of his pupils and in their achievements; and he was equally capable of talking resentfully of others who had done well but had strayed from the fold.

The complex charm of Schnabel included an unexpected sense of the ridiculous and a disarming delight in frivolity. He inherited a weakness—or strength, depending on how one views it—for punning. He got it from Brahms, via the latter's pupil and Schnabel's teacher in Vienna, Mandyczewski.

I once mentioned a pianist who was about to give an all-Mozart concert. "Oh," said Schnabel, "when he plays it, it isn't Mozart. It's Nozart." Particularly ingenious, I think, is the bilingualism: the English "notes-art" implying the pianist's inexpressivity, and the German "*no-zart*" (*zart* meaning tender or delicate).

One summer Schnabel had a telephone installed in his studio at Ann Arbor after his friends complained of his inaccessibility. In the midst of his practicing, someone phoned to invite him to dinner, adding: "Oh, it's wonderful that at last you have a telephone, isn't it?" Schnabel replied: "You know, with this telephone all serenity has gone. Life for me is a bell-hell."

Schnabel pulled a neat Spoonerism at the expense of his London dentist:

> *I paid fifty shillings*
> *For these shifty fillings.*

Not bad for a man using other than his mother tongue.

Whenever you made a reproving face over one of his puns, Schnabel always said: "A pun is the lowest form of humor . . . when you don't think of it first, yes?" He loved every kind of frank nonsense. One evening he diverted us by sitting down at the piano and singing *con amore* in a frog-like voice some songs he improvised. For texts he used a few of the delicious verses from Samuel Hoffenstein's *Poems in Praise of Practically Nothing*, most of which he appeared to know by heart. On this occasion he started off with

> *I could not love thee, dear, so much*
> *Were I not born to be in Dutch.*

He ended with

> *If you love me, as I love you,*
> *We'll both be friendly and untrue.*

Where serious music was concerned, and especially where his own standards were involved, Schnabel's humor deserted him. We are indebted to his close friend César Saerchinger for some early Schnabeliana heard at first hand.

In the days of player-piano rolls, Schnabel was invited by a company official to make some. "We have sixteen nuances," said the unfortunate man, who was promptly withered by Schnabel's reply: "Unfortunately, *I* have seventeen."

Recording was another story. Years later Schnabel had become an idol in England. He was asked to record. He refused again, but when questioned as to whether he thought that the machine was not worthy of his art, Schnabel replied: "On the contrary. I'm not good enough for the machine."

This is a revealing exchange. We can be certain that the question was not a sarcastic one, for Schnabel's artistic worth and integrity had been impressively demonstrated

to the British in several series of concerts which featured
Schubert's ten sonatas, then an entire Beethoven cycle,
and then all of the Mozart concertos. It is equally certain
that Schnabel's reply was neither false modesty nor rep-
artee. It was the considered judgment of an extraordinarily responsible artist who did not feel that his art had
yet attained sufficient maturity or excellence to be set
forth in permanent form.

Eventually—although with fearful apprehension—
Schnabel did reach the point when he felt, as he put it to
me, that he was "not so terribly far from artistic truth to
risk the venture." It was the beginning of an enormous
and invaluable catalogue that includes interpretations of
Beethoven sonatas and concertos, Mozart concertos and
solo works, and Schubert and Brahms works in the large
and small forms, none of which passing time can invali-
date.

Schnabel's playing had two primary qualities. It was
always nobly reflective and unobtrusively expressive.
Schnabel's concerts were like no others. He forced us to
forget the performer, the platform, and the piano. He
compelled us to give ourselves wholly to the music, to
share his own absolute absorption. There he sat, summon-
ing our faculties no less than his own to concentrate upon
the music itself, to feel all the emotions that lie deepest
and strongest in life and in art. Nothing he did ever had
the flavor of virtuosity or vanity.

During one of his Beethoven sonata cycles in New
York, there was a joke going the rounds: it did not matter so much whether or not you had a ticket to the series,
but if you did not carry a volume of the Beethoven sonatas under your arm you could not get into Carnegie Hall.
It indicated the atmosphere radiated by Schnabel's personality. There was no applause-seeking, no charm-let-
ting, no sweetmeat for an encore. All was sincerity, significance, and seriousness to the point of severity.

There were those who said that Schnabel was lacking in

showmanship. One might as well say that a glass of water was lacking in oil. Schnabel's concerts were never shows; they were invariably some kind of sacred rite. They were not calculated to ensure success with the mass public, and never did. In the days when his uncompromising attitude and programs took their toll of public demand, he told me that he had telephoned his manager, saying: "This is Artur Schnabel. Remember me?" I tried to lighten his despondency by saying: "You always have made the sharp distinction between artists and entertainers. Your concerts are always the highest form of art and the lowest form of entertainment. That's the way you want it." He answered: "I have never minded playing for a hundred people. I cannot even say that I'd rather starve as an artist than flourish as an entertainer. I have no such choice."

This man was not for this age. Artistic zeal burned within him, doggedness and dedication and pride. He had the will and the power to stir us to the best within us. We could not be more thankful.

In Retrospect

THE MEN I have been writing about worked their miracles more frequently and to a greater degree than any other pianists I ever heard. But not always, and not in all ways. These paragons had their limitations.

Hofmann's were least apparent because he knew them so well, and because he had the wisdom to avoid public competition with others on their ground. For example, he played very little Bach outside of the splendid organ works in stylistically absurd transcriptions by Liszt and Tausig. Hofmann realized that this was not Bach's language, that performances of the harpsichord and clavichord works on a comparable level with those works which fully belonged to him would take a special scholarship, one that had not been available to him in his youth. Attaining it would mean scrapping lifelong habits, starting afresh. This was clearly not for him.

His kinship to Mozart was confined to the dramatic fantasies and the Lisztian transformation of *Don Giovanni.* Although Brahms was not so conspicuously absent from Hofmann's programs as from those of his master Anton Rubinstein, Hofmann played mainly the three rhapsodies and the Handel Variations. He avoided the Paganini Variations and the monumental concertos and sonatas.

Even this greatest of Chopinists found stumbling-blocks among the *études,* especially the A minor, opus 10, no. 2, the studies in thirds, sixths, and octaves, and the prodigious "Winter Wind." No one claimed that he could not play them. No one, that is, but Hofmann. He had heard Backhaus, Lhevinne, Godowsky, and Friedman in these works. That was quite enough to keep him from performing them publicly.

Hofmann had a gigantic repertoire. As the years went by, he used it less and less, but his audiences must share partial responsibility for the stereotyped programs of the later years. They doted on certain "Hofmann pieces" in much the same way that men with a closetful of ties constantly select a few favorites. Especially did Hofmann's public anticipate encore time. Then they would get not only what amounted to a Chopin recital, but also a generous compliance with their shouted demands for Rubinstein's "Melody in F," Moszkowski's *"Caprice Espagnol,"* Schubert's *"Marche Militaire,"* Rachmaninoff's C sharp minor Prelude, Mendelssohn's "Spring Song," and many other less-than-profound items.

This post-recital ritual led to one of Godowsky's most acidulous remarks. After an hour of beloved war-horses had inflamed the Hofmann fans to an insatiable and hysterical pitch, Mrs. Godowsky started to leave. "Aren't you going?" she asked her husband, who gave no sign of rising from his seat. "I'm not budging from this spot," answered the naughty Popsy, "until Josef plays 'The Rosary'!"

Godowsky was a genuine paradox as the pedantic perfectionist and audacious iconoclast. The precisionist who would take your head off for the slightest deviation from a text was equally quick to point out, with the air of discharging a humanitarian duty, where Beethoven or Schumann had been careless or inept, and how we "owe it to them to correct their errors." Godowsky altered such "errors" with the conviction of a man who looks over your shoulder while you tally your bankbook and discovers a provable mistake in subtraction.

Stating that the classicists were only human and not above a fall from grace, Godowsky was fond of citing great musical material that had been transformed to advantage, from Bach's and Handel's free utilization of other composers' ideas to Ravel's orchestration of *Pictures at an Exhibition*. In Godowsky's words, "Ravel realized for Mussorgsky a fulfillment of ideals which Mussorgsky was obviously incapable of realizing for himself." If one ventured to point out the difference between a re-creation in which the transcriber assumes full responsibility and arbitrary "corrections" superimposed upon an otherwise original text, Godowsky said: "There are few things so flawless that they cannot be improved."

As he "improved" a classic, whether by slight or by radical means, Godowsky was confident that a composer whose solutions differed from his had committed at least a miscalculation, and perhaps even a downright blunder.

We used to say that Godowsky, like nature, abhorred a vacuum. The characteristic is less favorable to art than to nature, and Godowsky the transcriptionist was most vitally affected by it. In too many of his transcriptions—in Schubert's F minor *"Moment Musicale,"* Albéniz's Tango and "Triana," Weber's "Invitation to the Dance," Schubert's songs, and others—the over-luxuriant textures, the harmonic and contrapuntal complexities are such that the very character of the originals is all but lost.

As teacher, Godowsky unwittingly inhibited many musicians through his relentless insistence on the letter rather than the spirit of music. His inordinate demands drove them to a preoccupation with details, with fingers and notes. Convinced that anyone who could not "take it" would not amount to much anyway, Godowsky was ceaselessly picking blemishes and caricaturing weaknesses. I witnessed many painful scenes as gifted pianists became so tense and rattled that hysterics, nature's merciful device, finally released their overtaxed nerves. When that happened, Godowsky would punish himself severely, growing abjectly remorseful and showing it with deep tenderness. An hour later he would be at it again, helpless against his contempt for inadequacy, his frenzied pursuit of perfection.

Godowsky always said that he played best on the platform, stimulated by audiences. Perhaps this was true of his youth. But no public performance, no recording I ever heard matched the freedom and beauty of Godowsky's playing in an intimate atmosphere, in the presence of admiring friends and colleagues.

I am not alone in this opinion. One night he played for a few of us his newly composed *Java Suite*. It was sorcery, nothing less. Later, when I was walking Hofmann back to his hotel, he said: "Never forget what you heard tonight; never lose the memory of that sound. There's nothing like it in this world. It is tragic that the public has never heard Popsy as only he can play."

When I met Rachmaninoff, I was unprepared to have my faith in the omniscience of Hofmann or Godowsky shaken, for I knew Rachmaninoff admired them deeply. Yet, he started almost immediately to warn me that "academic theories belong to criticism, not to creation or interpretation."

"Your master," Rachmaninoff said, "is a pianistic genius, the greatest of all. Godowsky is another kind of genius, but both of them think that teaching can produce what it can only improve."

These were hard sentiments for me to swallow. They related to the first argument I dared to wage against him on the grounds that his refusal to teach was an indefensible abrogation of an artistic obligation. Apart from a few favorites among personal friends, Rachmaninoff had very little interest in musical education, in the musical scene generally. He was unconvinced that teaching could produce anything of vital significance, unaware of the damage done through the naïve faith that talent alone is sufficient to gain mastery, maturity, and inevitable recognition. Rachmaninoff's interest lay in the finished product, not in potentiality; in composition and performance. Period.

Rachmaninoff the pianist had a particular blind spot. Except for a handful of works, Chopin's language was

alien to him. Somehow the sham heroics one finds in the
unfledged composer of *the* prelude, the gushing sentimentality that saturates his *Elegiac Trio,* brooded over most of
his Chopin-playing. I have a melancholy remembrance of
his performances of Chopin's Twenty-four Preludes.
Throughout there was an amazing absence of Rachmaninoff's distinctive strengths. His rhythmic precision deserted him. The lyrical pieces sounded whimpering, the
bold ones inflated. The music and its interpreter both lost
their essential traits.

Later I heard Rachmaninoff play mazurkas, waltzes,
nocturnes, and études with a reckless loss of exactness
and elegance. They did not emerge even as inspired
misconceptions. They were stylistically artificial. I was
pained and puzzled, unable to realize at the time how
polarized were Rachmaninoff's Byronic romanticism and
Chopin's poetic classicism.

Artur Schnabel was often embarrassed by the
"anointed," who regarded him as their Messiah and his
every word as holy writ. Yet he indulged in assertive
oration and peremptory opinion that put a dangerous
strain upon the non-anointed, even upon their willingness, short of worship, to recognize him as a noble artist
and a candid man. "I am a simple musician," Schnabel
would say, and say it with the air of an emperor.

His book, *Reflections on Music,* alienated many who
were entirely disposed to succumb to the Schnabel magic.
Even the most spiritual appetites have been known to
acquire indigestion from the purple prose and the "let's-
get-down-on-our-knees, we're-on-hallowed-ground" attitude. I regret it because it is so contrary to the innately
modest man whose art at its greatest had an artless simplicity.

When it was less than that, Schnabel could be so careless about technical details that a performance or a recording would sound more like a *prima vista* reading than
a prepared execution. In lyrical movements he could be-

come introverted and meditative to the point of losing connective momentum, of producing unconscionable boredom.

Once, obviously aware that he had lost communication with an audience that coughed profusely during the music and applauded perfunctorily afterward, he rose slowly, bowed very slowly, and then fixed his public with a hard look. The look said: "You are unworthy to be in this temple." Schnabel was out to serve Beethoven and Schnabel's conviction about him, not to entertain the customers. He had laid down his life for this—they, only the price of admission. He made sure that they knew it.

In retrospect, I see the personal differences and distinctions between Hofmann, Godowsky, Rachmaninoff, and Schnabel as negligible in the light of their commonly assumed guardianship of standards and trusteeship of traditions. Each had the highest concept of artistic responsibility and very much the same instrumental and interpretative destinations. Each made his choice of the road to the journey's end according to his own endowment and environment. Each possessed abundantly the indefinable and incalculable elements of art.

We can also see that each knew limitation and frustration, and that these brought not only suffering but also the power of understanding which suffering can bring and the greater ability to illumine humanity's common struggles and ultimate hopes. Moreover, had it not been for the frailties of these superhuman singers, the gods might well have been sorely tempted in their jealousy.

Countersubjects

Concerning Donald Francis Tovey

AMONG THE men who, each in his way, revealed to me the very heart of the piano, only Hutcheson and Hofmann were my teachers in the sense of giving me consecutive lessons. Godowsky and Rachmaninoff were my mentors rather than my masters. Schnabel was more a symbol who represented the conscience of music. He was also an artist I revered, a teacher who generously offered to hear me several times and proffered invaluable comments, a man with whom I was privileged to associate on relatively few occasions but under unusually stimulating circumstances.

I assume that I share with many others the inability to place the exact moment when tutelage ended and independent judgment began. Despite my abject devotion to these giants, or perhaps because of it, I made many conscious and unconscious efforts to free myself from their vast authority, from the need of their assistance and approval.

But even more serious than the desire for independence, I was beginning to feel out of my depth. The priceless lessons and associations had stuffed me with a rich and heterogeneous stock of materials that I was unable to collate. My own identity remained concealed, my own problems remained unsolved. My ideas were not my own ideas, and they were in conflict. I felt that I had to work out my own salvation. I knew that I was somehow looking through the wrong end of a telescope—through interpretation to music, and that music was anything but clear to me.

This may sound strange, coming from one who had already composed quite a number of published works. But before that I had studied harmony, counterpoint, and form with Percy Goetschius, analysis and composition with Rubin Goldmark. Both were musical scholars, faithful teachers, and delightful human beings. Both had accepted and taught compositional theories as though they were scientific facts established before music existed. The fugue schemes I learned would not relate to any Bach fugue I played: the sonata-form doctrines rarely resembled the works I knew. The rules seemed to apply merely to textbook exercises. Finding them unworkable in my own creative efforts, finding them inapplicable to the masterpieces I loved, and finding myself tied up in knots of confusion, I stopped going for lessons.

My regained interest in musical analysis, my final ability to shift my emphasis from performance to composition, did not come about in one dramatic flash, or with the mere passing of time, or without further assistance. It crystallized slowly, following an unexpected encounter with a man—with a mind, I should say, a mind that let in a pure light, that took nothing for granted, that compelled me to re-examine everything.

During 1931 I returned to Europe to fulfill a recording contract and concert engagements. As good luck would have it, London was first on my itinerary, and there I found Donald Francis Tovey giving a series of recitals at the Wigmore Hall. Hearing him and meeting him affected my entire view of music. Later I shall speak of his unique playing. First I want to say that his was the most erudite and sparkling mind I ever knew. He talked exactly as he wrote, his wisdom peppered with unregenerate wit.

Learning that he planned to stay in London during his remaining concerts, I made a confounded nuisance of myself until he agreed to see me professionally, primarily to help me in compositional analysis.

"Very well," he said at last. "I suggest that you investigate a Mozart score in the Eulenburg edition and bring it along with a readable analysis."

When he saw the results of my "investigation" of Mozart's Piano Concerto in C, K.503, Tovey said: "Good heavens, it's almost fallacious enough to serve as a model text for one of your American music-appreciation rackets!"

That was only the beginning. Imagine the shock of a fairly established pianist, composer, and teacher on discovering that he had not yet learned to read a score, in Tovey's meaning of the term. Of course, my head teemed with hundreds of pages of memorized music, but it took no more than a few of his searching questions to tell me how lightly and uncomprehendingly I had skipped through them.

Analagous to the abrupt pianistic awakening that Hofmann's first words brought was the new awareness that I had been shackled by a statistical view of form, cowed into a servile faith in the printed word and in theoretical teaching that classified art forms as though they were geometric forms. Having been taught to expect masterworks of a species to conform to "the rules," to behave as though their structures had been rigidly determined before the music was conceived, I had fixed my attention on their familiar elements and obvious resemblances. In the process, I had overlooked their most significant differences. In fact, I had deliberately closed my eyes and ears to their uncomfortable existence in sublime ignorance of the primary point that virtually every great art work is a special case.

This fundamental fact and many others no less vital to an accurate observation of art forms had escaped me completely. The discovery was so humiliating and upsetting that I have confided this transient but momentous experience to few people. The wounds to my vanity were hardly healed by the excitement of learning. Roused to rescrutinize terminology, tonality, style, and structure, stimulated to reread textbooks and to restudy the works they "analyzed," I was painfully jolted to find how often the internal evidence of individual works contradicted the *a priori* generalizations of the academic orthodoxy that I had found innavigable but had not really questioned.

The largest part of my reading time was naturally spent in poring over every word from Tovey's untiring pen which I could find. His analytical work earlier that year had included program notes for Bach's B minor Mass in connection with an Edinburgh performance under his direction. When he showed it to me he said: "It's far from complete, but common sense forbids me to tackle every element involved. The truth must be faced that Bach scholarship is full of contradictions, especially regarding ornamentation. Now, *there's* a fruitful field for you. Why not investigate it?"

When he saw my enthusiasm for his suggestion, he said: "Let me give you one piece of practical advice. If you ever manage the time for research and find some of the annihilating things I think you'll find, don't discuss them with any pious professors. Present them only to your most scrupulously musical and intelligent colleagues, and to them with the rarest tact you can summon. Even then, I dare say, you'll often know how it must feel to slap a porcupine."

The comment was characteristically humorous, sagacious, and prophetic. I recalled it ruefully about a decade later when Serge Koussevitzky, who was to conduct the B minor Mass at Tanglewood, invited me to edit the score and parts and to give a series of preliminary lectures before his orchestra, chorus, and soloists. The orchestra numbered many faculty members of the school, the chorus many of its students.

It was at this temple of learning that I found the spirit of inquiry hailed with apathy or hostility by all except Koussevitzky himself, the scholarly harpsichordist Putnam Aldrich, and a handful of "scrupulously musical" members of the faculty and student body. I still cannot decide whether it was funny or sad to see the panic that

seized the soloists when those expensive warblers were
confronted with a tiny ornament and a discussion of its
expressive potentialities in the baroque style.

Those who howled the loudest were the "pious professors" from our most venerable universities, whose terrified resistance revealed the extent of their insecurity.
But the experience was not entirely unfertile. It persuaded a few that the topic held rewarding possibilities
and contributed considerably to my own understanding
of the fine art of institutional fraud.

Tovey, who took fiendish delight in piercing piety,
knew exactly what was in store for me. In fact, nothing
ever arose which he did not seem to know to its backbone.
Much of it, providentially, is available in his unparalleled
prose. Now I must return to that aspect of his career
which relates most directly to this book.

Tovey was in his middle fifties when I heard him, and
his playing did not show the mechanical command of the
ranking pianists. Although his busy life permitted limited
keyboard practice, he did not sound like one who had
ever been a virtuoso. But he had an imaginative insight, a
way of conveying the essence of a musical work in totality
which enabled him to stride past all but a few of the
greatest pianists.

He knew by heart practically every significant composition from the sixteenth century through the nineteenth. If
this sounds like a sophomoric exaggeration, read Mary
Grierson's biography of Tovey, wherein she relates that
Professor Newall of Cambridge once asked Tovey how
long he thought it would take him to play from memory
everything he knew, playing eight hours a day. Tovey answered: "Oh, about four weeks." Then thinking it over, he
corrected himself and added: "No. I think it would take
eight weeks, or seven at least."

Pablo Casals said: "Never did I mention one work of
the symphonic, operatic, choral, chamber-music, or solo
literature which Tovey didn't sit right down and illustrate

flawlessly from memory at the piano, starting at the exact point under discussion." When I mentioned Tovey to Georges Enesco, he crossed himself.

Everything Tovey played revealed his colossal musicianship, divulged something one had never before known or heard quite that way. When he played Beethoven's "Diabelli" Variations or the Handel-Brahms Variations, he produced a cumulative effect, a successive impetus that made every variation progress along one propulsive line with the structural inevitability and excitement of a detective story.

Tovey's belief in a masterpiece as a type of infinity, his understanding of the force and nature of its individuality, his intense desire to demonstrate the most important aspects of its structure, took your mind off everything but the music itself. You forgot the pianist, you could not think of "his interpretation." Here was not a performer, but an inspired medium proving the pure coherence and self-consistency of a masterwork.

Although I will not attempt here to discuss Tovey as a composer, the few works of his which I have seen (not heard) lead me to disagree with those who disparage his creative gift. I think it more likely that his laboratory and clinical investigations as an observer and author overburdened his imagination and impeded his own creative talent and activity.

It was inevitable that his greatest fame should rest on his intellectual powers, on the unique analyses he left, which enable us to discern more accurately and deeply the organizational originality of genius.

On Interpretation

"NOTHING HAPPENS in performance," said the realistic Toscanini, "that doesn't happen somewhere in the preparation—except the bad things."

Such a statement, coming from an artist whose power to summon the inspiration of the moment was unsurpassed, carries abundant implication that neither instinct nor luck can be relied upon to produce sustained excellence. Precise planning, conscious knowledge, and refined skills are all required to elevate muscular facility into technique, taste into judgment, perception into culture, and vision into conviction and communication.

Genius does not appear upon this earth in full bloom. In the beginning it is talent, and talent is not quite so rare as it is generally believed to be. Its fulfillment is the rarity, for fulfillment depends not alone upon the quality and quantity of talent, but also upon its direction and upon the degree to which talent is cultivated, guided, and utilized. Natural gifts are but the intuitive seeds of art. They must be carefully tended and prudently exposed to every fertilizing element if they are to flower. Otherwise, far more often than not, we find both creative and re-creative gifts stunted in their growth, withered, or dead.

But let us assume an ideal circumstance: a manifoldly gifted pianist is beautifully nurtured to become a performing artist of high caliber. Strange to say, the greater his imaginative force, the stronger his personality, the more he must face the most troublesome of interpretative problems: in what way and to what degree is he privileged to bestow his hard-won individuality upon the music he plays?

The mere fact that the problem can be stated in this way shows how far we have come from the days when the argument was waged whether a performer had any right to introduce anything beyond a faithful representation of the composer's intentions as indicated in the score. Although it is still being heatedly debated in certain metaphysical quarters, most of us recognize that the personality of the interpreter is an ineradicable fact, and therefore undebatable. The real problem—an eternal problem in art—remains one of proportion.

Before we tackle it, I must quote a pertinent remark that Richard Strauss made which keeps coming to mind. "A musical score," he said, "may have more or less than appears on the page, but it is always something not apparent on the page. A printed page is an imperfect blueprint of a conception. It is a lifeless diagram that awaits resurrection by an interpreter. His is the Last Judgment just so long as his re-creative powers remain relevant to the spirit and substance of a work."

The process of interpretation begins with an accurate observation of the printed page. It is the artist's first duty, but it is a minimum obligation. It has been absurdly magnified to become the major criterion of an artist's dedication. Far be it from me to deny that the average recital furnishes appalling evidence that precise score-reading is a skill obviously beyond the average player. Yet it is merely a starting-point, and the musician who holds "absolute fidelity to the score" as his highest interpretational goal holds an erroneous ideal.

It is erroneous because it is based on the untenable premises that music is born to the composer in a fixed and inflexible mold; that he is able to transcribe to the page the very sounds he conceived, in their entirety and with exactitude; and that there is but one authentic way to interpret a work of art.

No one knows better than the composer the limitations and imperfections of the printed score. Within the two centuries or so during which composers have been reasonably able to anticipate publication and performance, they have written and edited their scores with ever increasing care. Nevertheless, their most painstaking efforts are defeated by music's notational inadequacy and loose terminology.

No one knows better than the composer that the richest works of art are those with the widest gamut of expression, the greatest multiplicity of meanings. Only the composer knows the difference between abstract sounds as they spring up in the imagination and those same sounds translated first into symbols and later into performance.

The inability to transfer to the printed page exactly what the composer conceived in the mysterious ecstasy of inspiration leads us to contemplate what the effect on interpretation might be if it were possible to hear the old masters play their own works. What would we not learn, especially from composers such as Mozart and Beethoven who were also the greatest pianists of their day? The very thought makes one's head swim, makes one curse humanity's ill-luck that mechanical genius and artistic genius did not flourish simultaneously.

But apart from the sheer fascination of hearing a composer interpret his own music, apart from the stylistic and textual knowledge to be derived from the opportunity, the experience is a revealing lesson in music's unique dependence upon the interpreter. Many of us who love music have heard, in actual or recorded performances, Richard Strauss, Sibelius, and Stravinsky conduct their compositions, or Ravel, Medtner, Prokofiev, Hindemith, and Gershwin play theirs. Whatever was to be learned from the enriching experience, it was certainly not that a printed score is sacrosanct. And it was distinctly not—judging from how differently they played the same works at different times—that a composer's reading constitutes the inviolable tradition from which deviation is inadmissible.

The rendition by the great old masters of their own music must remain a matter of speculation. But we know enough about their works and about their improvisational procedures to conclude that nothing could be more audacious than to suggest that a Mozart or a Beethoven, for example, was not the freest of artists, or that they would ever have permitted anything to obstruct emotional truth as it arose spontaneously in performance.

Posterity will not have to rely upon speculation and deduction regarding the masters of our electronic age. In our lifetime, for the first time in musical history, there became available the recorded interpretations of an entire category of major works by a significant composer who was also a significant performer. Sergei Rachmaninoff was the one composer-pianist of our time whose interpretative gifts fully matched his creative gifts. His RCA Victor recordings as soloist with the Philadelphia Orchestra in his four piano concertos and *Rhapsody* are illuminating documents that settle some important questions.

Let us check the scores as we listen to these recordings and see what we can observe. Does Rachmaninoff rigidly obey his own metronome marks to the numeral? He does not. Do the composer and his favorite collaborators adhere devotionally to the printed dynamics? They do not. And when we hear so drastic a change as appears in the last movement of the Second Concerto, where the woodwind section, marked pianissimo, emerges fortissimo, it becomes obvious that public performance brings not only inspirational flashes but also practical realizations that demand anything from slight alterations to flat rejections of the text.

Finally, can we find symbols in the score which would enable an interpreter to achieve the glowing nuance, inner phrasing, and subtle accentuation, the exquisite transition from one tempo to another or from one texture or expressive range to another, or any of the other effects that ravish our ears? Not anywhere. There are no such symbols.

What we do find is that Rachmaninoff the interpretative genius brings to Rachmaninoff the composer the identical, disciplined originality that he brings to the communication of a work by Beethoven or Schumann. He has a way with music and with the piano which is all his own, right down to anarchistic mannerisms. The most personal and surprising effects emerge with such coherent relation to the whole that they stand vindicated as concomitants of the entire structure. Such playing is not performance; it is re-creation.

We now ask ourselves what are the applicable values of this authentic document. Is it to be regarded as the model for others to imitate as closely as possible? We see immediately, if we recognize individuality as the distinctive characteristic of a great interpreter, that imitation is impossible, even were it desirable. What, then, is to be extracted from the composer's approach to his own music? Before a performer's imagination can take flight, he must be in full possession of every possible fact relating to the music he hopes to communicate. Here is where the composer's interpretations become invaluable.

Rachmaninoff's performances of his own works provide the authentic basis on which we can verify compositional style, judge tempo markings and dynamic signs, correct misprints, and adjust miscalculations. The composer's readings show us what *not* to do; they chart the boundaries of our liberty; they disclose what would lead us too far afield.

Beyond that, the interpreter is on his own. He must go on to realize the music through his own image, his own truth. Of course it will vary from the composer's realization, just as it will vary from that of any other interpreter, for a work of art cannot mean precisely the same thing to two people. The richer a performer's imagination, the greater his command, the deeper his intuition, the more humane his culture—the more he will penetrate and fulfill the potentialities of the music he plays.

Should he seek to exploit himself at the expense of the music, should he distort its essential mood or meaning, he will fail. The music itself will give the lie to his deceit. But if he is a master of that art which conceals art, the music will appear to speak for itself. At this point I am pained not to be able to summon the name of the oracle who first said: "If music could speak for itself, it would cry out 'For Heaven's sake, interpret me!'"

I myself have lived through this matter on both sides. In my concert-playing days I played in private sessions to Godowsky, Rachmaninoff, and Ravel many of their works I had been practicing. With the brashness of youth I took interpretative liberties without apology; I did not hesitate to indulge in some fairly drastic individual ideas that I had concluded were suggested by the spirit of the music, but were not to be found in the text.

At no time did I hear any expression of indignation or any suggestion that my alterations were high-handed tamperings with their music. Their first reactions were always curiosity and interest. They did not consider each note or mark a deathless inspiration.

Rachmaninoff would say: "Yes, that does sound better" or "I think that change makes the idea clearer and easier to play" or "It is another way of treating my idea, but I must say it is an intriguing one." Once I brought Godowsky a composition of his and played it to him with meticulous observance of his metronome mark. He jumped up in agitation and said: "Oh, no! That's much too slow. Never mind the metronome mark. I put it down as I composed the piece, before I learned it!" Ravel, in response to certain pedal effects I had devised for his exquisite *Sonatine*, exclaimed: "Why didn't someone show me that such effects were possible with the sustaining pedal? How many more possibilities it would have suggested to me!"

On the other hand, I had the thrilling experience of hearing my own works transformed in "re-creations" by Toscanini, Stokowski, Hofmann, Rachmaninoff, and Horowitz, among others. To take two specific examples: a piano work of mine called *Narrative* presents some formidable difficulties. At several dramatic points the text directs the performer to slow down for widely dispersed and unwieldy octaves and chords. I played it that way, and so did every other pianist, because only such allowances of time enabled us to play the notes and attain the climaxes comfortably and clearly. One day Horowitz played it over for me at his studio. When he came to those bristling passages, he tore right through them at the prevailing speed, explaining that he had ignored my markings because he felt that the climaxes lost their power unless the momentum was maintained. The effect was overwhelming. It had never dawned upon me to ask for it, as I could not possibly imagine a pianist who could play it in tempo.

In 1931 Toscanini conducted a work of mine called *Parade*. At the first rehearsal I squirmed to hear how I had misgauged the orchestration of an entire section. It was not at all what I had imagined within me. Suddenly Toscanini turned around. "Chestnuts," he yelled (he never did learn to pronounce my name), "see me after rehearsal." As we rode in a cab to his apartment at the Astor Hotel, he said: "That middle section, Chestnuts . . . it is not what you want, is it?" The misery on my face answered him. When we reached his home, he sat down without a word and completely re-scored that section. At the second rehearsal I finally heard the orchestra play exactly what I had heard in my head but had been unable to translate to the page. My interpreter had to realize it for me.

The performer is not by accident called the interpreter. His first duty is actually to interpret what he sees on the page and translate the mute symbols into sound. Then he must envision what the composer really felt and thought, reaching far beyond the creator's ability to notate completely his expressive intent. Only then is the interpreter performing his highest function: to become the partner of the composer, to breathe life upon music through the power of his own vision and technique.

Guided by scholarship and integrity, not by willful caprice or exhibitionism, the interpreter develops ideas and ideals of his own and directs them to finding the best ways and means to communicate his acquired beliefs on behalf of the music's primal message. Should he conclude that its full realization requires him to depart from the text or to turn its directions inside out or upside down, he must do this. He cannot do otherwise, not with conviction. In the art of interpretation the power to create truth is the first law. Also, as Strauss said, it is "the Last Judgment."

Wherever I have experienced interpretative illumination, I have found it illustrated in the piano literature in greatest measure from the artists I wrote about in my opening sections. The ultimate proof of their principles was in their performances. Once we absorb these principles, once we consciously respond to their application, we become extremely sensitized to their absence and to the lowered artistic result it inevitably yields. In the hands of a master, we are tempted to think of them as platitudes rather than anything so grandiose as principles. It is primarily in their absence that we learn to what extent these principles in action are the life-blood that courses through an inspired re-creation.

Such re-creation is unique. It cannot be imitated. It cannot be adopted. It must vary from artist to artist. Therefore, we must accept every "originality," provided that it does not violate the essential style and character of a creation. How can we discover them, especially when they belong to the dead past? I can assure the reader that there is far more authoritative testimony available than most artists have ever been willing to examine.

Any performance that distorts the inherent evidence of a score is obviously deficient. One that displays textual fidelity, but little more, comes under the heading of honest workmanship. And damned lifeless it is, by itself. A performance that grasps and communicates musical material with conviction, individuality, and command is in the category of mastery. But more yet is possible, as possible as it is rare: the interpretation that illumines a composition through intensified meanings and freshly revealing views of its truths.

On Teaching

ALTHOUGH I find it hard to recollect my actual view of music as it kept changing through the years, I do know that before my exposure to each of the aforementioned men I had no means whatsoever of knowing any of the things they articulated or demonstrated.

Each new association initiated a magnetic conversion. Everything I learned made my brain spin; everything I heard burned into my heart. I realize now that I was far more alert to the insuperable sounds and standards before me than I was to their full import. Actually, I understood meagerly, just about enough to sense what understanding could mean. Hofmann said from time to time: "You won't really know what I'm aiming at for ten years."

The assertion turned out to be flattering. It took much longer, but I was further along than during my earlier studies when I had made no attempt to weigh what I was assimilating, when evaluation had been entirely beyond my equipment and my courage.

From the time I went to Hofmann I began to see—dimly at first—that this kind of teaching provided ultimate goals, not ways and means. I was expected to absorb rather than to accept ideas; to appraise them and to determine, apart from their validity, whether or not they were "for me." When it came to applying principles, developing physical skills, and realizing aims pianistically, I was on my own. How liberated I felt, how certain I was that at last I had gained artistic independence!

It was a thrilling but temporary illusion, and Hofmann

was quick to straighten me out on that point. Actually, I was retracing a familiar pattern—floating on clouds of contagion and identification, swept along by the inspirational force of great guidance. Few are the responsive pupils who do not identify at some point with glamorous teachers. In turn, teachers who awaken us, even when they claim no eminence, often become one with whatever they awaken within us.

The unsung heroes and heroines who guide our elementary steps rarely have the chance to stir us in this way. Confronted with untutored pupils, responsible teachers work to build a solid foundation. They try to create enthusiasm, or at least not to kill it, while they explain essentials, supply methods, and inculcate disciplines. It is a sacrificial and thankless task.

I had to teach for many years to appreciate adequately the angelic patience of Mrs. Tapper, the precise technical training of Epstein, and especially the erudition and lucidity of Hutcheson's mellow mind. Without their tolerant instruction and altruistic interest, I doubt that further opportunities would have come to me at all.

Artist-teachers can generate fervor. They can transform routine work into a passionate search. They can lead us to revel in realms infinitely more spacious than anything they or we have within us. They can catapult us into the imaginative life and quicken us to experience art as an ecstasy to be treasured and loved. With them we live in eloquence without syntax, in music itself.

If artist-teachers can provide such seminal force, why is there so lamentably large a percentage of casualties among their gifted students? There are many reasons. At the top of the list is the blunt fact that inspirational teaching can be a precarious as well as revealing experience unless the student is technically, intellectually, and emotionally ready for it. Otherwise, the vision that awaits him may be hopelessly beyond his capacity to approach; the challenges it poses may produce paralysis instead of liberation. The time must be ripe, the foundation firm, or the white light may be merely blinding.

When the "golden opportunity" arises, the last thing to enter the enraptured pupil's mind is the question of whether or not he is prepared to make the most of it. Such objectivity cannot be expected of a starry-eyed youngster. It is almost as unrealistic to expect it of the average ambitious parent. The temptation to grasp an opportunity prematurely is far more common than the ability to forgo it.

The artist-teacher alone must decide this vital question. The degree to which he assumes this responsibility is the measure of his integrity. No one can censure a master for removing himself from rudimentary processes and step-by-step supervision. He is fully justified in that. He has something else to contribute, something unique. It can work miracles. And it can also work havoc. The subtler it is, the greater the possibility that a student's inferences will misinterpret its implications. It can go frightfully wrong if it is not instilled under precise surveillance and constant adjustment.

The absence of vigilance is a form of malpractice, of course, and it exists on all levels of teaching. It is always reprehensible, but somehow it is most shocking when it comes from those who trade on their acclaim as performers to entice hopeful aspirants as pupils. It is explainable only in the light of a remark once made to me by an international merchant of music who sells inspirational "shots in the arm" *en masse* between concert engagements. "Teaching," he said, "is a very good biz-ie-ness."

Obviously, a frustrating aftermath of high-level study may be entirely the fault of a pupil who fails to assume his responsibilities. But even when everything is just as right as it can be—when a talented and well-prepared student goes to a conscientious master at the perfect moment —the results cannot be guaranteed. Many other matters are involved which I shall touch upon in later chapters.

To return to my own studies at alpine altitudes, I found Hofmann at a most fortunate moment. The circumstances of my first four months of lessons provided the leisure for him to keep an alert eye and ear on every phase of my work. Frequently I went off the deep end and he had to fish me out.

I recall at one point being so carried away by interpretative and instrumental principles that I was convinced that a firm grasp of these principles could enable anyone, no matter how limited his talents, to acquire emotional force and intuitive power. When I told Hofmann so, he became red with rage.

"You are dead wrong," he said. "There are no such principles." But immediately he qualified and amplified his statement, carefully explaining that what he said was quite another thing from saying that a consummate artistry is achievable without technical and intellectual resources. "Anyone who thinks that," he said, "anyone fearful of 'ruining talent' through exposure to disciplines and knowledge, is equally misled."

Although every artist tells of some inspiring personality, some dramatic encounter that first inflamed his imagination and made music come alive, another fact strikes me even more forcibly. It is the emphasis placed on sheer craftsmanship by almost all the artists I ever knew who had the divine fire, their insistence on the need for a musician to know what is knowable about his art and every relevant subject. I am almost equally struck, in an opposite way, to discover how many practicing musicians are loath to probe their art or to learn the salient facts of their profession. Those most lacking in instinct are always most resistant to ideas.

My own practical experience has shown that the finest artists have both feet planted firmly on the ground while they breathe the loftiest air; that they constantly maintain a self-imposed obligation to nourish their natural gifts with hard-earned scholarship and a ceaseless quest for technical and emotional freedom. Something in them or in their arduous lives may occasionally keep them, as teachers, from demanding as much from their students. Nevertheless, their philosophy, methods, and achievements are all there for the skillful and enkindled to observe and to emulate.

Observation and inference and deduction all need to be more heavily invoked in the pupil-teacher relationships of our hectic world. When I spoke of the galaxy of musicians who were not only watchful masters but also sympathetic friends, I spoke of another period. The environment was different then. There was more time, or there seemed to be: time to impart and to learn; time to linger, to consider and reconsider; time to lose oneself in the effort to find oneself. There was even time for fraternity, for great men and busy men to assist others patiently in their struggles and aspirations, and time even for human exchange and understanding.

So it was in the company of artists who were alien to the spirit of the changing world around them, whose unchangeable ideals were contagious and catalytic. Because our relations were so full, because as altruistic mentors those men were so near and dear and of such incalculable inspiration to me, my feelings about them can never be wholly objective.

Further, the degree to which the artistic principles and standards they exemplified are illustrated by others has remained the critical foundation of my pianistic thinking. I think it only fair to admit to these facts so that the reader may fully discount them as we go along to meet other artists, some also from the past, but mostly those who are playing for us today.

Development

Ignace Jan Paderewski

It was after the First World War at a conference of the League of Nations that Paderewski and Georges Clemenceau met for the first time.

"You are M. Paderewski, the great pianist?" asked Clemenceau. Paderewski responded with a modest and courtly bow. "And now," continued Clemenceau, "you are the Premier of Poland." Again Paderewski bowed. "My, my," said Clemenceau with a deep sigh, "what a come-down."

Although the Tiger of France was bantering, he could be said to have overlooked the crux of Paderewski's triumphant career. Had Paderewski been just a pianist, he never could have been the musician or the man he was, nor could he have aroused the frenzied adulation of his vast and international public. Apart from his piano-playing, this patriotic and glamorous Pole was a world citizen. To everything and everybody he brought a princely manner, a beautifully trained mind, and a broadly humanized heart.

Paderewski had all the ingredients of a public idol. No one found it possible to be coolly objective about him. No one ever said that he was merely a good pianist or a nice man. He stimulated either slavish devotion or bitter antagonism.

The American critic Henry T. Finck, who wrote of Paderewski as of a deity, once added a nervous and revealing footnote addressed to piano students: "If your teacher sneers at Paderewski, leave him at once." When someone raved to the pianist Alfred Reisenauer about Paderewski's remarkable versatility and general culture, his ability to converse brilliantly on any subject and in any language, Reisenauer said: "Oh, yes. Paderewski knows everything—except music."

Clearly, there was no middle ground. People either worshipped Paderewski or dismissed him as a musical charlatan. I became one of the worshippers, but not immediately and not at one of his concerts. I first heard him when I was a tot, and the experience meant nothing at all to me. Again I heard him when I was eleven, and though I was still too young to appreciate the man's art, I do recall fully appreciating the hysteria it evoked and being swept along in the mad enthusiasm.

A few years later I was invited by Ernest Urchs, an executive of Steinway and Sons, to play the traditional Wagner and Mendelssohn marches at his daughter's wedding. It was a brilliant occasion, and almost every pianist of note was there. I thought that everyone had arrived, and I was seated at the piano waiting for a signal to begin. Suddenly I heard a stir, felt something electric in the atmosphere, and noticed every eye riveted on something behind me. Turning around quickly, I saw Paderewski standing in the doorway. I shall never forget that leonine authority, that quiet dignity and regal poise—the way this man's presence illuminated that room crowded with his most celebrated colleagues, as though a blinding light had been turned on.

Immediately after the ceremony, the happy throng besieged the bridal party. Before I had a chance to rise from the piano bench, Paderewski came right over, bent and kissed me on the forehead, and said: "You played beautifully. I am deeply moved. Thank you, dear boy."

What courtliness! The sanctified spot remained unwashed for a week, and but for parental pressure would have stayed that way indefinitely. I shall never forget him, never stop loving that generous soul. That was the man's overwhelming power, and it poured into everything he played.

Paderewski generated that same quality from platforms to hundreds of thousands, perhaps millions, who never met him. Attending a Paderewski concert was a human rather than a musical experience. One felt like an invited guest at a palace soiree. Paderewski was the gallant host. He greeted you with regal grace. You, in turn, were caught up in a collective passion for this captivating personality who brought glory not only to himself but also to all who paid him homage. There were few present who were not mesmerized long before Paderewski placed a finger on the keyboard.

But this is not the whole story. Paderewski was never the pianist's pianist. His colleagues were too busy counting his "clinkers" and ridiculing his old-school exaggerations to catch Paderewski's world spirit. Moreover, a sorcerer who hypnotized his audiences, a hero whose reddish-golden locks were snipped by beautiful women and publicized like a patent medicine, a knight in shining armor who rode forth in a special railroad car built according to his own design and appointed with kingly splendor complete to grand piano, tuner, valet, secretary, and chef—such a man was bound to predispose many against his flamboyant victories.

What kind of pianist was Paderewski? It is a good question, and RCA Victor enabled us to answer it more objectively by issuing in 1956 "The Art of Paderewski" on an LP Camden disc containing fourteen performances recorded late in Paderewski's career. Chopin, Schumann, and Beethoven provided the bulk of Paderewski's repertory, and all are represented here.

Five Chopin works immediately demonstrate Paderewski's primary musical and pianistic characteristics. In the "Revolutionary" Etude, Paderewski's grandiloquent romanticism serves the heroic sweep of this classic admirably. The playing has irresistible vitality, momentum, and eloquence. The pianist who could play this way had a rich imagination, could think for himself and make things come out his way.

The A flat Prelude, C sharp minor Waltz, and the étude in the same key from opus 25 all emerge as examples of old-fashioned playing with its best and worst features. Largess, warmth, and the power of evocation are apparent throughout, and so are rhythmic distortion and maudlin sentimentalities that loom today as tasteless theatricalities. The "Black Key" Etude is heard at practice tempo. It is an attempt at a virtuoso piece by a man no longer a virtuoso, by a man, we ought to remember, who had sacrificed years of daily practice to found a republic, no less.

Schumann's *"Warum"* discloses Paderewski's beautiful tone and poetic feeling. It also discloses the unhappy traits of melodramatic expressivity—the agonized cantilena, the torn-to-tatters meter, the hands played one before the other.

The first movement of Beethoven's Sonata, opus 27, no. 2, is tonally luscious, and the treatment of the left hand is especially sensitive and meaningful. Yet, again there is present no small violation of sentiment and simplicity.

Stojowski's "By the Brookside" is completely authoritative and beautifully played, full of freshness and flow, as is Liszt's F minor Concert Etude with a voluptuously enchanting coda by Leschetizky.

Debussy's *"Minstrels"* finds Paderewski on unfamiliar ground. It is not his kind of piece. He labors over it and misses its humor and implications. Although stylistically not much more authentic, his performances of two pieces by an earlier French master, Couperin's *"La Bandolin"* and *"Le Carillon,"* are touchingly tender.

Paderewski's playing at its best was a dream of noble unity and tonal beauty. These attributes are most convincingly displayed here, complete with old-master effects, in a moving performance of his own Nocturne in B flat. Such quiet fervor and such gentle urgency are indeed rare.

Here, then, are the sounds of Paderewski. Musically and instrumentally they are reliable replicas of his playing when he was no longer in his prime. But the most important element is absent. Paderewski was the kind of pianist whose inspiring presence was essential to a fully realized communication of his art. So, I imagine, was Liszt.

Such magnetism is not to be shrugged off. It is an elusive and unique power, given to few. And it goes into the making of music as well as into the making of a career. It is not always artistic excellence that carries us out of ourselves, that makes us know we have experienced something, that something deep within us has been stirred.

If, as Duse said, art is the communication of ecstasy, Paderewski was a supreme artist. But he and you had to be at the same place at the same time for the communion to cast its spell.

Wanda Landowska

WITH THE completion of Wanda Landowska's recordings of *The Well-Tempered Clavier* for Victor in 1954—a project that she proclaimed to be her "last will and testament"—the musical world inherited a treasurable legacy. It was the harvest of over half a century of back-breaking work, the fruit of a Bach scholarship and a dedication rare even in a realm in which dedication is a way of life.

I am certain of the reader's willingness to assume with me that the "48" are representative of Bach's ripest musical thought, and that Landowska is a supreme harpsichordist. I am also fairly certain that none of us wants to become embroiled in that tiresome argument about piano versus harpsichord as the best instrumental medium for these works. As for the clavichord, there should be little doubt that Bach with a harpsichord at his disposal would hardly have preferred to entrust these full-fledged compositions to the more limited domain of the clavichord.

In any event, the entire range of these diversified masterpieces has been realized on Landowska's Pleyel harpsichord with a variety of registration, color, sonority, and touch achievable only on the harpsichord. And this has been accomplished with imagination, eloquence, and rhythmic inspiration that prove once again Landowska's absolute stylistic sovereignty in the baroque sphere.

The cause of music would be greatly advanced were it possible to prevent all but a handful of performers from playing or recording another note of baroque music until they absorb and put into practice what can be learned today by anyone who wants to learn it.

This seems both the time and place to say firmly and publicly what is usually spoken *sotto voce* in scholastic conclave: with appallingly few exceptions, the performances of Bach's music in the concert hall and on recording disclose that the baroque scholarship of most performers is still in the dark ages. This is an exceptionally dismal fact because illumination has been available for some time now, and any real artistic integrity would acquire it. The sources, no longer inaccessible, include such recordings as the Landowska discs of the *Italian Concerto* and "Goldberg" Variations by Bach, and of many works by his French, English, and Italian precursors and contemporaries. Had they alone been properly evaluated, studied, and assimilated, some of our most famous conductors, instrumentalists, and vocalists might have saved themselves from innocently exposing an encyclopedic ignorance when taking baroque music to the platform and to disc.

How is this plausible, and how did it come to pass? Briefly, because of musical, theological, and social changes around the time of Bach's death, almost all of his music lay scattered and forgotten for nearly a century. Most of it was reassembled by nineteenth-century musicians who had the best will in the world but who knew little of seventeenth-century music and less about the man who synthesized it. So it was that Bach's music was revived, compiled, edited, and performed by a generation that spoke a musical language entirely different from his. A "tradition" stemming from the wrong century is responsible for the ubiquity of the unreliable editions and stylistically distorted performances generally accepted today. Accepted, that is, by all except a small band of scholarly musicians, Landowska among them.

Whoever regards the pursuit of stylistic validity as an academic activity unrelated to the emotions will quickly discover his error if he listens scrupulously to a few of Landowska's realizations in the "48"—when he hears in

Book One the rich five-part polyphony that emerges from
the constant arpeggio figure of the very first prelude, the
rhythmic vigor of the C sharp major Fugue, the beautiful melodic lines of the B flat minor Prelude, the tragic
tension of dissonance driving upon dissonance in the last
fugue. In Book Two, let him hear such eloquent achievements as the spaciousness of the A flat Prelude, the powerful climax of its fugue, the sonority of the three-part A
major and B minor fugues, and, above all, the declamatory freedom of the A minor Prelude.

Such freedom of the heart stems from the severest discipline of the mind and body. It demonstrates a complete
grasp of that improvisational age in which publication
was rare and expensive, in which manuscripts were prepared mainly for the composer himself or for pupils and
disciples. All of which, in addition to the figured bass
notation, led to the labor-saving and time-saving device
of writing scores in a musical Morse code for those
thoroughly familiar with the common practice of the
day.

This left the performer free to ornament the skeleton.
But how? That touchy subject inevitably brings forth
the cliché that immediately stamps the uninformed: "It
is purely a matter of taste." In all aspects of art, taste is
certainly an essential, but taste not based on knowledge
can go woefully wrong. Many important things about
ornamentation can be learned from hearing Landowska,
by listening and observing hard enough and long enough
to discover the harmonic, rhythmic, and melodic basis of
seventeenth-century embellishment. The hearer may
hand himself a diploma from the first moment he feels
the desire to change the name "ornamentation" to "ex-
pressimentation."

Landowska's performances and recordings have always
exemplified the least-known and most salient facts concerning the baroque period. They demonstrate that baroque scores, as originally set down, were rarely more

than outlines of the composer's intentions; that ornamentation was *not* a device for prolonging sonority, but an improvisational element that determined such crucial matters as harmonic consonance and dissonance, melodic progression, and rhythmic design.

Further, they compel us to realize that baroque appoggiaturas have no relation whatsoever to modern grace notes; that their typographical placement and smallness were intended only to isolate them from the harmonies as indicated by figured basses. Landowska again shows her comprehensive stylistic knowledge by supplying embellishments omitted from the text but demanded in the formulas that Bach so frequently utilized and often did not bother to notate because of their familiarity to his contemporaries.

Landowska enables us to discover that, although the manner of executing ornaments in an improvisational period was necessarily flexible, the shapes of those ornaments were schematically inflexible; that trills never, but *never*, begin on main notes, and that inverted mordents, as we know them and as they deluge most nineteenth-century editions, were unknown to Bach.

She shows that there is no such thing as "the Bach style." Bach had many styles, and Landowska reveals their broad and subtle differences as the composer alters his vocabulary to conform to his French, Italian, English, or German models.

Landowska's performances also disclose Bach as the Gothic architect. She expresses his edifices in broad acoustical designs: the music "rises in broad terraces, like primitive temples." The animation and independence of Landowska's phrasing further enable her to communicate both the structures and the details within, and to keep them equally clear.

Were Landowska's re-creations merely definitive disclosures of the essential differences between baroque styles and all others, that alone would make them sig-

nificant. But she reveals those differences not only histor-
ically but also as they affect the most rhetorical and dramatic aspects of music—those aspects which make the
difference between living interpretation and moribund
abdication of all but routine responsibility.

Bach—above all composers—exposes those performers
who hardly deserve the name of musician because they
have not assumed a decent minimal responsibility toward the composer they pretend to worship; he exposes
those lesson-sellers who do not deserve the name of
teacher. Landowska's art could do a lot for them, but
only if they were stimulated to do more for themselves.

In addition to stylistic scholarship and instrumental
mastery, Landowska possesses magical individuality and
expressiveness. Even when an interpretation or a tempo is
at drastic variance with one's preconceived ideas, her
convictions are so solidly grounded, her intentions are so
clear, and the force of her personality is so overwhelming,
that one is ready to grant her conception or, more usually,
to succumb.

On one matter alone I am not willing to succumb, but it
has not to do with Landowska the artist. It concerns the
commentaries that she supplied for the record sleeves.
She first states that "Bach's Fugues and also the Preludes are masterpieces of the science of counterpoint."
Later she refers to "The Fugue—a high and involved art
form." And still later: "the relationship between these
Preludes and Fugues is often undeniable" and "it is
plain that Bach selected and coupled them on account of
the relationship they show."

First, counterpoint is not a science; it is entirely an art.
Next, there is no such thing as a "fugue form." Fugue is
not a form, but a texture with no power whatsoever to
determine the shape of a composition. As for the relationship between the preludes and fugues being "often undeniable," I deny it completely unless Landowska meant
that the Bach who selected and coupled these works was

a man who valued the relationship of dramatic contrasts above far-fetched resemblances. I know only one case in which a prelude and fugue—the twenty-third in Book One—show more than a casual thematic relationship.

But the playing's the thing. Forever are we grateful for the heart and the labor that produced an art that is an indispensable key to the baroque style; for the way in which Landowska utilized the opportunities to become the creative partner of the composer—opportunities that this style not only provides, but actually necessitates.

Landowska's work is therefore far more than interpretative. It is the classic demonstration of the principles upon which Bach's art was founded. I infinitely prefer to think of her "last will and testament," and everything else she plays, as Bach's will and Landowska's testament. And not as an end, but as a new beginning.

Wilhelm Backhaus

IT WAS a source of poignant pleasure to attend the triumphal return of Wilhelm Backhaus to the American scene in 1954 after a twenty-eight-year absence, to witness the excitement of an audience that jam-packed Carnegie Hall and welcomed Backhaus as a beloved master and public favorite. The occasion was especially significant to those who saw it in perspective, who brought memories along.

When the blond, stocky young Nordic we remembered appeared before us as a venerable, slightly bent, and white-haired man of seventy, we were reminded sharply how many years had passed. When he began to play—and he had to begin with the wild applause still echoing around him—we were astounded and stirred to find his gigantic technical command unimpaired by time. But now it was guided by a gentler and more meditative spirit, molded by an authoritative maturity that comes only after a lifetime of devotion to art. When he had summed up the all-Beethoven program with a towering performance of opus 111, thousands of thrilled men and women responded with a blazing ovation.

My memory roved back to the early twenties, when Backhaus played year after year to row upon row of vacant seats in the modest spaces of Aeolian Hall. Essentially, in the incredible ease and naturalness of his pianism, in the unassuming simplicity and absorption of the man, Backhaus was much the same artist and personality then. And he was far from unknown. Even before he won the Rubinstein Prize in 1905, Backhaus was internationally celebrated as a prodigious virtuoso. How, then, can we reconcile an early public indifference and the electrifying acclaim that a substantially similar experience later produced within substantially the same generation?

I was careful to say public indifference because Backhaus never failed to win a *succès d'estime* among professional musicians. They always knew his qualities, always marveled at his instrumental perfection, his titanic mastery that scorned every complexity, his unsurpassed freedom and endurance. There was never a time when Backhaus could not toss off any or all of the Chopin études or the Brahms-Paganini Variations with an imperturbable calm, an implacable security that left one open-mouthed. Not everyone, for only the pianists really knew what was happening before their eyes and ears, knew how to measure such achievement. There they all sat, in breathless astonishment and envy and despair. But pianists do not fill concert halls and rarely buy their tickets.

The paying public stayed away in droves. Onstage, Backhaus was a shy, unaffected, recessive personality whose sensational capacities were so unsensationally projected that lay audiences remained totally unconscious of his fabulous accomplishments. Offstage, this pale, modest, silent man was an unlikely drawing-room lion, especially in the early twenties, when anti-German sentiment ran high.

Backhaus's preoccupation was with music. His was the European tradition in which the music comes first, the artist afterward. The extent to which this is still true was illustrated by an incident told to me by my wife, the pianist Constance Keene. While touring in Germany, she heard a famous orchestra in a Mozart concerto with a piano soloist who could not possibly have survived the preliminaries of our major contests. The audience applauded madly. Puzzled, my wife later asked a member of the orchestra how such a musically educated public could respond so warmly to so dreadful a performance.

"Oh," he answered, "they weren't applauding the soloist. They were applauding Mozart."

Backhaus observed that in America, too, they were willing to applaud Mozart, as well as Bach, Beethoven, Brahms, and Chopin. But only, he ruefully noted in the old days, when these composers were played by Paderewski, Hofmann, Godowsky, Rachmaninoff, Lhevinne, Gabrilowitsch, Bauer, Rosenthal, Levitzki, and still others who were less acclaimed but today would loom as titans of the keyboard. These latter, Backhaus among them, were not numbered among the elite during the golden age of pianism.

Not only was the competition overpowering, but Backhaus also learned that there was no middle ground. Whether it was flagpole-sitting or piano-playing, a man was on top or nowhere at all. Backhaus left our shores a great pianist and an embittered man resolved not to return.

Almost thirty years passed. Our people had become more and more musically experienced and cultivated. All of Backhaus's former rivals had vanished, their loss lamented by the older generation. Meanwhile a new audience had arisen. It was buying recordings, and so discovered Backhaus to be the possessor of pianistic maturity and virtuosity not easily found today.

At that moment Herbert Barrett, a public-relations counselor with no little taste and courage, expanded his activities to include concert management. What awaited him was anybody's guess, but one thing was certain: unless he could find a few stars to represent, he would be beaten before he started. He confided to me that he was thinking of bringing Backhaus back, and asked what I thought of the idea. I said that Backhaus was certainly a phenomenal pianist; that his recordings had made his name better known and more widely admired than ever before in our country; and that particularly in view of the dearth of pianists of comparable stature, his return struck me as an entirely happy and promising idea. Shortly thereafter, Barrett persuaded Backhaus that the American stage was set for a proper appreciation of his art, that the timing seemed perfect.

The rest we know. But I must confess, despite my optimism, that I was totally unprepared for the magnitude of Backhaus's success. Of course, he played all the notes, and brilliantly. But he always had. There were no tricks, no follies. There never had been. Everything emerged with a consummate polish, from dainty delicacy to granitic power. When had it not? What Backhaus had acquired in the interim—and it was to be expected from such an artist—was a mellower spirit, a deeper understanding brought to a more profound repertoire.

That is a great deal, a very great deal. But essentially Backhaus has been the same kind of pianist throughout his entire career. A meticulous craftsman, he is more expert than rapturous. When music demands dramatic utterance, melodic expressivity, and poetic ardor, his gaze does not reach from earth to heaven. Consequently, in precisely the most magical and moving moments of the serious music he plays—in the sonatas and concertos of Beethoven and Brahms—we miss the glow of the "fine frenzy." And we always did.

But among contemporary pianists, Backhaus emerged as a complete colossus, and it is another sign of the times that an artist who does not evoke romantic drama from a dramatic literature holds a supreme place among us. As an executant, Backhaus eminently deserves this place. As an inspired interpreter, as a visionary, he is victorious today by default.

One aspect of his emotional appeal, however, is a positive one. Although Backhaus the musician may have lacked romantic fervor, Backhaus the man who returned in his seventies to conquer had a strong romantic appeal.

Our imaginations are deeply stirred by those who remain undefeated by time. Our sympathies are aroused by injustice, our esteem by tenacity.

An artist, and a truly distinguished one, who embodies the musical history of more than half a century is bound to evoke romantic awe. Backhaus must know this, but the intellectual honesty that he has maintained throughout his time-honored career makes us know that he would be the last man to exploit it.

Artur Rubinstein

JUST AS my taxi drove up in front of Artur Rubinstein's house, he dashed out of the entrance, hat in hand, sprinted to the cab, and bounced into a seat, his face glowing beneath the frizzled halo of his silver hair. It was January 1956, a few days before Rubinstein launched his Herculean series of five Carnegie Hall concerts within two weeks, playing seventeen concertos with an orchestra conducted by Alfred Wallenstein. During the same period, Rubinstein was committed to seven rehearsals and two recording sessions. The day I called for him, we were on our way to judge a dozen young pianists for *Musical Talent in Our Schools,* an annual project sponsored by *The New York Times* and its radio station, WQXR.

"Considering everything that's going on," I said, "I really feel guilty about asking you to serve on the jury this year. But I'm so glad to find you looking so well and vigorous."

"My dear," he answered, "it is not really so difficult. After all, I've played all these works all my life. Never well enough. Now, before it's too late, I want to play them all together, and perhaps more decently. I won't make a penny, of course. But maybe I'll be able to feel that I've accomplished something better than just pounding keys for fifty years."

As we approached the Times Building, Rubinstein reached for his wallet. "What's that for?" I asked.

"Why should this be on you?" he asked.

"It's not on me," I answered. "It's on *The Times.*"

Suddenly the driver turned around and said: "Nope. It's on *me.* I heard Mr. Rubinstein on TV last night, and it's an honor to have him ride my cab. Wait'll I tell my wife about this. Boy!"

The driver's generous impulse was not accepted, but the incident remained in my mind to illustrate the power of Rubinstein's warmth to arouse reciprocal warmth in all who encounter him.

The auditions are frequently preceded by a luncheon to which publisher Arthur Hays Sulzberger invites his executive associates in honor of the guest judge. Rubinstein's appearances are eagerly anticipated, and invariably stimulate a thorough relaxation of the individual and collective dignity of that thoughtful group. Rubinstein is a free spirit, free of the constrictions that enwrap most of us. His love of laughter is contagious. He delights in sharing his fabulous experiences and his endless fund of stories, which he tells in any dialect of almost any language, complete with graphic grimaces and gestures.

Short and stocky, and anything but a beauty, Rubinstein has every grace of manner and speech. One tilt of his head, and you see imperious Nero; a blink of an eye, and you see a Hollywood cutie. One arm flung out, a sudden lurch, and you would swear he was a matador averting an onrushing bull. At luncheon that day he told many hilarious stories. In one of them he impersonated the tall King Haakon of Norway by standing on a dining-room chair, imitating, in a commanding voice, the monarch's speech of welcome to tiny King Victor Emmanuel of Italy. He then imitated Victor Emmanuel's response by dropping to his knees, his chin barely visible above the tablecloth, his voice a plaintive chirp. Rubinstein's humor is rooted in the accuracy of a deep perception. What is so compelling, so characteristic, is his exuberance, his irrepressible joy of living and giving.

Between stories, Rubinstein's conversation grows serious until something touches off another funny story. During one interim the talk veered around to international matters. I think Elliott M. Sanger, co-founder of WQXR, music critic Howard Taubman of *The New York Times,* and I were the only ones not surprised to find Rubinstein impressively informed. We three knew of Rubinstein's profound concern with political conditions, particularly of his indignation over artists who boast of "not mixing" politics and art.

"What kind of people are they?" he asks. "What moral responsibility can they have to remain aloof from humanity's constant struggle against oppression? Bah—they simply have no capacity to think or to feel! Their world is their own size; and they sound like it."

At the auditions, Rubinstein was no longer the fighter or the raconteur. But he was no less lovable. Gallantly rising to shake hands with each youngster, he would listen intently, showing each one a courtly interest and respect, offering sober advice and humor. "You know, my dear child," he said to one trembling participant, "you are very musical, but you cannot afford to be as lazy as I was when I was your age. How I hated to practice! And I never did until I came to your country—may I say *our* country? I am a proud citizen now, you know. But this country is so difficult for us pianists. They expect us to play every little note. Dreadful. Now I practice very hard. Please promise me you will, too, yes?"

Later that afternoon, when the auditions were over, I hailed a cab and we got in. When I asked: "Artur, where may I drop you?" and he answered: "Steinway's," the driver's head spun around, as he exclaimed: "Have I the pleasure of driving the great master in my cab?" It developed that we had struck another fan, but a sad one, who immediately confided that for weeks he had been trying unsuccessfully to buy a seat for one of Rubinstein's concerto concerts.

"My dear friend," said Rubinstein, sighing in despair. "How I wish I could get one for you, but I really can't.

For the past few weeks our phone hasn't stopped ringing. We've discovered a hundred relatives we never heard about. It's awful. I'm sorry. Please forgive me."

After we let Rubinstein out, the cab-driver said: "I guess he'd be a great man no matter what he did. You know, my wife and I go to everything, but that man gives us the biggest thrill we get from anybody. I don't know if he loves music more than other musicians, but he sure makes you feel he does, and that he loves to play it for you. Great guy. Wait'll I tell my wife about this!"

It was funny to take two cabs and to hear the same phrase from the drivers of both. It sounded planted. It was life being stranger than fiction, a typical Rubinstein incident. I was frankly amazed, and thought to myself that this sort of thing happens only in such cities as Vienna. Perhaps I underestimated Rubinstein's fame. Anyway, it brought home to me that Rubinstein occupies a unique place. To his friends he is more than a fascinating companion, to the public, more than a pianist. He is a symbol of warmth, of life lived in gaiety at an exhilarating pace, fortissimo and *con amore,* as none of us others can possibly live it. Just as he gets to the heart of the music he plays, so he reaches the hearts of people.

Rubinstein lives up to the public's dream of a celebrity's life. You are likely to meet him in any corner of the globe constantly surrounded by admirers. He is at home everywhere. If he takes you out to lunch or to dinner, you find yourself in one of the world's finest restaurants seated before a Roman feast, inhaling the voluptuous scents of magnificent wines and glamorously perfumed women. Everyone stares at him or comes over for a word or an autograph.

In his own lovely homes, whether in New York or Paris or Beverly Hills, the red carpet has never been known to be rolled up. The same royal treatment awaits a distinguished celebrity and a nobody. Their host rushes around tirelessly, sampling champagne to see that it is properly cooled, replacing a cheese that has not quite reached the right age with one that has, anxiously watching to see whether a guest has everything or wants more or something else.

The man is a dynamo, driving himself around the clock. After one concert in which he had played the Brahms D minor, Beethoven B flat, and Tchaikovsky B flat minor concertos, plus encores, the inexhaustible Rubinsteins gave a supper party for some thirty guests. The dining-room tables were covered with an international cuisine especially prepared by Mrs. Rubinstein, who furnished the recipe of every delicacy as she heaped the goodies on the plates. Rubinstein kept circling around the other rooms helping everybody to drinks and smokes, all the while talking charmingly and incessantly. After a few hours, people started to leave, one by one. At two a.m. my wife and I rose to go. Rubinstein, jumping to his feet, would not hear of it. "But you have a rehearsal at nine tomorrow," I protested.

"Look," said Rubinstein, "as a professional you should know that I can't possibly sleep now. I want to be with my friends. I want to talk. Only amateurs think artists get tired at concerts. We are tired before. We yawn, we are sleepy. But the concert revives us completely. Come on! Let's have another glass of champagne. I feel wonderful!"

His physical and spiritual stamina, his unquenchable ebullience, have yielded not only their artistic rewards but also their artistic punishments. For many years Rubinstein rode entirely on talent, spending his incredible energies recklessly. In his youth he had not invested in the performer's old-age-security plan: the acquisition of a solid technical foundation. He allowed himself to make appearances for which he was inadequately prepared, trusting to luck. With him, luck is the inspiration of the moment. He has on occasion dropped enough notes at a concert to make up another one. Despite these costly blunders, he won his share of adoring audiences, but not everywhere. The critics went after him, and conductors shied away from him, especially in the United States and England. Eventually it was Rubinstein himself who squarely faced up to the fact that he was not properly fulfilling his gifts. But he did not face it alone.

At long last he met the right woman, Aniela Mlynarski, a sensitive beauty with good hard sense. When they married during the early thirties, after Rubinstein had batted around the world since the turn of the century, he began to assume the full responsibilities and disciplines of a serious musician and performer. For five years he buckled down to the hardest work he had ever done. Then Sol Hurok came along with an offer to take Rubinstein under his management for another try at the United States market.

"You'll lose your shirt," Rubinstein warned, mindful of his previous failures here.

"I'll take the chance," Hurok said.

They did not sign a contract. They never have signed one. Hurok is no flesh-peddler. An artist in his own line, he has an acute sense of quality and timing. The last of the impresarios, he regarded Rubinstein as the last of the romantic pianists. They made a perfect pair. But success came slowly. Rubinstein played many great concerts before anything big started to happen—many concerts at which the proverbial cannon could have been shot off without hitting a soul. It was ten more years before Rubinstein sat solidly on top of the heap.

Rubinstein's career has paralleled the career of the phonograph, most coincidentally since the depression, in its steady rise to public favor. More than those of any other pianist, Rubinstein's performances have been perpetuated on discs, right from their earliest experimental days. As artist and medium grew in mutual ascent, Rubinstein's recordings undoubtedly aided in converting his reputation as a brilliantly gifted *bon vivant*, a man of impeccable taste in the arts and in wine, women, and cigars, into that of a sovereign pianist.

One is compelled to approach an artist of Rubinstein's stature with an individual measuring-rod. His own originality and courage compel it. In his youth, musical Europe was still smoldering from the war that revolved around Wagner and Brahms and embroiled all their cohorts. In Rubinstein's early teens he was a protégé of Brahms's great friend Joseph Joachim. Yet, Rubinstein already had the daring and musical curiosity to steal off to hear the Wagner operas at the risk of offending Joachim and of losing his protection. Into the homes of Rubinstein's fellow students the youthful nonconformist smuggled *Lohengrin, Meistersinger,* and *Tristan,* carrying them all in his phenomenal memory.

When one takes exception to a performance by a musician of Rubinstein's caliber, equipment, and experience, it must be from the broadest point of view. For here is a man with undeniable genius. And genius can conciliate anything. "When I go wrong," he once said, "I go way off the deep end. Yet, it is not so bad as timidity. What troubles me about so many of the younger musicians I hear is that they think small and act small. They are afraid to feel, afraid to make a mistake. Who cares about that if you say something, say it with passion and pleasure? Piano-playing is a dangerous life. It must be lived dangerously. Take chances, take what comes. The world hates a coward. Who can always play safe? Who wants to? Plunge, give yourself entirely to your art and to your audiences. No one can resist that." He opened his arms wide, wide enough to embrace the globe. "And," he concluded, shaking a raised index finger for emphasis, "if you don't lose five pounds and ten drops of blood, you haven't played a concert."

Man and artist are of a piece. Whether he is the melodramatic actor lifting his hands from keyboard to ceiling as he plays Falla's "Fire-Dance" or sits with noble dignity

before Beethoven's *"Appassionata,"* he is the incarnation
of expressivity and emancipation. He can be maddeningly
careless, but nothing is cheap or mundane when he does
it. He can fly in the face of every convention and conviction, yet manage it with supreme elegance, manage to
arouse enthusiasm and to preserve our respect. His memory is dazzling, far beyond the scope of the standard
piano literature. Without score, he can play the orchestral parts of most violin and cello concertos, the piano
parts of the most important vocal and chamber-music literature. One night, happy about his performance of the
Brahms B flat Concerto earlier that evening, he sat down
and played the entire second act of *Carmen,* singing every
aria and every word.

"When I was a boy," he says, "I had a fiendish talent
for learning. In a way it was a curse. Never did I have the
patience to polish anything, to work at it over and over.
Often I had the nerve to play music I hardly knew and
had no business playing. Do you know that I first performed the Franck *Symphonic Variations* in Madrid after
studying it for thirty-six hours on a train? I don't try
things like that any more. Now I work. But at heart I am
still a gypsy. Music is in my blood, and it is more important to me than my piano-playing."

This is the characteristic that always gave Rubinstein's
playing the quality of inspired improvisation. Today it
is still there, but in moderation, tempered by greater artistic repose and maturity. His playing can be uneven, but
it is always unmistakably Rubinstein. Regardless of his
fettle at a given moment, whatever he elects to play from
his gigantic repertory reflects an incomparably rich and
imaginative personality. Even the expression on his face,
the flashing eyes beneath the bushy brows, the head
thrown back heroically or bent forward as a gentle smile
lifts the corners of his mouth—everything about Rubinstein contributes to his fascination.

Largess has been one of the primary motifs of Rubin-

stein's life. No other pianist of our time has done more
to discover and further the music of his contemporaries
or given so much to encourage the creative spark wherever he found it. Rubinstein was the self-appointed "attaché" to *Les Six* when that youthful group of French
composers was struggling for recognition. He excavated
Villa-Lobos from the orchestra pit of a motion-picture
house; he was the first to perform and, in some cases, to
transcribe music by Szymanowski, Albéniz, Falla, Stravinsky, and others. Although he may not always have assumed the entire responsibilities of his gifts pianistically,
he has never ceased to devote all his remarkable resources
and all of himself to the service of music itself.

It follows that no musician has given more happiness or
drawn more from his life in art.

Walter Gieseking

EVERY NOW and then one attends a performance that casts a spell of enchantment. It does not happen often. But Walter Gieseking's all-Debussy program at Carnegie Hall in 1955 was such an occasion. From the first note of the *Suite Bergamasque* to the fourth encore, *"General Lavine,"* it was an evening of magic. Few of the many musicians present would have challenged the publisher's right to print on the music: "Private Property of Walter Gieseking. No Trespassing!"

He evoked excitement, transparency, and movement throughout. Occasionally he would choose to hold his audience hypnotically suspended through an ethereal pianissimo or a section of tremulous repose. With endless refinements of touch and pedaling, one phrase grew out of another. Climaxes developed with the inevitable force and upward sweep that stamp the musician and the architectural master. In each piece we perceived an artist living in the very sound he was creating. He painted, so to speak, with fingers dipped in the hues of Degas, Renoir, Manet, and Bonnard. The sum was a tableau of surpassing beauty, color, and poetry emerging from a Baldwin.

Sometime later I turned to the Columbia LP recordings of Gieseking's 1951 performances of Debussy's two books of preludes, *Children's Corner,* and *Suite Bergamasque;* the reissue of the artist's 1939 playing of *Estampes* and *Images;* and, finally, to Gieseking's Angel recordings of Ravel's piano works. These, too, confirmed the fact that Gieseking clearly ruled the domain of impressionism.

I found myself listening time and time again to one piece after another, enthralled and mystified. Mystified that the unearthly sounds could possibly come from a piano or from any determinable instrument set into vibration by human energy. This is disembodied aural beauty, the intoxication of sensuous perfume, the blaze of sunlight, the shimmer of moonlight on water.

And how is this done? It is done with love, with knowledge, with vision. It is also done with a technical equipment adequate to the demands of a glowing imagination. Only the perfect co-ordination of the strongest arms and the most independent fingers can produce such delicate suavity. Arms and fingers are not all, for Gieseking's pedaling was a miracle. He could pedal throughout changing harmonies, retaining for each its own identity; he could pedal throughout a melodic line, yet keep the progressive action of the cantabile.

The most kaleidoscopic mixtures of colors paradoxically emerge spotlessly clean and clear. Releases are as precise as attacks. Gieseking could increase or reduce dynamics in the space of a split second, from the subtlest pianissimo to the most sonorous fortissimo (and the other way around), and have it sound absolutely inevitable, all of a piece. He had unique command of suspended motion with vibration, like that of a hummingbird hovering over a flower. One hears a perfectly spaced, pearly articulation for some figuration, and above or below it another figuration will come through as undulation produced as though by a boneless and muscleless hand. And always the music came first, always the motion of the drama was carried forward. Such playing is the ultimate in mastery and sensuous elegance, the result of a scrupulous care that marks genius. Everything is present to the nth degree: knowledge, precision, tonal color, radiance, iridescence, limpidity. And their balances and blendings are luminous and wondrous.

In somewhat the way that people's difficulties make life more bearable to others, it was a source of encouragement to many pianists to discover that Gieseking did

not possess a comparable corner on every style. Especially
in his recordings of the complete piano solo works of
Mozart, issued prior to the Mozart bicentennial, quite
another Gieseking was disclosed.

One had anticipated that the matchless knowledge,
interpretative subtlety, and emotional inspiration that Gieseking lavished upon the music of Debussy and Ravel
would now be bestowed upon Mozart. One had expected
that the same artistic responsibility would be directed in
the same measure of devotion to the woefully misunderstood genius of geniuses. One was therefore doubly astonished and reluctant to find that Gieseking lent his
great gifts and prestige to further the fictional nineteenth-
century tradition of Mozart as a miniaturist. "Most people," Edward Fitzgerald said in essence, "cannot believe
that Mozart is so powerful because he is so beautiful." It
is even harder to believe that in the hands of a Gieseking
Mozart could emerge so divested of both power *and*
beauty.

Mozart's masterpieces of piano writing are principally
confined to his concertos and chamber music with both
string and wind instruments. The exceptions, the sublime handful among the sixty-three solo works, are the
three fantasies, K.394, 397, and 475; the B minor Adagio
K.540; A minor Rondo K.511, and Little Gigue K.574; the
Mannheim sonatas K.309 and 311; the sonatas in A
minor K.310, B flat K.333, C minor K.457; and, finally,
the public's favorite in A, K.331, with its famed theme-
and-variations opening and "Turkish March" finale.

The larger part of Mozart's piano solos has less aesthetic interest, for it consists of improvisations by the
child prodigy which were later notated, such other interesting but innocent compositions as the Sonata in C,
K.545, labeled by Mozart a "Little Clavier Sonata for
Beginners," and some pot-boilers with which the mortal
immortal paid off publishing debts. Most of these works,
to put it harshly, were written with three of Mozart's fin-

gers while the rest of him was occupied with inspirations of overwhelming potency and perfection.

Nevertheless, there is no question that, from the historical and musicological points of view, there were high merit and justification in issuing Mozart's complete works for solo piano. But Gieseking was not the man for the project.

Seldom, if ever, have I been so baffled and confounded that such an artist, like so many lesser colleagues, could have been so misled. Where in these performances are the Gieseking vitality, variety of touch, and singing tone? No one expected even him to convert the hack works into great works, and it is perhaps too much to ask an interpreter to bring a spirit of sanctification to weak themes and routine structures. Nevertheless, the degree of an artist's sympathy and skill can be tellingly demonstrated by his ability to bring luminosity to pale material, to discover, intensify, and extend meanings. And no artist met this test more convincingly than Gieseking. But not here.

The miniature frame persists even through the powerfully inspired works of Mozart at his most Beethovenish, as in the Fantasy K.475. The playing here is as angular and static as it is wonderfully rounded and forward-moving in Gieseking's Debussy and Ravel. The notes themselves are all there, clear and dry, but they take us nowhere except right back to the mute symbols on the page. Metrical quantities are also all there, but the rhythm lacks tension in big moments and flexibility in simple song. The suppression of Mozart's intensity, color, brilliance, and wit perpetuates an all too common stylistic error that the most superficial curiosity would destroy instantly. Even a casual observation of available manuscripts, tables of ornaments, and letters by Mozart and his contemporaries would help an artist to render an overdue service to authenticity.

In one letter Mozart enlightens us by reporting to his father a performance of one of his symphonies: "It went magnificently! We had forty violins, ten double basses, six bassoons, and all the woodwinds doubled." Mozart's own words demonstrate what to him constitutes a magnificent Mozart performance, disclosing it to be in sharp opposition to musicians who believe they serve him faithfully through reduction and repression.

The essence of the Haydn-Mozart-Beethoven styles is drama. It comes as a shock to hear the strange, deeply tragic B minor Adagio emerge as a far less emotional, far less evocative work than, for example, Ravel's *"Le Gibet"* as only Gieseking played it. Furthermore, Mozart's mature keyboard works were not written for either the clavichord or the harpsichord. They were written for a piano; not our modern grand, of course, but one whose clanging brilliance compensated for less sonority. And it had a pedal, that soul of the instrument which no pianist used more imaginatively than Gieseking. On behalf of Mozart, he used it sparingly or not at all.

A fragile sonority for Mozart the dramatist is damaging enough, but a curtailed expressivity renders him lifeless. One can shrug a shoulder and smile sadly at some uncomprehending pianist who will take a visionary and passionate Mozart masterpiece and treat it with the cool efficiency of a respectful robot. But from Gieseking, whose flaming power in the French repertoire is a lesson for all, it is impossible to accept a strait-jacketed Mozart, a Mozart without Italian color or Viennese sparkle.

Beethoven, Brahms, and Schumann emerged closer to the summit of Gieseking's interpretative realizations, but they too were not wholly his composers. He was not so comfortable, not so convincing or enlightening in this repertoire. The sounds that came out of his piano were no less lovely; it was the music that often lost its inherent emotional content and ceased to become a spontaneous communication.

As a Bach interpreter, Gieseking was more ingratiating than authentic. I heard him play the G major French

Suite, the D minor English Suite, and the E minor Partita. They sounded fluent, airy, and beautifully polished, except when the treacherous contrapuntal figuration occasionally caused an impairment of clarity. Everything was deliberately held within a reduced dynamic frame. Consequently, there was never a moment of harshness. Neither was there a moment of drama or declamation. Pianistically, they were superb. Stylistically, quite false.

It is obvious that almost nothing that an artist of Gieseking's stature would do in music could be totally devoid of interest or of some commanding trait. But inevitably we are forced to recognize that his final and full powers were summoned on behalf of one style alone, that of French impressionism. Its range of resplendent expressivity extracted from Gieseking a rare state of inspiration, the kind that depersonalizes an artist and enables his auditors to catch glimpses of eternity.

For this we can forget what there is to forget. For this we can remember, and even revere.

Guiomar Novaës

No woman pianist has ever become celebrated in quite the glamorous way that Liszt or Paderewski or songbird Jenny Lind became celebrated.

For more decades than a gentleman has any right to compute, Guiomar Novaës has been a pianist of the first caliber. Yet I think it is accurate to say that she is not among the famous figures of our time except to musicians and to a limited, loyal audience to whom she is an idol, for whom she can do no wrong, on whom her superb pianism has had a consistently secure hold.

These are her just rewards, for Mme Novaës is a pianist to the manner born. She has talent, ease, dignity, and elegance that have long made her a royal executant. She has never stooped to conquer. And she has never lessened her devotional absorption in music since the day of her brilliant debut in Paris at the age of sixteen.

Such is her simplicity and lucidity at the piano that one grasps instantly what any piece she plays is all about. At the same time one discovers what Mme Novaës is all about. We discern a modest, deeply dedicated artist, a woman proud to be a woman, and so fully in command of herself that she is also in full command of her music, her instrument, and her public. Her expressivity is entirely personal. It has been that of a consecrated wife and mother and musician who sees life whole, who speaks from the heart of joys and sorrows she herself has known. Her playing reveals intuition, emotional sensibility, and personal discipline, all fused in an art that, for all its sensuous beauty, has a highly moral and spiritual quality.

Away from the platform, Novaës has a Latin politeness

and formality. In her musical opinions she is usually taciturn. But whenever she chooses to speak, she speaks frankly—sometimes ruthlessly, as some young pianists who have sought her advice can testify. She will not curry favor. Nor is she inclined to give quarter in the interests of expediency. Managerial and recording officials admit that Novaës can be worrisome and even denunciatory, yet most of them agree that differences and difficulties are easily outweighed by artistic rewards.

Her teacher, Isidor Philipp, told of one of Novaës's first lessons with him when she was thirteen. She played a Chopin piece. Beautiful it was, but subject to pedagogical suggestions. Philipp explained his ideas. "I understand," said little Guiomar. She sat down and played it precisely as before. Patiently, Philipp again explained. "I understand," said the prodigy. Again she played it, exactly as before. After a third repetition of this episode Philipp gave up, utterly convinced that her way was best. Certainly for her.

Evidently at an age when her contemporaries were still playing with dolls, Guiomar already showed signs of the most effective of all artistic elements: individuality. She has always made her own laws and almost always has justified them. There are undeniable moments when she does not succeed, when one is puzzled, when one has to stand on one's head in reorientation of convictions in order to understand her premise. But it is often worth it, just for the pleasure of observing how imagination and authority—no matter how capricious—can produce a fascinating and provocative example of re-creation. Pianistically, Mme Novaës has an effortless and spontaneous approach to the instrument. Therefore her tone always sings. Therefore limpid articulation and luminous gradations of color pervade everything. All with crystalline clarity. All with humanness and an abiding faith.

Both were demonstrated at Novaës's 1954 recital in New York. Once she missed the final top note of a deliciously played piece. For a moment she looked askance, then impulsively stuck out her tongue at the offending note. Everyone roared. In her opening work, she played a particularly exposed wrong note. Later she explained: "God wanted to keep me humble for the rest of the concert."

The fervent applause that Novaës earned from this recital seemed to me more than a testimony to her subtle artistry. Somewhere in the quality of the response was the expression of a pent-up revolt against the bang-bang, faster-faster pianism of our concert colts. Novaës's taste and finesse restored to the piano its inherent harmoniousness, soulfulness, and transparency.

Novaës has spent her years in constant refinement of a basically romantic literature. She is less at home in the classic and modern worlds. Her classics disclose a disinterest in musicological facts. Her service to contemporary creation has been mainly confined to that which emanates from her Brazilian environment. Her genius lies in doing naturally what comes naturally. Her entire nature is evidently as stimulated and enhanced by audiences as they are by her presence, for it is primarily on the platform that the full force of her personality is freely expressed and significantly revealed.

In her numerous recordings we often encounter another Novaës, one who rarely equals and nowhere heightens the sorcery of her counterpart. Side by side with the poetically precise Novaës at her best, her recorded performances also divulge her limitations—limitations on various levels, scarcely apparent when we are beguiled by her effortless pianism, captivated by her handsome demeanor and dimpled smile. I suspect that Novaës's realization of the permanency of discs is partially responsible for the frequent lessening of her justly famed spontaneity, vibrancy, and freedom.

Happily, these qualities and still others are fully present in Novaës's recordings of Beethoven's sonatas opus

81a and opus 27, no. 2, Schumann's *Kinderscenen* and *Papillons*, Chopin's F minor Concerto, Twenty-four Preludes, and certain other small-form works by this composer and others. Toward other recordings I tender qualified enthusiasm or none. Of course, a pianist of Novaës's caliber, unless faced by insurmountable challenges, is never less than a solid and interesting artist.

To her playing of the two Beethoven sonatas, for example, Novaës brings child-of-nature faith, tenderness, and impetuosity extremely favorable to their expressive substance. But in her readings of the sonata opus 31, no.2, and the Fourth Concerto one thinks back to the insight, drama, and spaciousness of Schnabel. One cannot even say that Novaës's depths of feeling outweigh depths of conception, for in these works she sounds uneasy and coolly remote.

In her interpretation of Mozart's concertos K.271 and K.466, sonatas K.283 and K.331, and the rondo K.511, she keeps scholarship at a distance, inappreciative of its blood relationship to the most vivid elements of the classical styles. Just contrast the mistaken timorousness of Novaës with the knowledgeable luxuriance of Landowska, in whose hands Mozart springs to life with such vibrancy and breadth.

In the Chopin concerto she again becomes the great Novaës: expressive, subtle, and captivating. She wisely eschews the heroic frame. This music responds perfectly to her exquisite treatment because its subject matter transcends its design and its subject matter is emotion.

The Schumann Concerto is another ideal vehicle for Novaës's taste and her ability to sing lyrically without insistence. I find her performance lacking only in tension and brio, and feel the same about her way with the Grieg Concerto, with one added point of esteem. Novaës approaches it without any sense of that condescension or relaxation of musical standards so frequently encountered when performers play "hollow war-horses" in a manner demonstrating their basic disrespect for the music. Not so Novaës, who also lends her seriousness and refinement to Falla's *Nights in the Gardens of Spain*. But this opulent score demands a voluptuousness and virility not wholly present in her performance.

Novaës endows Schumann's *Carnaval* with color, variety, and many ingratiating details. Heard beside the complete conviction and perfection of her *Papillons* disc, however, it is far less impressive. Heard beside the masterly unity and imaginative power of Rachmaninoff in the *Carnaval*, Novaës sounds innocent.

There is no getting away from it: physical power is a compelling power. I have never heard any woman—not even Teresa Carreño—who had it in sufficient degree to extract from the piano its fullest grandeur. I have therefore never yet heard the woman pianist able to command such works as the Beethoven E flat Concerto, the Brahms, Tchaikovsky, Rachmaninoff, or Prokofiev concertos.

Mme Novaës does not perform these works. She is a wise woman. Mainly, her selection of compositions to play and to record proves that her ability to choose is not far behind her ability to perform. Occasionally, more often in recordings than in the concert hall, she has been persuaded to play works for which others disclose considerably more affinity and authority.

When Novaës essays Chopin's B flat minor Sonata, F minor Fantasy, and B minor Scherzo, we become aware of her femininity. There are many pages of luscious tone and fluent passage-work, but everything is essentially small-scaled. Breadth, bravura, and architectural continuity are the additional resources required for these dramatic canvases. Just sample the flaming triumph of Horowitz in the coda of the scherzo. And is there anyone in the house who recalls Hofmann in the sonata and the fantasy? He will understand.

In the Chopin études, recorded complete, Novaës appears musically and technically divested of her most treasurable assets. With the exception of the third, fifth, and twelfth études of opus 10, the first three and songful C sharp minor of opus 25, and the *Trois Nouvelles Etudes,* Novaës seems overwhelmed by the task. Her characteristic ease, accuracy, and polish are often absent, and there are many disconcerting pages, as throughout the very first two études. It is only right to add that no artist has ever been adequate to the mechanical and poetic requirements of the formidable project. It would take an artist of Hofmann's all-encompassing art, and he never had the slightest intention of playing the complete set.

This last statement, originally made in an article I wrote for the *Saturday Review,* elicited a revealing letter from Hofmann's friend and mine, Alexander W. Greiner, manager of the Concert and Artists Department of Steinway and Sons:

"Your statement," wrote Mr. Greiner, "brought to mind a conversation with Emperor Josef quite a few years ago. I mentioned to him that before I depart this vale of sorrows, I would like to hear him play all the Chopin Etudes. He looked at me and said, 'I'm surprised at you. You know better than that: there is no pianist, and there never will be one born, who can play all the Chopin Etudes equally well. I can only play perhaps a half dozen.' There we have it again," concluded Greiner, "the degree to which the sense of responsibility belongs to the chosen few."

Novaës's performances of all the Chopin nocturnes, complete, show her high gifts and her unpredictability, too. She plays one phrase like an inspired cherub, the next as though she had not the faintest notion of its significance and cared less. The nocturne played with the greatest mastery, with breath-taking beauty, sustained thought, and expressive intensity from beginning to end turns out to be the profoundest and most difficult of them all, the tremendous C minor! In the waltzes, also recorded complete, Novaës does marvelous things, commonplace things, ravishing things, and pedestrian things, all in one piece, and in many of them. Here, as in so many of the nocturnes, one hears an impersonal and often uncommunicative Novaës hurtling through melodic figurations with indifference to their interior poetry, struggling for expressiveness by playing one hand before the other, or just abstaining from realization or involvement.

Joyfully, one again greets the spontaneous, rhythmically buoyant, and authentic Novaës in her performances of eleven Chopin mazurkas. Unburdened by the demands of completion, playing selected works that she commands absolutely, Novaës exhibits compelling artistry. She does not seek the Slavic verve of Rubinstein. Each work is marked by her own unique style and dignity.

From one point of view it is possible to maintain that Mme Novaës's frequent inability to match her concert standards on discs is evidence of her high sense of responsibility. The word "record" itself explains a true artist's trepidations. The recording performer literally puts himself—the self he seeks to perfect and perpetuate—"on record." Anyone who can approach the task without deep apprehension is no artist. Few musicians have the authority, the prestige, the bargaining power, to insist upon conditions commensurate with such responsibility. Mme Novaës has. She is in the well-earned position to accept or refuse an assignment. She has the right to select from a number of "takes" those which are representative of her fullest artistic intentions, and to reject those which are not. Presumably her recordings were created thus.

Recordings made under such circumstances by such an artist invite estimation on the highest plane and in direct comparison with those of other sovereign artists. It is the old case of *noblesse oblige*. I am certain that Mme Novaës, a queen among pianists, would not have it otherwise.

Robert Casadesus

THOSE WHO maintain (and I among them) that the art of romantic piano-playing has suffered a decline are closer to fact than to fanaticism. And though this has been an undeniable and serious blow to a large part of the keyboard's most treasurable literature, it would be a mistake to contend that the general level of piano-playing itself is therefore inferior to that of former times.

Actually, in my opinion, it grows more and more proficient decade after decade, corollary to the continual upsurge in scientific attainments and the industrious acquisition of facts so characteristic of our empirical age.

Genius is another story. In the full furious flight of imagination the man of genius is unique, no matter what his generation. He creates his own world, makes his own laws, and justifies them. He wears a halo and casts a magic spell. There is no arguing with that, and one does well to avoid comparisons of incomparables. I am now thinking of that century from about 1825 to 1925 during which interpretative giants personified by Paganini and Liszt conquered the world of music-lovers. They strode regally across the platform, tossed back their leonine heads, and poured forth hypnotic vibrations of sullen passion and tender compassion, leaving their hearers shaken and swooning. But these were not concerts. They were battles in which heroes marched with banners flying to shattering victories on the fields of the Grand Old Tradition.

For every artist of such caliber there were dozens of others, flourishing fakes who had only the manner, and rode helter-skelter to artistic disaster, violating every aes-

thetic law of taste and textual fidelity en route. I know of
only one such who has survived into our generation, an
exception to prove that the phony part of the old tradition
is gone.

Today classic clarity, quiet demeanor, solid scholarship,
authority, and craftsmanship of a very high order are
the qualities of an extraordinary number of interpreters.
And if there are few or virtually none who dwell on
the summit, the hills are richly populated with pianists in
whom technical skill and intellectual curiosity are at an
all-time high. They work and look like successful businessmen and businesswomen, possess a powerful grasp of
form, and exhibit a strict devotion to the text. From their
playing we conclude that most of them subconsciously
rate knowledge above drama, reverence above passion,
and depth of thought above depth of emotion. And they
have certainly brought the art of piano-playing to a new
gauge of professionalism.

When Robert Casadesus made his first American appearance in 1935 with the New York Philharmonic he
was immediately recognized as a distinguished representative of this modern era of pianism. In addition, he was
a charming, balanced, and realistic man. His success
changed him not at all. He never stopped learning, and
he never posed as a prophet. He continued to be a hard
worker who loved his work, cultivated a versatile and
adult mind, and followed a simple, straightforward life
revolving around a devoted family with home bases in
Paris and Princeton.

Casadesus exemplifies the admirable executant musician. He has taught and composed. His playing shows it.
No man who has had to explain, analyze, and articulate
principles of technique and interpretation can fail to be a
much wiser man after repeated experiences of this sort.
Only a teacher with platform experience as well as pedagogical experience can impart anything worth learning
about communication, audience reaction, or acoustic phe-

nomena to a pupil who aspires to a public career. An executant who composes is always the best of musicians because composers know more about the basic materials of music than anyone else.

Celebrating Casadesus's twentieth concert season in America, Columbia records issued his album of the bulk of Debussy's solo piano compositions. It also includes the *Six Epigraphes Antiques* for four hands as well as *En Blanc et Noir* for two pianos, in which the French pianist is joined by his gifted wife, Gaby. The assignment was a formidable one, for Debussy's piano style exploits the instrument's maximum resources of dynamics, variety of touch, and combinations of color and pedaling. Further, the French genius of impressionism, that phase of musical reaction against post-romanticism (notably Wagnerism), discovered expressive means that demand special concepts of technique and interpretation. They also demand of the interpreter worldly experience coupled with intuition, for their subjects range from legend to literature, from architecture to personalities.

Mr. Casadesus meets these demands squarely. His interpretations reveal a scholar, a thoughtful man who knows the world, a musician, and a technician through and through. Clarity and taste are his most impressive qualities. These and his ability to maintain a musical line and basic tempo. He has individual ideas about Debussy which fit perfectly the framework of his artistry, even though they may not always fit the framework of the music.

Some of the strongest examples of Casadesus's solid musical culture are to be found in Debussy's unique Twenty-four Preludes: the unity maintained through the snatches of folk tunes and tarantella rhythms of the gay *"Les collines d'Anacapri"*; the cold desolation of *"Des pas sur la neige"*; the full revelation in *"Ce qu'a vu le vent d'Ouest"* that a west wind to a *musicien français* like Debussy (and Casadesus) is not what it is to an American

Easterner. To the Frenchman it is a sweeping and fearsome element that has gathered terrifying force on its violent journey across the Atlantic. Much to be admired also are the broad humor of *"La sérénade interrompue,"* particularly in the final despair of the frustrated serenader; the skillful management of the problematical architecture in *"La Cathédrale engloutie"* with its two climaxes, the second usually emerging as a disappointing anticlimax; the crystalline impishness of *"La danse de Puck";* the rhythmic exactness and pliable texture of *"Les tierces alternées";* the sharp pianistic display of whirling sparks and soaring rockets in *"Feux d'artifice."*

Debussy's renunciation of romanticism was the revolt of a child against a loved parent whose influence can never be eradicated. It is precisely in the interpretation of this aspect of Debussy's art that the modern school of playing leaves one yearning for *"les sons et les parfums"* of sensuousness, suggestion, incense, and poignant expressivity. And for mercurial irony and piquancy, too. Such atmospheric subtleties and emotional opulence are in shorter supply than the pianistic brilliance and musical maturity that Casadesus brings to *Estampes, Images,* and particularly to the captivating *Children's Corner* and to a scintillating performance of *L'Isle joyeuse.*

Perhaps that is why I hold his playing of Ravel's piano music in higher esteem, for Casadesus's precision, suavity, and fastidiousness are better applied to the music of the neo-classic master whose equilibrium was of that order which posed clear-cut problems and admitted of no ambivalences. Casadesus is a skilled and authoritative interpreter of Ravel despite one of the severest handicaps that can befall an interpreter: he was a close friend of the composer. Nevertheless, Casadesus is a powerful and lucid protagonist of "the Swiss watchmaker" (Stravinsky's name for Ravel), with special affinity for *Miroirs, Gaspard de la Nuit,* and *Le Tombeau de Couperin.* He richly deserved the Grand Prix du Disque awarded him for his recorded collection of Ravel's piano music.

My all-out enthusiasm is reserved for Casadesus as the superlative interpreter, from the first to the last impeccable notes of his recordings, of Weber's F minor *Konzertstück* (with George Szell's perfect conductorial answer to a soloist's prayers) and of Saint-Saëns's C minor Concerto (with brilliant support from Artur Rodzinski).

In these works, Casadesus is completely at home. Their urbane stylishness draws his fullest powers. They are custom-tailored to his dispassionate ardor. Applied to melodramatic delicacies, his taste, dispatch, and sophistication are the perfect catalysts for extracting sentiment from sentimentality, pathos from bathos, elegance from ostentation. Casadesus's identity with this music is definitive, and the coloristic variety of orchestral instruments, and especially the warm expressiveness of string sound, provide the happy aids and complements to his other artistic amenities.

Rudolf Serkin

It took nearly twenty years of playing in the United States for Rudolf Serkin to be able to draw large audiences and command large fees. But there was never a time after his 1936 debut in New York with the Philharmonic under Toscanini when he was not unquestioningly accepted among the leading pianists. Through the years Serkin not only maintained but also increased his prestige. He accomplished this in defiance of almost every proven requirement for pianistic success.

Serkin is not a "born" pianist. Not having the born pianist's innate equipment, he is awkward at the instrument and struggles against it. If he does not practice incessantly, he cannot perform. His body moves around in agonized contortions. He seems to be performing a self-imposed penance, a tortured ritualistic dance, before the implacable images in white and black ivory.

He is not a natural platform "personality." Not at home there, he walks nervously onto the stage looking away from the audience, throwing quick glances backstage with the desperate air of a man who wishes he had never left there. Wearing dark-rimmed glasses and a worried expression, appearing not to know quite where he is or in what direction he should go, Serkin is the cartoonist's absent-minded professor.

What, then, has made this man one of the most persistently admired, beloved, and influential musical figures throughout the entire world?

Just as you conclude that he is no virtuoso, he will play a Brahms concerto or the Beethoven Fourth or Fifth or Schumann's *Symphonic Etudes* with the ease and note-perfect security of a natural technician who disdains difficulty. Just as you conclude that here is an artist who makes his appeal to the mind rather than to the heart, that his forte is the classic rather than the romantic literature, Serkin will play Schumann's *Abegg Variations* or the Mendelssohn G minor Concerto with a glowing tenderness and springtime ardency that convince you that this is the very first time you have ever really heard these works. Just as you decide that Serkin's art is most favored in intimate surroundings, and especially in chamber music, he will play a concerto at the Lewisohn Stadium, riding over every spatial and acoustic obstacle and hitting the most distant standee squarely in the midriff— an achievement denied many a block-busting virtuoso engulfed by the orchestra and blown away by the breezes.

I came to an understanding and appreciation of Serkin only slowly. Not that I failed to sense instantly his vibrancy and stature. I was distracted by his disturbing mannerisms, which made his fervency emerge suspiciously like misdirected energy caused by faulty technical schooling. Later I was troubled by the wide disparity between Serkin's playing when he was at his best and when he was not. He would play one phrase or piece with a poetry and mastery second to none, and then attack the next with a curious blend of harshness, hysteria, and inexpressivity which would make you shake your head in bewilderment. I know now that I was often missing the forest for the trees.

Gradually, with eyes closed and ears open, I began to discern that Serkin played not only with his whole body but also with his whole soul. I began to perceive what music means to him. Finally, I became vividly aware of the sheer exaltation that music arouses in this man, and at last I realized that his muscular agitation reflects a compulsive bodily response to what he hears and feels within him and struggles physically to transmit.

As anyone can sense when Serkin succeeds in creating inexorable logic and beautiful sounds, what he hears within him is unsurpassed in purity and nobility; and what he feels is felt with the utmost sincerity and selflessness. When he does not succeed—no matter how out of hand and unbeautiful his playing may become—he is never less than the dedicated musician totally incapable of courting applause, totally without vanity.

Serkin shuns any aspect of publicity. Actually, he hardly has to contend with it, for there is little about him or his activities which inspires it. He lives a hard-working professional life and a close, secluded family life with his wife and five children. He is shy and unpretentious, even recessive. He holds the highest moral and humanitarian principles, practices them unswervingly, but avoids being put in the position of having either to state them or to fight for them publicly.

Everything Serkin does is seriously motivated. His artistic ideals and personal modesty have made him a symbol rather than a pianist. He is listened to as a searching mind, as a voice of conscience. This is his power, in spite of the fact that he himself has not always found it easy or possible to fulfill the dictates of that voice. But it is always there in some way, this ethical force which has placed him in a rare category among contemporary pianists. It is in the man himself, in Serkin the music-lover, the teacher, and the human being. It is still there when he plays much less well than he knows how to play.

Serkin's seriousness, his faith and hope, his character and musicianship bear the unmistakable stamp of great tradition and significant association. One influence in particular shaped his life, every phase of it. At the age of seventeen, he aroused the interest of Adolf Busch. Together, they toured in violin-piano sonata recitals; Serkin appeared with the Busch Quartet and with chamber orchestras under Busch's baton; eventually he became

Busch's son-in-law. It is therefore no accident of talent, but unremitting conditioning and experience that make Serkin the greatest chamber-music player among pianists. And he is certainly the greatest pianist among chamber-music players.

Serkin's pedagogical work has also been considerable, though the demands of world-wide concert engagements have made it necessarily sporadic. Nevertheless, he directs the piano department of the Curtis Institute in Philadelphia, and during the summer guides the Marlboro School of Music in Vermont. He is a teacher in the inspirational tradition.

At Curtis, his students are gifted and hopeful young soloists. At Marlboro, the entire emphasis is on the ensemble playing, from duos to chamber-orchestra works. Students, teachers, artists—good, bad, but none of them indifferent—all come, and all are welcome if they but render homage to the treasurable literature that brings human beings warmly and closely together in common ideals. For from six to eight weeks everyone there makes music with the unique joy derivable only from playing chamber music informally.

Adolf Busch provided the original incentive in 1951. Serkin is now the guiding spirit. Since the inception of this extraordinary project, Rosalie J. Leventritt has done most of those "necessaries" without which dreams remain dreams.

This dream has come to fruition, and I suspect it to be Serkin's deepest love and most absorbing interest. He is father confessor to his own brood and to hundreds of others. There, in the heart of the Vermont forest, he and his colleagues and pupils and neighbors can make music and hear music far from the madding crowd and the madder critics. In near-by Brattleboro, Serkin has a farm. He is a good man at the hoe or at the wheel of a tractor, a more relaxed and sanguine man than the one who appears at

Carnegie Hall in white tie and tails. Yet, as always with Serkin, it is music—man-made music—that is enshrined amid Nature's green temples of Vermont.

Many a brainless speed demon has gone up there and come back entirely transformed at the end of a summer, thinking less about his fingers and more about music. In any event, thinking. And loving "Rudi." Everyone who has ever met him finds that easy to do.

My own regard for Serkin began in 1944. In that year Station WQXR, on behalf of the War Financing Program of the Treasury Department, initiated a series of symphony concerts featuring distinguished soloists in concertos with the National Orchestra Association conducted by Leon Barzin. The audience was to consist entirely of war-bond purchasers.

Seeking to launch the project effectively, I made a small list of eminent artists who could get the series off to a successful start. I first telephoned a famous violinist, inviting him to play the opening concert at Hunter College Auditorium. "You want me to play for nothing?" he shouted. "This telephone call has to be paid for, and so do the printed programs and the electric lights, but artists are supposed to play for nothing. I won't do it, it's against my principles!"

I telephoned Serkin. "I cannot tell you how much I appreciate this opportunity to serve in my small way," he said. After the concert, a splendid and triumphant one, I wrote to Serkin thanking him for his appearance, and especially for the fervid spirit he brought to the event and communicated to an audience that had purchased nearly a million dollars in war bonds to attend. Before I had a chance to mail it, a letter arrived from Serkin.

"In this terrible struggle against those who would destroy everything we cherish most," he wrote, "the artist has a hard time turning his art to account, finding ways to make what he is able to do directly helpful. I am truly grateful to you for giving me this chance to feel that perhaps I am not so useless to my adopted country as I feared. When and where may I again do my little bit?"

There is no need to say more about a man like this, for everything he is deep down at the core of him is expressed in his music.

Vladimir Horowitz

JANUARY 1928 was a memorable month in the life of Vladimir Horowitz. When he singled it out, I immediately assumed that its significance derived from his sensational New York debut. But I was mistaken. Horowitz had already tasted success; he had already vanquished audiences in great cities. I am not saying that he was casual about his American triumph, but that something else happened. It happened a few days after his arrival in the city that was to become his home, and one day before he was to conquer it in a flaming performance of Tchaikovsky's First Piano Concerto with Sir Thomas Beecham, who also took his first American bow that night. The memorable event was the realization of an even greater dream: Horowitz met his musical idol, Sergei Rachmaninoff.

At that first meeting in Rachmaninoff's apartment, there was no music, just music talk. In one hour they were fast friends. The following evening Rachmaninoff attended Horowitz's debut, as did Hofmann, Lhevinne, Moiseiwitsch, Levitzki, and every other pianist in town. The audience went wild, and the critics groped for fresh superlatives to describe the triumph. But it was a letter from Rachmaninoff containing warm praise and sober advice which proved most deeply satisfying to Horowitz.

"If he had written me that I played miserably, I would still have been happy," Horowitz said.

Some weeks later he was scheduled to play Rachmaninoff's Third Concerto with Walter Damrosch, who had fathered its *première* almost two decades earlier, with Rachmaninoff as his soloist. When Rachmaninoff learned of the concert, he offered to accompany Horowitz in a rehearsal, playing the orchestral part on a second piano. They met in the famed basement of Steinway's piano salon. Horowitz modestly reported that Rachmaninoff said very little, that he merely made a few suggestions. But Rachmaninoff told me that he was completely over-whelmed, that he listened open-mouthed as Horowitz pounced upon the fiendish work with the fury and vora-ciousness of a tiger.

"He swallowed it whole," said Rachmaninoff. "He had the courage, the intensity and daring that make for great-ness."

These capacities were not always recognized, and Ho-rowitz's career had not been a series of unqualified suc-cesses. Following a modest and uneventful debut at the age of seventeen in his native city, Kiev, Horowitz played in Moscow, Tiflis, Odessa, Kharkov, and other Russian cities for two years without setting fire to any of them. Recognition of his superior gifts came in Leningrad when he played twenty-three concerts during the 1923-4 sea-son. Recognition, but no money. He left Russia in the fall of 1925 for Germany, accompanied by his manager and friend, Alexander Merovitch. In Berlin, three recitals were booked on borrowed money, to take place early in 1926 within a two-week period.

"At the first concert, I was very nervous," Horowitz said. "I didn't play well, but I was fortunate. No critics came."

Three days later he played again.

"It was better." One critic attended—an important one. He wrote: "With Horowitz, our pianistic culture is again awakened."

Horowitz was gratified, but startled because he had been hearing Schnabel, Backhaus, and Edwin Fischer during the months before his own appearances. He was given an extra date and the chance to play the Tchaikov-sky Concerto with a small orchestra. The third recital finally covered expenses, but nothing much happened.

Hamburg was next on the itinerary. Two recitals were booked in the ballroom of the Atlantic Hotel. Few people came to the first one, but the critics were there.

"A good artistic success," admitted Horowitz. "But, as usual, no money."

Several days later, anticipating nothing more than an idle afternoon, Horowitz and Merovitch went to Hamburg's famed zoo. They spent the afternoon walking around. When it began to snow, they turned back to their hotel. They were dead tired and chilled from the outing. Near the entrance of their hotel they caught sight of the local concert manager. He began gesturing wildly and shouting in a stream of German, not a word of which Horowitz understood. Merovitch translated excitedly that the manager had been searching for them all day because a woman pianist who had been scheduled to play a concerto that night at an orchestral concert had fainted during the rehearsal. Would Horowitz substitute?

The concert in question, Horowitz told me, was comparable to a Saturday night at Carnegie Hall with the New York Philharmonic.

"It's the chance of your life!" exclaimed Merovitch. "What do you say?"

Horowitz hesitated. Exhausted and cold, with no practice, no food, and no shave that day!

"What time is the concert?"

"It's going to start any minute with the symphony."

"All right. Tchaikovsky Concerto. Has the orchestra got the score and the parts? Get me a glass of milk," Horowitz said all in one breath.

A phone call brought assurances that the music was in the orchestra's library. Horowitz ran up the stairs to shave and dress. Mentally, he practiced the score while shaving, for he had not touched a note of the concerto since he had played it at that little concert in Berlin ("With result, zero," he said).

The trio arrived at the hall just as the conductor, Eugen

Pabst, was finishing the symphony—not knowing whether he had a soloist or, if he had, what music was to be played. When he walked into the artists' room during the intermission, he was quickly informed of the situation. He nodded and, without a word of greeting, gave Horowitz a cold stare, opened the score, and started right off in French:

"Look, you. I conduct like this. This is *my* opening tempo. Here, I take it this way. There, I take it that way."

"*Oui, monsieur, oui, monsieur,*" Horowitz repeated, bowing from the waist, thoroughly intimidated.

"Just watch my stick," said Pabst, "and nothing too terrible should happen."

After the orchestral opening, Horowitz started. Upon hearing his first crashing chord, Pabst spun around in amazement. At the second, he jumped off the podium and sprinted to the piano, staring incredulously at Horowitz's hands. He stayed right there until the conclusion of the first cadenza, his face a study in disbelief while his arms beat time—Horowitz's time. When it was all over, the piano lay on the platform like a slain dragon and the whole house rose as one, screaming hysterically. Pabst grabbed his soloist and hugged him repeatedly, while the audience tore the place apart. The leading critic reported that "not since Hamburg discovered Caruso has there been anything like this."

"That was my big break," said Horowitz. "Who knows? If not for this concert, maybe my career would never have amounted to much. Today, if one plays well, it is not enough. My Russian success meant nothing at all to Europe or America."

The second Hamburg concert was hastily rescheduled, moved from the Atlantic Hotel Ballroom to a concert hall seating three thousand. Within two hours of the announcement, the hall was sold out. Horowitz was on his way. Paris was next: two recitals booked in small halls. His artistic success was such that he had to play five, cul-

minating in a last recital at the Paris Opéra, an event duly
recorded in the annals of Parisian triumphs.

I heard the glamorous story of that recital from friends
who were there in 1926 and witnessed the wild excitement that night. They recalled the arrival of vanloads of
gendarmes summoned to control an inflamed audience
that refused to leave the hall and was breaking up everything not nailed down.

Thirty years later Horowitz told me a sequel to the
event which would have shocked any member of that be-
witched mob. It seems that their hero left Paris later that
evening for his debut in Rome, sitting up all night in a
third-class coach, meditating wryly on the exuberance
of their ovation—and munching on a tired cheese sand-
wich that had taken his last sou.

I was reminded of a similar story told by Paderewski,
who said that it always amused him to be typed as the
Admirable Crichton of the keyboard, pocketing fortunes
from houses packed with worshippers. "They forgot," he
said, "but I never have, the long climb, the years of slavery which yielded only a lot of experience, but small audiences, little response, and no money."

"My early successes followed a similar pattern," Horowitz agreed when I told him this story, "Prestige galore,
but only enough money to pay off some of my debts, to
cover the expenses of halls, hotels, transportation, and
food. But in Paris I had an unexpected 'break' that had
a long-term result. Arthur Judson was there." A contract
was signed for twenty-five concerts in America—a tour to
be launched in 1928 as only Judson could launch it, in-
cluding a debut with the New York Philharmonic and appearances as soloist with Koussevitzky in Boston and
Stock in Chicago.

"New York was all right," Horowitz said, "but Chicago
was a second Hamburg. Isn't it curious that in three countries my success came in other than the first cities? In Russia it was Leningrad, not Moscow; in Germany, Hamburg

instead of Berlin; in America, it was Chicago, not New York. The major cities came later."

The pattern was broken in Italy and England. London became a "Horowitz town," though not at once. A Wigmore Hall recital in 1926 "brought nobody and nothing." On Horowitz's return in 1930, he took the city by storm, playing Rachmaninoff's Third Concerto at Queen's Hall with Mengelberg conducting. Ernest Newman grappled for adjectives. The Londoners had found a new idol. Earlier, Horowitz had added Rome to his conquests. First came the usual artistic success with small financial returns; then came the invitation to reappear the next season, starting with a command performance for the Queen of Italy.

Ten years after his career had been launched, Horowitz's fame had spread throughout France, England, Italy, Germany, Belgium, Holland, Switzerland, Scandinavia, and the United States. Then in 1936, following an appendix operation, Horowitz withdrew from the platform for two years. "I had a lot of things to think about," he said. "One cannot go through life playing octaves."

It was a modest comment. Horowitz's octaves are not just octaves. Nor are his scales and double notes just scales and double notes. They always dramatize the music he plays. They have a controlled intensity unmatched by any other pianist. They are played with flawless honesty and accuracy, with speed and volume that make his rivals sound tame and timid by comparison. The subtle restraint of his pedaling, the variety of his touch and accentuation, his relentless rhythm in bravura, and the sheer excitement he generates have been worth anyone's price of admission. A Horowitz recital was always an experience, but it was rarely a deep experience. His playing of the intellectually and emotionally profound literature revealed his limitations. He was unhappily aware of it. It was one of the things he decided to think about.

Horowitz's "comeback" was staged at a charity affair in

Zurich, at which he shared a program with the Busch Quartet, playing a group of Chopin solos. He returned to the United States in 1939 under the immigration quota before the outbreak of the Second World War. Since then he has left our shores but once for a two-month European tour in 1946. Through the years, audiences continued to react to his devastating mastery, but were able to note an ever growing human and musical sensitivity. His climactic power never lost its terrifying quality, but he was now able to play meditative passages without restlessness, lyrical passages without tampering with their simplicity. He was even able to smile occasionally. The full expressivity and charm of maturity which began to accrue to Horowitz were most noticeable during what to date have proved to be his last public performances—in 1953, marking the silver anniversary of his American debut.

Will Horowitz play publicly again? I do not think he knows any more than we do. I went to see him, and during the evening I asked him this question.

"I still love music. I practice. I am making some records. I read. I love to talk with friends, to look at my pictures, to listen to recordings, to study a great deal of vocal and symphonic music I never previously had a chance to know. I don't know, but I don't think I will play again in public."

Retiring at the height of one's popularity and powers is unusual. The thing I find even more unusual about Horowitz is the way he is now working, the intensity with which he is seeking greater fulfillment within himself. He has not "let down" at all. He is more dedicated than ever. He played for me that evening. Along with the intellectual and emotional enhancement of his personality has come a richer, more serious, more communicative artistry. The fabulous virtuoso has unexpectedly become an introspective musician.

Absence from the concert platform could well account for his greater philosophic serenity, for the virtuoso who captured the public imagination never gloried in that part of his musical life. Concerts terrify him. People *en masse* frighten him. He always found it easier to learn five new compositions than to attend one social gathering. Today he seldom goes out except to take a walk. Exercise has always been important to him.

"Rachmaninoff once told me," he said, "'if I don't walk, my fingers won't run.'"

Not only do Horowitz's fingers run with miraculous speed and accuracy, but also the man himself moves at a very brisk, decisive pace. Even in moments when he seems completely relaxed—and they are rare—he is half-coiled and ready to spring. When you visit him, he is full of vitality and cordiality, fueled by an enormous energy. Withal, there are shyness, simplicity, and genuine modesty.

Superficially one could conclude, from Horowitz's quiet charm and diffidence, his wide-eyed wonder about everything, that he is unworldly and naïve. He is anything but. He is aware and astute about the world and people. He has a distinguished collection of French impressionist paintings that he himself has selected with unerring taste and at minimum cost through shrewd evaluation and negotiation.

When he plays canasta and is certain that he has no safe discard and is bound to hand over a fat frozen pack, he will turn toward his opponent looking like a pathetic child, hold out his cards helplessly, and whimper: "Take it. Take any card. I cannot bear to put it down myself." Many an unlucky pick has saved him from the disaster of a bad decision.

He is not always so ingratiating. Socially, Horowitz can be a difficult guest . . . when he shows up. But professionally he is among the most generous of colleagues. If a musician for whom he has little regard is being discussed, you can hardly drag a word out of Horowitz. If an artist he respects is under discussion, even one he may dislike personally, Horowitz will always find something highly complimentary or kind to say, and will mean it. Once we were talking about recorded versions of the Rachmaninoff Second Concerto. There is one that has always aroused me to strong language. "Yes," said Horowitz, "it is not at all good, and it is not right for any artist to allow himself to be so misrepresented. But, you know, I am sure that he left immediately for Europe and never heard the play-backs, and that some stupid engineer finished the job."

Horowitz now lives in a spacious private house in mid-town Manhattan, surrounded by his pictures, two Stein-way concert grands, and a fine library of music, books, and recordings. His solo discs are made in his living-room. He also teaches a little, his interest confined to promising young artists.

Mrs. Horowitz, the former Wanda Toscanini, is a re-markably understanding and devoted companion. Their daughter Sonia has become expert at record-editing and tape-splicing, and she works on her father's and grand-father's discs and tapes of their concert performances.

Should Horowitz announce a public concert tomorrow, it would cause a riot at the box-office. Never before has he had so much to give and to get. He can command any fee and any appearance he wants. At the moment, and it may not be true of the next moment, he does not seem to want. Let us hope he changes his mind. Unblemished perfection brought to meaningful maturity is uncommon to any gen-eration, especially to ours.

... and *Others*

In NEARLY fifty years of a life spent in music, I have naturally heard and known a great many pianists. The list is large, too large to present full-length impressions of them all. The fact that I am not able to devote individual chapters to the pianists I am about to mention is no indication either of lack of esteem on my part or of their place in the artistic hierarchy.

Among my earliest remembrances is a crystal-clear recollection of Ossip Gabrilowitsch in every facet of his active career—as recitalist, soloist with orchestra, and copartner with Harold Bauer in two-piano recitals; as collaborator in chamber music with the Flonzaley and Kneisel quartets; as conductor of his own Detroit Symphony and guest conductor of the Philadelphia Orchestra; and even as the clement accompanist to the singers Hulda Lashanska and his own wife, Clara Clemens Gabrilowitsch.

The piano sang under Gabrilowitsch's fingers. Curiously, despite the prestige and admiration he enjoyed, he played his recitals in small halls to select audiences. He was, in much the same way as Georges Enesco, the musician's musician, regardless of the role in which he was cast.

His production of Bach's *St. Matthew Passion* at Carnegie Hall in 1928 remains for me perhaps the most poignant impression of my concert-going life. Gabrilowitsch not only led his orchestra and choristers entirely from memory, but also sat down and played all the clavicembalo accompaniments to the soloists' recitatives. Never have I seen an audience more profoundly moved by music. It was no less stirred by the compelling passion, the devotion and dignity that Gabrilowitsch brought to the noble drama and extracted from his inspired players and vocalists.

I have further treasurable remembrances of the series in which Gabrilowitsch played sixteen concertos in five concerts with the National Orchestral Association under Leon Barzin during the 1934-5 season. In a "survey" of piano concertos that included the towering examples by J. S. Bach, Mozart, Beethoven, Brahms, Schumann, Chopin, Tchaikovsky, and Rachmaninoff, Gabrilowitsch made musical history. He also managed to do equal justice to every period and every composer through his stylistic mastery and all that this implies of mental and imaginative endowment. Twenty years elapsed before this formidable feat was comparably accomplished by Artur Rubinstein.

Personally, Gabrilowitsch was a self-effacing, erudite gentleman whose aristocratic manner, speech, dress, and bearing derived from a gracious earlier era. He had a delicious wit, and as I write this a characteristic remark of his brings a chuckle to my memory and takes me back to a dinner given by the "Bohemians" in honor of Bauer and Gabrilowitsch. Bauer, whose artistry and drollery closely paced Gabrilowitsch's, made a delightful address, in which he ascribed "Gabby's" and his friendship to "our inability to agree about anything." Gabrilowitsch then rose and said: "Harold has again made one of his usual and glaring misstatements. The fact is that we are invariably in total agreement except, of course, on those lamentable occasions when he is wrong."

Every account of Gabrilowitsch must mention his professional generosity and courtliness. I know them well, for it was under his benevolent baton that I made my debut in 1929 as soloist in my own First Piano Concerto with the Philadelphia Orchestra. I have ample cause to honor the man as well as the artist.

. . .

One Saturday morning early in the thirties I took a train with Josef Hofmann from Philadelphia to New York, and we headed straight for Leopold Godowsky's apartment in time for lunch. When we arrived, our host said: "I have a box for Pachmann's recital this afternoon. Who wants to go?"

Hofmann answered first: "I can't. It's too painful."

"And I don't dare go," said Godowsky. "Heaven only knows what he'll do this time if he hears I'm there."

Godowsky was referring to an embarrassing experience he had endured many years before at a Pachmann recital in Berlin. After the customary period of quasi-comical, quasi-pathetic vaudeville stunts, Pachmann finally settled down at the piano to play the first number. He made a few false starts, and then seemed to change his mind about playing. He rose and advanced on tiptoe to the edge of the platform. Peering into the darkened hall and beckoning coyly with an index finger, he called out: "Godowsky, Godowsky!" Godowsky froze, then snuggled deeper into his seat. Three times more Pachmann called. Getting no response, he returned to the piano, banged down the lid, and said, with finality: "No Godowsky, no music."

With that, the audience began to participate in the ridiculous business, staring at Godowsky and urging him to obey Pachmann's summons. Poor Popsy was trapped. Unable to withstand the pressure, he got up and waddled down the aisle. Pachmann, leaning over the platform and smiling benignly, took Godowsky's face in his hands and kissed him smack in the middle of his large bald spot. The audience collapsed with laughter; Godowsky was mortified.

Nor was that the end of it. Making a sort of mock obeisance, Pachmann announced: "I bow. I bow to the greatest pianist in the world! Oh, yes," he said, raising himself and his voice and addressing the audience, "Godowsky plays even better than Pachmann. But," added the wily showman, "Pachmann plays more beautifully!"

We had all heard that story so many times that Godowsky did not have to explain his decision to stay away. Holding up the tickets, he turned to me with an inquiring look.

"Should I go or not?" I asked. "You know I've never heard Pachmann."

"I'll tell you," said Godowsky, "if he plays for one minute the way he used to, it will be worth while being miserable for the rest of it."

I went. The hopefully awaited minute never arrived. The whole thing remains a nightmare, and I wish that I had never gone, for now the mere mention or sight of Vladimir de Pachmann's name makes my heart sink and flashes before my mind's eye a sickening picture of a senile, tragic old man.

Around that time and a year or two later I heard Moriz Rosenthal on two occasions, one sadder than the other. That unhappy and bewildered veteran being sadistically pushed out onto the platform was the most pathetic thing I have ever seen. Not a trace was left of his distinction. Having heard from everyone of Rosenthal's wizardry, of his daring exploits in his prime, I am deeply and frequently haunted by the vision of him as a lost, helpless, and terrified man.

Returning to pleasurable recollections, I wish that discs had been made of a Carnegie Hall recital I heard during the 1926-7 season given by an artist I had somehow missed. His recordings and reputation had prepared me for a major experience. Instead of yielding the more usual anticlimax, it surpassed my highest expectations. Later that week I saw Hofmann. "Your Majesty," I said, "I think I've just heard your heir apparent." Without hesitating a second, he said: "Ah, so you heard Moiseiwitsch. Now *there's* a natural pianist in the romantic tradition. From here in it only remains to see how much *Sitzfleisch* he has, and how much he is willing to give up for the solitary confinement his kind of talent demands."

Exquisite sensitivity and sculptured phrasing, bold sweep, and a tonal beauty that can never be taught—all belonged to Moiseiwitsch. Whenever he has played in top form, as he did on that day I first heard him, he has drawn from the piano sounds of entirely individual elegance and eloquence.

When I met him, I instantly sensed the man's deep feeling, his need for and adoration of people, which he tried hard to conceal behind a barrage of wicked puns and acidulous barbs. No one could ever have been fooled for long. His tender eyes and whimsical smile were evidence that way down inside of him this man had the warmth, imagination, and charm of his playing. Moiseiwitsch also had the gift and imagination for life and a zest for living it to the hilt which carried irresistible temptations for time-consuming interests outside of music. These, together with tragic personal losses and sorrows, militated against the consistent maintenance of Moiseiwitsch's abundant capacities.

Another admirably endowed artist with charm and magnetism and the tendency to digress was likewise headed for a pianistic supremacy that did not fully materialize. When José Iturbi was in good form and in the right mood, his playing was beautifully proportioned and polished. I use the past tense because it is a long time since I heard him play this way. His attractive personality opened the door to film stardom. A man should go the way he wants to go. But he cannot travel every road simultaneously, and Iturbi's pianism and prestige have been seriously impaired. The conductor stays intact.

Apart from the strong likelihood that a man and his

art are one, I have also noticed more than a subtle connection between a man's art and the environment in which it is nourished. Personality and talent contain so many elements in such varying degrees that their nature and effect are often mysterious. But there is nothing mysterious about an artist's culture and his main stream of thought. Both are instantly apparent to an audience. Professionals are constantly baffled by the public's unconscious grasp of what they *are* more accurately than of what they *do*.

Perhaps this explains the inequality between Alexander Brailowsky's public and professional standing. From my own experience and according to reliable hearsay, there has rarely been a professional argument that concerned the relation between an artist's qualities and the worldly success he enjoys which was not promptly stymied by the question: "What about Brailowsky?" The caliber and extent of his engagements, recording assignments, and public following have made Brailowsky a mystery to the profession. Not the mystery man, for he has always won the warmest personal affection from his colleagues.

What I have been able to discover about him proves again how much a man's essential personality can contribute to or mitigate against public support. Brailowsky's earnestness, modesty, and gentle charm are very winning. It is also instantly apparent that he wants to play the piano more than anything else in the world. This might appear strange in a man who has so little natural ease and affinity for his work, but it accounts for a sincerity, an enthusiasm, and a kind of fierce intensity that carries genuine force and vast appeal.

Brailowsky works harder at the keyboard than anyone else, but despite his hectic battles he gets through every time. It causes me to wonder whether some of his appeal may not derive from the kinship we feel for one who struggles as we all do in some way or other, from the pleasure we get when we witness a final victory over obvious difficulties. It may also be that his audiences prefer to hear the bare bones of a work without being involved in its subtle or profound meanings. Certainly Brailowsky has posed few intellectual problems to himself or to his auditors.

Here, then, is a man who loves what he does and has made his public love it, year in and year out. Brailowsky may not be a pianist's pianist or a musician's musician, but he is a people's pianist. There is no doubt about that. And it is something to ponder.

So is the public reaction that Gina Bachauer arouses by her execution of the masterpieces of the piano literature. I was not present at her debut, which mesmerized the New York critics. But I made it my business to hear her second recital, most of her subsequent concerts, and all of her recordings. I observed some of the qualities ascribed to Mme Bachauer—her instinctive pianism, fulgent tone, and genuine magnetism. What I could not observe was enough utilization of these qualities on behalf of music itself, enough devotional attention to the styles and subject matter of the masters she elects to interpret.

Her Bach, Haydn, and Mozart are innocent of too many vital and determinable facts concerning their texts and textures. The romantic repertoire is undermined by metrical accentuation and blurred pedaling. Bravura finds her hurtling rashly while the music loses its profile; lyricism invariably finds her in a brand-new tempo and mooning rapturously while design and momentum are sacrificed.

In short, Mme Bachauer now presents more pianistic and personal than artistic distinction. But she seems both serious and ambitious, and the day that she applies these attributes to scholarship will find her undeniable gifts splendidly fulfilling the first obligation that gifts impose on their possessors: discovering what is discoverable about great works of art. She and we could be richly rewarded.

I am fully aware that scholarship is an unpopular subject with the musical public. Audiences base their judgments on emotion, and their judgments have been excellent
in the long run. But that only proves that they evaluate
artists better than they evaluate themselves, for, whether
they know it or not, their greatest support and adulation
have gone to artists whose spontaneous emotions were
matched by technique and intellect. Audiences lend their
ears and even respect and affection to others, but they
know the difference almost unerringly.

All of which leads me to a group of pianists who display
a patrician schooling fast fading from our frenetic age;
and all within this gracious assemblage have long
breathed the reposeful air of England. I am now thinking, in addition to Moiseiwitsch, of Dame Myra Hess,
Solomon, Clifford Curzon, and Louis Kentner. Nowhere
in their art is there anything vulgar or hasty. In each we
find cultivation, dignity, and maturity, which most of
them have demonstrated most of the time for close to half
a century.

Mind you, no one who lives in the real world, no one
who has observed the course of piano-playing, expects or
demands today the luminous standards of individuality
and conceptual grandeur of other days when pianistic
giants roamed the earth. I am now referring to such qualities as composure and contemplative serenity and still
other admirable areas of modern man's squandered estate.

I have been charmed by Myra Hess and her art ever
since I first went to London. On only a few occasions has
her playing been that of a great pianist. She has warmth
rather than burning temperament. She plays easily but
carefully. Of soaring declamation and technical daring,
there is almost none. But never has she sounded less than
a great lady. The way she plays and talks and conducts
herself reveals the breadth of her intelligence and the refinement of her spirit and emotions. Her personal convic-

tions and mettle were demonstrated daily at the free concerts that she organized at the National Gallery in London throughout the terrors and hardships of the Second World War.

Dame Myra's platform manner is entirely enrapturing. When she plays, she seems to be saying: "Isn't this a lovely work? I am so very glad we can share it together." Her whole attitude brings her audiences a satisfying kind of participation and relaxation. It also brings her the kind of relaxation and freedom from self which enable her to do her best comfortably.

Solomon has that quality, too. In addition, he has a grand sense of momentum and musical design. Although he is most persuasive in the less gargantuan compositions, his playing has such proportionate grandeur that instead of seeming to lack power, he appears not to desire it. I can remember few performances from him that failed to produce something enchanting in the way of insight, elegance, or distinction.

Clifford Curzon is an unusually cultivated musician, much more a master musician than a master pianist. Basic tranquillity and sensitivity, personal modesty, and love for music are his most telling qualities. But his playing in works he cannot command is a far cry from his playing in works he can. He reads few works from beginning to end with sustained expressive or technical power; yet nothing he does is without its distinguishing earmark, especially when the music thoroughly becomes his style.

The public and journalistic reaction to Louis Kentner's first New York recital in 1956 bore witness to an appreciative discovery of another star in the British constellation, one all too long missing from the American scene. Kentner is no thundering lion, no dazzling virtuoso; nor is he one to break your heart.

The fact is that his art reflects the trend of this generation in that the whole state of inspired artistry and dramatic fire is replaced by incontestable musicianship and stability. Kentner is a solid, sincere, and unostentatious musician with impeccable taste. He will play the most difficult works with a well-bred effortlessness that conceals the extent of his technical mastery from all but the professional listener. He makes music with a depth and lucidity that place him firmly among the elect of contemporary pianists.

The same rank and some of the same attributes pertain to Claudio Arrau. Chilean by birth, German-trained, and now a United States resident, Arrau has a prodigious repertoire and a prodigious pianistic command. His German schooling is unmistakable in meticulous phrasing, technical precision, and devotional attention to the text—also in his cool restraint and chiseled angularity among the poetic treasures of the romantic literature. But in music tailored to his temperament, he is a master craftsman, whether or not you agree with everything he does. I feel especially indebted to him for a consummate performance he gave of the Sonata opus 2, no. 3, during a Beethoven sonata series in New York. Arrau alone awakened me to its fullest beauties in an inimitable interpretation to which he brought the utmost in style, grace, and inspiration.

I have another happy Beethoven recollection in a performance of the Third Concerto played at a concert of the New York Philharmonic by the Czech-American pianist Rudolf Firkusny. He endowed it with a glowing intensity that is unusual for the work, and unusual for him. Firkusny has come a long way up the pianistic ladder on his intelligence, honesty, fluency, and charm. These amenities, together with the polish and refinement of a diplomat, belong to the man and to his music.

If anyone is interested in what it is I look for, I shall tell him exactly. I want to feel something and have something revealed to me. I do not care whether I am made sad by tragedy or joyful by triumph, but I just cannot react to, cannot summon either love or admiration for, an experience that leaves me where I was before. In short, I want to be quickened. That is what I want from art. No. That is what I demand.

But there is a hitch. What quickens me now is not what quickened me twenty or thirty years ago. We are all inescapably conditioned by the standards that surround us. They may be beneficial or harmful. I am certain that the pianistic premises of the last two decades have unconsciously influenced me, and harmfully. Here is an instance.

In the old days I faithfully attended the annual recitals of Josef Lhevinne. They were easy to enjoy. Every piano-lover could revel in his fabulous technical equipment and ravishing tonal palette. His style was refinement itself; his sounds glittered and flowed. Even so, we looked for more in those palmy days: for intellectual profundity; for new concepts and meanings; for an imaginative transfiguration of the music we knew backward and forward.

Well! The other day I replayed the LP disc of Lhevinne issued by Victor in 1955. I felt like an utter fool. At first I was humiliated to remember that I had once dared to sit in critical judgment of Lhevinne's art and to regard it as incomplete. Then I realized what had happened to me and my standards—how I had unconsciously been seduced and persuaded to yield to contemporary criteria of piano mastery.

Now that I have unbosomed myself, I will merely say that in comparison with what Lhevinne demonstrated on that disc, all but a handful of today's pianists playing the same pieces resemble a litter of squealing kittens trying to sound like ferocious tigers.

The reader can find signal proof of what I am saying. Please hear this disc. I defy anyone not to be cumulatively enchanted by Lhevinne's delicacy and double-note perfection in Chopin's study in thirds; by his blazing performance of the octave study; and by his reading of the grandest of all the *études*, the "Winter Wind," in which he displays a daring in lightning speed which matches the boldness of the rising and falling waves of Chopin's figuration. There is much more to hear—particularly his transcendent playing of the Schulz-Evler transscription of the *Blue Danube* waltz—all teeming with skills that seem to me, after all these years, to border on the supernatural. The disc also contains the Debussy-Ravel *Fêtes* played by Josef and Rosina Lhevinne, in which duo-pianism realizes ultimate standards of taste and technique, of coloristic beauty and stylistic precision.

Words are poor instruments for describing sounds, and whenever I make an assertion about an artist of the past, I am grateful when it is possible to refer to discs, no matter how old or inadequate they may be. I am prayerful that somehow or other they may be heard, for in this way the reader and I can share certain sounds that he may not have experienced, sounds that my memory can never erase.

I am therefore resentful that there is not yet one LP record at the moment to document the pianistic genius of Mischa Levitzki for those who did not hear him. Those who did will smile in vivid recollection of Levitzki's winsome, boyish grin, of the warmth and chivalry and magic that poured from him and his playing alike. His compelling force resided in the greatness of his talent and the greatness of his heart. He had, in counterbalance, a small repertoire and a small opinion of himself and of his truly superb art. Within his limited repertoire, however, he was a vibrant, master workman: everything was pure radiance; every note shone like a sunbeam. Nevertheless, Levitzki was sure that just about everybody who played the piano knew more and could do better than he. If the reader cares to measure this modesty, I urge him to beg, borrow, or steal one of Levitzki's obsolete discs, any one —Schumann's G minor Sonata, Liszt's E flat Concerto or

Sixth Rhapsody, it does not matter. They are electrical, and the word does not describe only their mechanical process.

Equally electrical, and yet in totally different ways, was the art of Simon Barere, who reached the heights of sheer pianism more often than he failed to reach the heights of musicianship. He had flawless fluency. He was a humble and retiring man who never won the public success his playing deserved. Undismayed, he continued on to the last moment. He died with his boots on, in 1951 at Carnegie Hall, in the midst of playing the Grieg Concerto with the Philadelphia Orchestra under Ormandy. He is remembered by his colleagues with deference and affection.

We could ill afford to lose an artist of his stature, for ours is a pianistically descending epoch. Few pianists will agree. I can assure the others that the fact is no less painful to me. That is why I revere every remaining trace of aural beauty, and treasure any musician to whom art is not a way of life, but life itself.

Theme and Variations

Also With Us

SOME OF the pianists we have met in these pages are either no longer living or are no longer playing, while others, though no longer young, are happily vigorous and are maintaining established careers. If the reader has noticed that there has been no discussion of certain renowned artists such as Alfred Cortot, Edwin Fischer, and Clara Haskil, I should like to explain that it is simply because I know their playing only through recordings.

Now we come to the largest group, those pianists whose abilities exceed their public recognition, who are not only executants but also educators, ensemble players, accompanists, and teachers who contribute importantly to the entire musical scene. They are known by students and by the thousands of the music public rather than by the millions who know only "the champ" and perhaps the chief contenders.

I list alphabetically those who have made regular or occasional appearances and recordings throughout several decades, and whose performances I have heard personally and in some cases frequently: Clarence Adler, Webster Aitken, Artur Balsam, Jeanne Behrend, Jorge Bolet, Grace Castagnetta, Shura Cherkassky, Ania Dorfmann, Maria Luisa Faini, Sidney Foster, Dalies Frantz, Rudolph Ganz, Robert Goldsand, Sascha Gorodnitzki, Gunnar Johansen, Harry Kaufman, Muriel Kerr, Wiktor Labunski, Eugene List, Leopold Mannes, Nadia Reisenberg, David Saperton, Frank Sheridan, Leonard Shure, Abbey Simon, Bruce Simonds, Jan Smeterlin, Rosalyn Tureck, Alexander Uninsky, and Beveridge Webster.

A younger group whose artistry I have also heard

demonstrated impressively in performances and recordings includes Jacques Abram, Leon Fleisher, Vera Franceschi, Ruth Geiger, Frank Glazer, Herman Godes, Gary Graffman, Cor de Groot, Friedrich Gulda, Leonid Hambro, Grace Harrington, Eugene Istomin, Byron Janis, Grant Johannesen, Julius Katchen, Constance Keene, Jacob Lateiner, Raymond Lewenthal, Seymour Lipkin, Moura Lympany, Ozan Marsh, Frederick Marvin, William Masselos, Leonard Pennario, Menahem Pressler, Marisa Regules, Zadel Skolovsky, Leo Smit, and Sylvia Zaremba.

These are imposing lists in anybody's book. They contain no infant prodigies, for artistry is not built in a day and there are very few who show very much while they are very young. Yet, there is an up-and-coming, exceptionally talented group from whom we should rightfully expect outstanding consummation (God, the Draft, and the Age of Anxiety willing). Among its members are Daniel Abrams, Kenneth Amada, Paul Badura-Skoda, David Bar-Illan, Thomas Brockman, John Browning, Van Cliburn, Philippe Entremont, Malcolm Frager, Glenn Gould, Lillian Kallir, Theodore Lettvin, Russell Sherman, Claudette Sorel, Maria Tipo, and Sigi Weissenberg. And others I have neither heard nor heard about are surely preparing to capture pianistic laurels while this page is being written.

There is no question at all that there are many pianists among us with the musical qualities to continue a tradition of great piano-playing. But it must be realized that musical qualities are dependent upon extra-musical factors for fulfillment, and that "a tradition" of great playing does not necessarily mean "the traditions" of the past.

This is the point, and there is no avoiding it, at which I must bluntly state my belief that the forces that have inexorably affected every aspect of life in our epoch have conspired to make ultimate artistic fulfillment less attainable now than in former epochs. Our subject is the pianist. But what has happened to him, what is happening to him, is symptomatic of the predicaments that are streaked throughout the labyrinthine patterns of our day.

When Hofmann used to tell me that the emotional intensity and imaginative insight of his leonine master, Anton Rubinstein, made every other pianist sound like a midget (and this included Hofmann and his contemporaries), I really did not believe him. When he described the elemental power, the orchestral storm that raged over the keyboard, the hands crashing down on the ivories as Rubinstein growled in despair: "It's too small for me. I could use twenty like this!"; when Hofmann further depicted an audience so moved, so lost in the ethereally expressive quiet of Schumann's "*Warum?*" that it sat hypnotized, forgetting to applaud—I ascribed it to his cloudy remembrances or to his overimpressionable youth.

And all of us have heard and read fantastic tales about Rubinstein's idol, Liszt. Every account, from enemies and admirers alike, attests to the gaunt, handsome sorcerer whose magical playing, from gossamer grace to demonic force, overwhelmed his hearers, brought them to a delirium of emotional excitement. The verbal history of that heroic era, backed by its creative history, seeks to illustrate how fabulous a period it was, and what men it produced. Yet, for a long time I found these accounts hard to credit.

But now I know that the wide disparity which Hofmann cited between his master's qualities and those of his own generation was no figment of his imagination. It existed. And it signalized the changing values now fully revealed to us in the disparity between the older pianists of our day and the younger pianists who are everywhere compelled to find new solutions to old problems.

Where is this disparity? There is no decline in the quantity of talent. Technically our best young artists are brilliantly equipped. Many show fine standards of musical taste. Some show scholarship, the American musicians particularly. Some even have genius. What they lack is the environment that generates a broad outlook and patient confidence, that enriches the spirit and nourishes greatness of heart. They lack the concept of knowledge and technique as the means for capturing emotional and spiritual truth, the most permanent forces in art.

This is an observation, not an indictment. I am merely trying to identify the forces around us which have affected our artists, and to separate those they cannot control from those they can. I hope to make it clear that I am not the kind of hidebound fossil who holds that all excellence has vanished from the earth or that all the great artistic principles are the exclusive property of the dear, extinct past. Sound principles are invariably present whenever we encounter vital interpretation, but beneath vital interpretation there must be strong, whole, and pure affinities based on culture. And there lies the artistic stumbling-block for our generation.

On more than one of these pages I have betrayed my opinion and sorrow that the grand traditions of piano-playing are decaying. Here and there they still appear, but they are uncommon, and are growing more so every day. The works that emanate from them are still vital. But they are being presented to us in restyled performances that falsify their truth.

It is not new for surveyors of one period to observe the loss of some enchantment of a former period. It is not new or ingratiating, and it is always met with considerable disbelief, if not with open resentment. This is inevitable, for in effect such observation calls for confessions of present blind spots and makes demands on behalf of former ideals.

But such observation would be less needed and less general were its demands made by performers of themselves. Some part of the decline in art is chargeable directly to the artist. Nothing marks great artists more than the ability to lift themselves above their milieu. In our frenzied time, William Kapell and Dinu Lipatti somehow managed to transcend their environment. They dedicated themselves to relentless inquiry into historic styles; they saved themselves through an absorbing passion for artistic truth. These are the areas in which we can make demands of any artist at any time.

What exactly are those demands? A respect for old forms by those who use them, an understanding of their language, and a sense of their spirit. Would this not appear the precise measure of an interpreter's responsibility, the test of his regard for the character and content of his materials? Is it not a basic gauge of culture itself?

Such is our artistic decline, such is our day's denial of traditional values, that historic authenticity is a matter of growing indifference even to those whose substrative materials derive entirely from other epochs. With but a handful of exceptions, today's artists are unaware that unless they can transport us to those epochs, or at least differentiate for us one from another, they cannot convince us. Were they at all aware, their pragmatic sense would propel them to acquire from any and every source whatever might contribute to definitive and persuasive interpretation.

But they go blithely on in a continuous series of abdications. They are rarely called to account by criticism. But they could learn, if they would, from the musical public. Despite the fact that listening habits become implanted, concert-goers have been indirectly but forcibly registering their instinctive judgment. They have little or nothing to say about those who appear at an orchestral or recital series to which they have already subscribed. They have their say when an artist hires a hall. And for whom do they turn out in droves? For less than a handful of survivors of the golden age of pianism—silver-haired patriarchs who assuage the hunger for traditions vainly sought in the younger pianists.

Our contemporaries handle the virtuosic and dance elements of the eighteenth-century music admirably, but few (Rosalyn Tureck is a shining pianistic example) have the morality or the interest to discover its expressive and stylistic facts. These are best known and protected by harpsichordists, notably the scholarly Putnam Aldrich, Ralph Kirkpatrick, Fernando Valenti, and Sylvia Marlowe. The general musicianship and technical efficiency of our younger pianists enable the best of them to handle Schubert, Brahms, and Liszt with skill more structural than emotional, but almost always comfortably and commandingly.

They manage French impressionism knowingly as regards its design and harmonization, but their metrical view of rhythm endangers its subtle pulsation, just as their atmospheric playing has a tendency to become spineless. Their meat is the atomic repertoire of the twentieth century, and they gobble it whole.

The romantic literature is what stops them cold. Not so much the exhibitionistic glare of a Liszt or the ironic sentimentality of the moderns. That they wield stunningly. What defeats them is the real thing, the classically poised romanticism that was in music long before the emergence of the romantic movement itself.

This comprises a great solo literature: from Scarlatti sonatas, through Bach's and Mozart's fantasies and concertos, to Beethoven's sonatas and concertos. Now add the entire output of Chopin and Schumann, and calculate what proportion of the piano repertoire finds most of our current interpreters on weak ground.

The performer probably never lived who was not somewhere on weak ground. I certainly never heard one who could interpret all music equally well or wisely, and artists of former days had less literature and fewer styles to contend with. How did the giants of the past deal with the problem? Is there a lesson somewhere in their procedures? I think so.

Those I knew studied just about everything. While they studied, they performed only what they could feel spontaneously and perceive exactly enough to bring significantly to life. Quietly and persistently, they continued to unriddle whatever they could about the music they were unable to penetrate with equal ease. Their final decisions followed long periods of soul-searching. Whatever remained unfathomed was ruthlessly barred from their programs. Never did they forget that interpretation is no less accurate a portrait of the interpreter than of the music he selects and plays.

This process takes time. It takes reflection and humility. These are hard things to extract from our turbulent age. The more thoughtful pianists certainly ask themselves: "Can this music serve my particular gifts?" Few ever ask themselves the more pertinent question: "Can my particular gifts serve this music?" The proof lies in the innocence, ignorance, or entrenched conceit evidenced today throughout concert programs and recordings, superabounding in works that instantly show themselves alien to the temperaments of their performers. And the intrepid fledgling is not the sole source of this occupational immodesty. One has only to recall a widely accepted "Chopin specialist" of our day to re-define a specialist as one who does everything else worse.

When the pendulum swings full to those who do not hesitate to do anything and everything, we are let in on woeful things that should have been concealed.

Above all else we observe an inappreciation of the full significance of great works of art. Glenn Gould, for example, came to immediate and deserved attention with his first recording, Bach's "Goldberg" Variations, wherein his playing revealed exceptional maturity and accomplishment. The music was a challenge, the performance firstclass, and the critical response unanimously approving. Clearly, this called for another disc from the twenty-one-year-old pianist, and quickly.

Mr. Gould then promptly tackled, if you please, Beethoven's last three sonatas. Whatever soul-searching went on emerged only in a written commentary for his own record in which Mr. Gould ventured, regarding these sonatas, that "Perhaps they do not yield the apocalyptic disclosures that have been so graphically ascribed to them." There is no "perhaps" about it, not after hearing what his record disclosed. There was a time, though, when we were deluded into believing that these sonatas were full of profound and inspiring ideas. I blush to remember how hoodwinked we were in our youth, especially by a wily old fox named Schnabel, and we are no end grateful to Mr. Gould for awakening us to Schnabel's sharp practices.

But there is a postscript to this strange adventure which makes me think it was not without benefit to Gould. A member of the New York Philharmonic Symphony Orchestra tells of an incident during the 1956-7 season which is informative. After a rehearsal of Beethoven's Second Concerto, with Gould as soloist and Leonard Bernstein as conductor, the latter is said to have proposed spontaneously that they record the work "while it is hot." We are told that the soloist declined. "Why not?" the conductor asked. "Because," Gould answered, "Bernstein isn't ready."

The remark, if made and accurately quoted, is certainly reprehensible. For all the precocity of Bernstein's career, his is an adult musical mind and he is equally in command of the piano literature and of the orchestral literature. Although the story was told to exemplify a lack of humility which is keeping some talents on our side of the Atlantic from artistic maturity, I regard Gould's alleged comment as that of a greatly gifted youth manifesting a dissatisfaction with himself by projecting his own artistic uncertainties. This indicates anything but complacency. (P.S. The disc was finally made.)

Simon-pure complacency seems to me far more common abroad these days, where artistic talent is a hopefully fostered national resource, where opportunities to record are so prodigal that virtually none of the foreign pianists remains unknown to us. Some of those recordings, as well as the subsequent appearances here of those who perpetrated them, even suggest that practically anyone who finally masters "Chopsticks" is promptly marched into a studio to immortalize his exploit. Far be it from me to denigrate national pride. But I have often wondered why, when the local virtuoso gets to the studio, he is not asked to record "Chopsticks" instead of something he has *not* mastered.

This situation was candidly highlighted by my esteemed colleague Paul Henry Lang in a New York *Herald Tribune* review after Eugene Istomin was soloist in Beethoven's Fourth Concerto with the New York Philharmonic under George Szell. "Of late," Mr. Lang wrote, "we have heard a good many pianists who came to us with enormous reputations sworn to on a stack of phonograph records. Well, I would not trade this young man for the whole slew of them."

Before this, Mr. Lang and the rest of us had sat in on the appearances with major orchestras of Geza Anda, Samson François, Lelia Gousseau, Witold Malcuzynski, Gonzola Soriano, Daniel Wayenberg, Anna Xydis, Ventislav Yankoff, and a bevy of others who played without displaying a commensurate proficiency. How their engagements and re-engagements by our most important orchestras took place concerns a double standard, and discloses a malignant national sense of inferiority about our art and our artists unheard of in any other American walk of life.

Not that we do not have plenty of home-grown pianists who could match all comers in unvarnished incompetence. But ours do not ordinarily get hired. Not unless some skulduggery is afoot. More usually, they just pay Carnegie Hall or Town Hall for the privilege of committing artistic suicide. And it is a good thing that orchestras, artist series, and recording companies rarely sponsor American mediocrity. Any day now, our merchants of music may learn to recognize mediocrity in any language and treat it accordingly. At least, some recording firms are beginning to identify and espouse excellence even when it is home-grown and before it has become encased within a thoroughly disenchanted and embittered human frame.

It is precisely within such a frame that the bulk of American pianistic potentiality resides, for it dwells in a world that values many things above art. When its masses value art at all, it is as entertainment and decoration. Few regard art as a reflection of the nobility of the human heart or of the beauty and dignity of the human mind and spirit. The tiniest segment of all acknowledges art as a vital element of its history.

I am aware that I have borne down heavily upon our contemporary pianists. But I am equally aware that they have been cruelly impinged upon by extra-musical matters, oppressed by psychological and economic forces, and depressed by a sense of isolation and futility. And I think it high time for us to take a good hard look at the rude realities that coerce our pianists to fail in their full duty to themselves, to their art, and to their public.

The Expendables

Despite the cliché that history repeats itself, our age is unique. It is unique in complexity and anxiety and competition. Its inexorable demands have conditioned man to become an expedient and efficient animal rather than a foresighted and reflective one. Evolution has attained the speed and shock of revolution, bringing its changes at an unprecedented and bewildering pace. There are gains, there are losses. Everyone is affected, and the artist most of all, I would say, for the artist's environment influences not only his physical state but also the basic convictions, emotions, and ideals at the core of his work.

From 1914 on, the twentieth century has been a pretty hectic time. Its new generations, not without justification, became convinced that unconscionable old reactionaries and their obsolete ideals were what had got us into a mess and that it was up to the young people to clean it up. So an awful lot of things got thrown out and thrown over— and good riddance to most of them. But the day when the whole past became irrelevant was an evil day for art. What pertains to a work of art must pertain to its interpretation, and what pertains to an interpretation pertains to what the interpreter is, as man and as artist.

He is today, whatever else he may be, the most expendable member of our society. It is a tough world for him. It always has been tough for him in some way or other. But our world is toughest because it holds cultural values and artistic standards as anything but immediately useful and far-reaching. History has always cheerfully seen the artist on the bottom rung of the economic ladder. But formerly it provided him with psychological compensation in the tacit recognition that art is a noble calling which enables exceptionally endowed men to turn chaos into order and meaningless experience into significance.

This is the era of and for those who supply our tangible daily needs, from food to escape—those who make our gadgets and keep them functioning. The heroes of this society are those who get there "fustest with the mostest" and no questions asked. And today's gauge of the mostest is far less the extent of a man's vision than the length of his car. The artist, and this includes the cream of American talent, lives on his knees, challenged, indeed goaded, to die on his feet.

Please do not mention the astronomical sums earned by Las Vegas entertainers and television luminaries who sell honored names to vulgarize everything that made these names honorable. I am now referring to artists, pianists specifically, whose names are no more negotiable than their art, who are not counted among "the champs," but who cling to artistic ambitions and standards in the face of heartbreaking odds.

It does not aid their morale to read in Jacques Barzun's *Music in American Life* that their country "spends more money for music than the entire rest of the world." What they know, despite such murky and optimistic facts, is that hardly one of them can make a living playing concerts. And it does not aid their sense of pride and usefulness to perceive what any child learns instantly: that what matters greatly in this age of the survival of the slickest is material success.

It is a fact we would all like to mitigate, rationalize, or dodge. But make no mistake. In the midst of an economic and scientific boom, we are witnessing a cultural depression. True, man has never before been so knowledgeable. But if knowledge is power, how is it that man has never been so incapacitated to manage or manipulate the world around him?

All but the few top artists have been undermined and

alienated, their confidence and hope shaken by a generation which has regarded the frank expression of poetic feelings as weakness and which views uncompromising ideals with indifference or overt contempt; a generation which prides itself on its emancipation from sentiment and whose solvents have been not in art or philosophy, but in charts and graphs. And it wants to see results. In cash or its equivalent.

The poetic age in which visionaries flourished was hardly an easy or tranquil one. But side by side with its problems were incentives for intellectual and spiritual quests, opportunities for leisurely reflection and informal exchanges of ideas—large ideas, dealing with the nature and destiny of mankind and art.

Today's artist is on a treadmill, the same treadmill as the television-service man who one morning charged six dollars for a six-minute visit which produced his expert opinion that his client needed a new set. With this difference: that the increase in the amounts paid the technician and the butcher and everyone else has no more applied to the concert artist than our higher standard of living has applied proportionately to our cultural climate.

The artist therefore gets it coming and going. His society's emphasis on figures and facts, and its indifference to all but a chosen few who seek abiding values have discouraged him on idealistic levels. The sheer business of keeping financially afloat in this economy has made it impossible for him to live the life a musician should lead, that any intellectual worker must lead.

It is self-evident that the public's enthusiasm for music and its principal experiences with it derive primarily from performance of one kind or another. As the creative and interpretative past fades into time, the status of the contemporary artist assumes vital importance. Each threat to it is a threat to the continuing life of music and to our cultural resources. An environment that compels an artist to do less than his best work, or even other work, in order to exist destroys his spiritual and emotional fiber and menaces his power. It makes him substitute the immediate for the absolute, cynicism for faith. He is not the only loser. We are all in this thing together. We all pay a price. And so does our nation when its artists lose faith, lose the very reasons for faith.

Almost every artist of every nation has at some time and to some degree suffered in this way. And always it has taken a superior man to overcome a social environment incompatible with cultural ideals. But heretofore his place in the community has been measured and established by what he gave to the world, not what he got from it. His work was spiritually fused with his society. A man can endure many privations when his faith in the far-reaching good and usefulness of his chosen work remains unshaken. But when it is neither rewarded nor prized, he is finally driven to ask himself: "What am I doing this for? Why am I killing myself?"

Should many more of our artists than those who have already surrendered conclude that the most valiant battle is futile, we shall be in a bad way. The currents of our epoch are so chaotic, so conducive to uncertainty of purpose and jumbled canons, that even some who are successful by every outward standard demonstrate frustrations that are not easy to explain.

In the summer of 1956 we found Friedrich Gulda, one of the greatest talents among today's classical pianists, playing an engagement with his own "combo" at Birdland, one of New York's flashiest jazz clubs. Clearly, this was no case of a concert failure seeking success elsewhere. This young Viennese had made a big noise in the musical world through his remarkable musicianship and striking virtuosity.

In the classical world Gulda is right on top. In the jazz world he is nowhere near it, and his deliberate excursion into that field provokes conjectures. Perhaps it provides some release from concert tensions, some needed chance to indulge in interpretative expression on a less exacting level. That I can understand. Or perhaps its fascination lies in its improvisational opportunities. Although I wish a pianist like Gulda would seek those opportunities in the works of Bach and Mozart, I can still understand how rewarding that aspect of jazz can be.

What is hard to understand is why a fully recognized young master of an infinitely rich milieu is driven to find satisfaction in another environment on a professional basis rather than as a pleasurable avocation. There is only one way that it makes sense to me. It is just a fact of our time, a symbol of the rootlessness that makes it hard for the artist to know where he belongs.

There is no question that musical activity of every sort flourishes throughout our country at an unprecedented rate today. But this frequently made and accurate observation can only be more disheartening to artists of unwavering ideals who see that, though they are the masters of an art that is truly popular and no longer esoteric, they are still unable to make firm places for themselves.

Most concert pianists teach, not only to earn money but also because teaching is both an enhancing experience and an artistic obligation. But what chances are there in this frantic world to create an atmosphere that enkindles the spirit and imagination of both teacher and student?

The art of teaching lies largely in the ability to enlist the pupil's ardent co-operation in a combined, calm quest after truth. Our way of life makes it equally difficult for master and student to indulge in the spontaneous adventures of reflection and discussion, of digressions from the music at hand to other music, to literature or painting or reminiscence in pursuit of first principles. Indifference to the clock is a prohibitive luxury. There is very little room in the crowded corridors of our precipitous existence for a teacher, no matter how dedicated, to exert an all-inclusive influence on the student's life, to develop his love for learning, to animate his imagination and quicken his desire to expand and control and express his powers.

But even so, the honest teacher who does the best he can is more deeply rewarded than he is as a performer. He gives what he has to give, and it is usually appreciated. He gets respect and he gets paid.

As a player, and ironically at a time when the demand for his art is at its height, his artistic resources are being squandered. Never before has the soloist been so seriously threatened from so many sources. But from none more lethal than the managerial system through which his "unique and induplicable services" are first sold, then worn down, and gradually buried.

Buried? Yes, buried. But surely that is not even good business. Assuredly, it is not. But it fits perfectly the unscrupulous myopia and the impracticality of practical men whose creed is expediency. Yesterday we saw it in blind and profligate recklessness in the use of our rich forests and precious soil. Today the same blindness and profligacy imperil our artists and artistic standards.

The Chains of Management

THE PLAIN FACTS of concert management are a scandal, but not an open scandal except to musicians, especially to performers, whose relations with chain managements are comparable to the labor-capital struggle of pre-unionism. Of course, there are always the few who benefit too greatly from malpractice to renounce or denounce it.

All the principled businessmen and professionals in other fields who learn the managerial facts of the music business find them beyond belief. Most of them say that such ethics and tactics would not be tolerated in any other endeavor, that did they pertain to law or medicine, we would soon be left without lawyers or doctors. All of them say that it makes no sense for anybody in the long run.

They are dead right. It makes no sense. But it makes life, the exacting and arduous life that almost every serious artist of our generation has had to endure. If he cannot endure it, he can quit. And many have. If he does not quit, he finds himself forcibly retired or buried alive.

I am now referring not to aspirants who could not make the grade, but to recognized talents with impressive histories. Over one hundred of them within the past twenty years emerged successfully from the brimstone and fire of competing for the most significant piano awards of our time. All went on to make important appearances that accrued from these coveted awards, and a good many earned unstinting approval from the implacable metropolitan press. Yet their names will be unfamiliar except to their colleagues and friends, for most of them have all but vanished from the concert scene. Genuine talents all, and finely schooled too, but where are they and what has happened to them?

Exactly three have been able to build and maintain what we might call careers. That is, they are with an influential management, they play some of the best orchestral dates and recital series, and they have recording contracts with dominant companies. They are not big names. They are not big-time. They do not command large fees. At least they are practicing their art and growing in it, and they have managed to keep their heads above the treacherous waters.

As for most of the others I have not named, don't ask. But I should like to tell you anyway. The majority never got inside the doors of any management. Some actually got on the lists of the Big Two, which in those days were called Columbia Concerts Corporation and National Concert and Artists Corporation. After playing a few years, most of them too have disappeared from the American platform. Others pried contracts from independent managers and in fairly short order folded up together with their agents. A few have found a haven abroad. A few others go doggedly on in their own country, skimping and struggling to give New York recitals periodically at somewhere close to two thousand dollars a throw.

Why do musicians pay for the chance to play a New York recital? For many reasons, but chiefly for press notices. Notices that a debutant hopes will enlist a manager's interest, that an artist already represented trusts will stimulate managerial action and results. Their expectations are pathetically unrealistic. Performers who have been regularly pilloried by knowledgeable critics have been booked widely, whereas performers who have caused the same critics to rhapsodize have been rudely awakened to the fact that good notices can mean nothing. They rarely motivate a management either to accept a new artist or to improve the status of one it represents. Favorable reviews are helpful to a career only when a powerful management utilizes them aggressively. In the great majority of cases, enthusiastic reviews actually jeopardize the continuing relations between artist and management. On the face of it, this sounds utterly absurd. But in a moment we shall see why a compelling success by anyone but the "champs" is a threat to the vitals of the managerial system.

Around 1930, two organizations acquired a subtle stranglehold on the concert business of our country: Columbia Concerts, Inc., and the National Concert and Artists Corporation. More recently Columbia Concerts was renamed Columbia Artists Management and the NCAC still later became the National Artists Corporation. From the reports of their solo artists, the deletion of the word "Concert" by both organizations was an unintended omen of things to come. Originally, Columbia was financially linked to the Columbia Broadcasting System, while its rival had some similar rapport with the National Broadcasting Company. Within ten years the Federal Communications Commission got around to asking questions about these liaisons that some evil-minded people viewed as possible restraint of trade. Whereupon the principals undertook a voluntary divorce between their radio and concert interests.

The concern and power of the FCC lay in the broadcasting sphere. It did not inquire into the nature of Columbia's partnership with Community Concerts, its booking network that extends throughout the United States and Canada, or into its counterpart called Civic Concerts, created by National to meet competition.

The plan of both Community Concerts and Civic Concerts promised to provide wide cultural benefits, vastly expanded opportunities for artists, and an economically sound mechanism that would enable a lot of people to hear a lot of music. It was a combination of the old

Chautauqua idea and the package concert series initiated during the early twenties in Chicago by Ward French and Dema Harshbarger. Anyway, the concept was a venerable and admirable one. The same could be said about the wheel until it was attached to a cannon.

The two chains organized more than one thousand towns, among them many which had never seen a real live musician and whose good citizens became eager converts to Culture. In each case, a cultural missionary came unto them whose sideline was to sell a galaxy of artists managed by his organization. The town leaders and their brethren then went forth to wage a subscription drive. And when they brought the fruits of their green pastures to the managerial messenger, he said they would have music, and he left in peace.

Say that the town raises five thousand dollars. For that it may have a series of three or four concerts. One features a big-name artist who will draw the public and a fee of around thirty-five hundred dollars. After incidental expenses, some two hundred to three hundred dollars are left for each remaining soloist or ensemble.

Now let us meet the artists who play the series. There is no need for concern about the big name. With few exceptions, his fame and power are deservedly secure. He is in the enviable position of writing his own ticket. He is a *rara avis*, required and desired. He has the bargaining power to dictate to the chain managements. All other artists tremble before them.

I know the case history of dozens of young pianists, hard-working, richly endowed, and fully ready to utilize the chance to perform, to gain precious experience, and to build a following. Each and every one of them who managed to get a coveted contract from one of the Big Two was gullibly certain that he was on his way to a career. All but the three I mentioned previously have had identical unhappy experiences.

They started on the Community or Civic circuits as

filler artists in perhaps five to ten towns. Gross annual take, maximum, twenty-five hundred dollars. Outlay for circulars, pictures, postage, hotels, transportation, and fifteen per cent for managerial commission left a net of zero or minus. *Next year,* muses the artist. *After all, I played well, got good reviews, and the audiences liked me.* Next year, twenty dates. *Now I'm on my way.* But the routing this time eats up profits in long jumps and in hotel living between engagements. Gross, five thousand. Net, if one is frugal, twenty-five or thirty per cent. *Next year,* the artist thinks, *maybe I'll play better towns and get more money.* A few better towns, perhaps. Or the windfall of an unexpected substitution for an indisposed star. In such a case, incidentally, the pinch-hitter gets his usual two hundred and fifty regardless of how many thousands were set aside for the celebrity's appearance.

On occasion, such a substitution may result in a spectacular success that produces national press coverage. The artist is convinced that he has hit the jackpot, that he has now become a salable personality. Has he not had the break that every manager tells every artist is essential to catapult a nobody into a somebody?

Now come the realities. He must first make a huge investment or throw in the sponge. Thousands of circulars are printed and mailed. Spreads are purchased in the trade journals. Expenditure, several thousand dollars. But now he can *really* expect something to happen next year. The booking starts. Instead of two hundred and fifty, he gets three hundred. He even gets a few more engagements.

Suddenly the light dawns. He realizes that it matters little what he does or how he does it. He remains rigidly frozen in his niche. He is in the same fee bracket. He cannot develop a public following, for re-engagements are not encouraged. He is still a filler artist, getting nowhere fast.

Nevertheless, merit becomes known among professionals. That way, more than through management, some of our young artists have won important engagements. Fortunately, there still are among us some conductors with artistic ideals, some board members of orchestras who resist managerial pressure. Such men provide another way through which young artists have had the chance to show their mettle. The bitter fact remains that these isolated successes, in one case after another, became the straws that finally broke their backs.

Mustering some of their ever dwindling confidence, artists go to their managers and furnish proof of their ability to deliver when an eventful assignment comes their way. Does this not indicate, would it not seem fair that more effort should be made to book them with other orchestras or for some straight sales dates, and perhaps for higher fees?

Wham! That is when they learn the facts of an art that has become a ruthlessly curbed business. There is room at the top, which they can never reach from their pigeonholes, and at the bottom, from which they cannot escape. In between is No Man's Land.

Some call it a day there and then. Others linger on, defenseless and disheartened. If they are "lucky," they continue to play for a few years, reconciled to their plight and to the discomforts inherent in traveling from one small town to another. Suddenly, when they have played all or most of the towns available to them, their dates evaporate. This is the point at which the "luckier" ones are invited to stay on if they can form their own ensembles or will become anonymous members of a group attraction. It is the point of no return.

I hear the unindoctrinated reader asking impatiently: "Why in blazes did they not leave the chain managements and go to independent managers?"

The answer lies in the starched phraseology of the United States District Court, dated October 2, 1955.

The plaintiff was the United States Government *v.* the defendants Community Concerts and Civic Concerts.

"The defendants combined and conspired in unreasonable restraint of the aforesaid interstate trade and commerce in the management and booking of artists and in the formation and maintenance of organized audience associations and have combined and conspired to monopolize, have attempted to monopolize and have monopolized said trade and commerce in violation of Section 1 and 2 of the Sherman Act."

Now perhaps you can see what the independent manager was up against, unless he had an artist like Horowitz, who needs a manager less than a secretary to acknowledge the dates he will accept.

The defendants pleaded *"nolo contendere,"* which my lawyer friends tell me meant, in effect: "O.K., Uncle, we won't contest your charges." A fine was imposed, a consent decree was signed, and time marched on. From what I can gather, the situation has not changed much. Theoretically, the independent manager was always able to sell his artists to Community and Civic courses. But the mechanics of chain management put him at an impossible disadvantage. It still does, although the consent decree stipulated that every artist of every management must be made available to every town. The independent is not in the picture while the season's concert plans are being formulated. The chain representative is in there first. After he has booked the main attraction, the cream is off the top.

But his work is not yet finished. He has other problems and primary obligations. He represents not only his company, not only its soloists, but also group attractions that have to be booked solidly if they are not to eat up the organization's investments and potential profits. If he does not sell them consistently, he endangers his job, for such groups represent large investments of time and money. That is why chain managements are willing to buy group attractions from independent managements and to book them on their own courses. But this hardly pertains to the soloists.

Say that an artist under independent management is insisted upon by a concert committee. There are many ways and incentives to divert this interest, especially as the independent has neither the sales force nor the physical ability to be on the spot to represent his artist on an equally competitive basis. There is the further fact that such dates are often not worth fighting for unless by accident the artist happens to be booked within a reasonable distance around the time of the proposed date. Despite all the fine talk, therefore, the independent manager still faces an impossible situation, even when he represents an artist in some demand.

This is how the managerial system affects artists—even artists under chain managements, for they must take what is left after the groups are booked. Now let us see how artistic standards are affected, as disclosed in the chains' shocking disinterest in music itself.

Our chief concern relates to pianists. In town after town they have been sold before anybody paused to inquire whether an adequate instrument was available to them. Think of a tennis-player attempting to play a match on a half-size racquet with a warped frame and broken strings, and on a rain-soaked court. Now consider pianists who have devoted thousands of hours to developing precisional evenness, subtlety of nuance, and beautiful tone quality. Time and again they encounter out-of-tune and unregulated baby grands with missing strings, defective actions, and jagged keys. Under these circumstances the greatest skill is hopelessly handicapped.

For years the programs of concert artists were subjected to scrutiny and censorship by men who were musically illiterate. Their decisions, no matter how absurd, were obeyed to the letter. Or else. The way things are going, artists will not even have to face this problem much longer. Today the push is for group attractions. The more people on the stage, the better. And if it keeps up much longer, all but a select few soloists will go the way of the horse car.

Salesmen have sold artists they knew nothing about. Managements have given contracts to artists they have never heard, products they have never tested even in audition. Why? They needed a new face to play in an old place, a face that was willing to show itself anyplace at any fee. So it has been and so it shall be that whoever and whatever courts easy success *en masse* becomes compromised to pragmatic ends and to the lines of least resistance.

What I am describing has forced most of America's greatest talents of the last quarter-century to abandon all hope that within their lifetimes either their government or their fellow creatures would become sufficiently interested, informed, and indignant to act and improve their lot. Once and for all we should realize that the great majority of soloists vegetate within a regime that denies them fundamental rights that belong to all others—the chance to do their work, the chance for advancement in recognition of a job well done and of long and loyal service.

Our nation's industrial and domestic workers have for many years enjoyed the highest living standards ever known to any country in any century. It is an uneasy prosperity that affords peak opportunities and compensations for all provided that they are not artists.

Recently, I undertook an informal little survey on concert pianists. Except for four pianists, all in their sixties or seventies and whose careers were molded in a former era and in other countries, I found none able to maintain themselves and their families entirely from concerts. All must depend on supplementary income derived from one or more of the following sources, listed in order of frequency: teaching, being married to partners who work, accompanying, receiving regular aid from parents or patrons, or periodic assistance from organizations.

A treasurer's statement from a musical foundation lists 1957 disbursements for grants-in-aid to five pianists. I know them well. Two are former Naumburg Award winners whose debut recitals reaped exceptionally fine reviews. Two others also captured significant awards and have been playing the circuits for several years. The fifth had won a prize that provided the most promising opportunities of all. Artistically, he had come through. But he had returned from a tour of eleven concerts with less than the amount of the rent bill that awaited him. The Foundation saved him from the embarrassment of borrowing money just to keep a roof over his head.

Behind all this are many greedy people who neither love nor value music, who have capitalized on it and on the artistic provincialism and lethargy of the public to exploit and sacrifice talent to their own financial interests. It must be said, however, that within their organizations are many men and women who had no part whatsoever in creating company policies or practices, and who do not like them any more than we do, but who can no more afford to give up their safe berths than anyone else can today.

But the system under which they operate is ruthless and crushing, and its undiminished ability to depreciate and manipulate our musical resources is to be counted among our worst failures.

High Fidelity—High Fatality

A WHILE AGO I scanned a music magazine, and an advertisement leaped out of the page. "IMAGINE!" it screamed, "ALL THE SO-WHAT SONATAS ON ONE LOW-COST DISC!"

I did not have to imagine anything. I had heard it, and had it. Before that I had received a letter while I was in California from the agonized pianist who recorded what I call the So-What sonatas out of sympathy for an assignment that was doomed from the start. But let the pianist's letter explain.

"Although I can hardly hold this pen, I must unburden myself, ask a favor actually, or go quite mad. I finally landed a recording contract. It hinged on my consent to do all the So-What sonatas. I had played only one of them, the shortest and best. The others are for the birds—the birds who want hi-fi, an LP filled to the brim, and to hell with everything else but the discount. Yesterday, the murder started. I can already see critics and people like you sharpening your pencils and inventing smart cracks like 'Old pianists don't die. They just fake away.' Please do an old friend one favor. Please find the mercy in your heart not to review this record."

Actually, the record came out better than I had expected after reading that letter. The playing had no little grace and technical fluency. What it did not have was interpretative conviction, architectural coherence, and the poise and polish that come from the mellowing processes of leisurely preparation and public experimentation. It was a characteristic modern piano disc, full of music that never had a chance to settle, full of splices that did not adhere to the rest. In short, there were areas of excellence surrounded by acres of deadwood.

Theoretically, wholly successful devices should produce improvements on all levels, not on one at the expense of another. In music, when mechanical progress is isolated, when it becomes the end rather than the means, it is bound to yield a diminution of artistic standards.

Recently I reheard a number of acoustic and electrical recordings made during the "Golden Age." Having heard so many LP discs in recent years, I understand the term better now than I did when I was hearing newly made recordings by Caruso, Journet, Ponselle, Chaliapin, Onegin, Flagstad, Kreisler, Casals, Schnabel, and Rachmaninoff, to name a few.

These records bring home some truths worth cherishing. Great artists are great artists, no matter how you splice them. They are severely self-critical and therefore selective. They choose to interpret only those works for which they have surpassing affinity. They spend long years of loving labor in the effort to mold their repertoire meticulously and to see it whole. Most of them could not recall the day when the music they recorded was not in their hearts or ears, long before it was in their throats or fingers.

These distinctions are precisely what the recording realities of our day conspire to prevent. LP, like TV, is a material-devouring monster. The public demand for complete packages and categories is insatiable. A recording company today that does not produce a large and continually increasing catalogue cannot compete in business.

What to do? The companies naturally try to get their best artists to do as many recordings as possible. They also make whopping blunders in the erroneous assumption that great artists are great no matter what they do. Great artists are great in what they choose to do, not in what they are sometimes coerced and seduced into doing under the undermining influences of a dynamic economy. Unless top-flight artists have particular areas of rapport and scholarship, as Schnabel for Beethoven, or Landowska for baroque music, they rarely play every work of a collection. Why? Because there are few collections that contain equally powerful and impeccable masterworks from first to last.

So, with children's shoes costing what they do today, with the necessity of making either a disc with a lot of music on it or none at all, we are beginning to see artists prodded and instigated to record works they do not respect or have not digested, and even works they have no business playing.

Every new record catalogue brings fresh evidence that this is happening more and more frequently. It is an inevitable result when mechanical quality competes on an equal basis with artistic quality, when bulk enjoys parity with distinction. The competition becomes fierce, for there are slews of pianists ready to accept any assignment at the drop of a hat, and without much more time than it takes to drop a hat to "master" their assignment. And here is where another mechanical "blessing" aids and abets such projects. The technique of splicing and patching tape has been pressed into service to assist more than one performer inadequate to the formidable requirements of LP recording.

To illustrate, let me reconstruct a series of recording sessions I witnessed when a pianist was engaged to play a complete category of over thirty works. Exactly three were already in his repertoire, and on the concert platform he had demonstrated a substantial incapacity for their style. His unpreparedness for the task was as nought to the record company's "artistic" director, who rewarded it with a contract to perpetuate the whole batch for posterity.

Fortunately, the project did not start as one of those

harrowing sessions where the studio turns out to be a dud
no matter where the instrument or the microphone is put.
Nor did a piano leg collapse at the first arpeggio. It was
just a nice, normal session with the usual number of mis-
eries. But our artist had walked in visibly fearful of the
assignment. By the time the microphones were placed,
the maximum and minimum volume calculated, and other
problems of acoustics solved, he was already unnerved.

The pianist made the first take. The playback disclosed
rhythmic unsteadiness and a loss of power toward the end.
He tried again. This time the rhythm was better, but
something of the first fine rapture had been lost. The
next try revealed the presence of improved tonal control,
but at the expense of considerable accuracy. Moreover,
the pianist's endurance began to fail, so an attempt was
made to play section by section, with rests between. Just
as in the good old days of recording large-form works on
78 rpm, except that he played for about two minutes at
one sitting, rather than for four and a half minutes. And
he had the comfort of knowing that a "fluff" could be
"corrected."

A fast section of finger passages turned out to be practically note-perfect but constricted and devoid of any performance excitement. For a person of emotional sensitivity, there is always the danger of getting to a point where
something snaps within, where a fuse is blown, where the
source of power fails. Our pianist was now overcome with
fatigue and discouragement, the recording company with
overtime. So everybody went home.

The next day further attempts were made with very
much the same result. Science was now compelled to come
to the rescue. The technicians rolled up their sleeves and
got to work. In the first piece they extracted section one
of take three, with its poetic gradations of tone, tacked it
to section two, with its rhythmic verve, spliced it to the
third part of take four and its effective passage-work, and

so on. The same ridiculous business went on with each and every other piece, day in and day out for weeks. When the album emerged, it had all the coherence of a birthday party for a mob of three-year-olds.

Mass production by its very nature is incompatible with the superlative craftsmanship of a creative work of art. And a transcendent performance, like a transcendent composition, is an individual case. Most of the time art is an ever receding horizon. Few indeed are the times when great artists are able to say: "This is it. This is what I dreamed. And now I have realized it."

It will be readily understood that no one has a right to expect this kind of unique achievement to occur often. I certainly do not. But what we all have a right to expect from any pianist who accepts the obligation of performances to be preserved more or less permanently is basic and minimal qualities: the ability to play a melodic line that does not disappear under the piano, to lend grace and recognizable rhythm to dance movements, to display logic in relationships, and to play any confounded four bars in the same tempo.

The sheer number of recording artists needed to fulfill the repertoire needs and the sheer amount of music consumed by an LP disc are sufficient causes for a ruthless decline in the pianistic standards of recording.

What we hear in the finest recordings, old or new, is the venerable ideals of variety within unity, technique at the service of expressivity, and the fixed purpose of an adventurous spirit unafraid to bend the knee in obeisance to creative genius he seeks to serve. Music yields its treasurable secrets to no others. Only when it does can we feel the inevitability of a great work of art as a glimpse of immortality. The difficulty of achieving it is so enormous that we are lucky to have as many examples as we have.

They are indeed wonderful, and we are not unmindful that high-fidelity enables us to hear them more wonderfully. But they will become rarer and rarer until our artists assume a higher fidelity toward music and toward their interpretative responsibilities. Then we may even hope for unimagined wonders.

State and Art

I HAVE POINTED out behind the decline of pianism the sociological, economic, managerial, and mechanical factors that provoke especially the American artist's disinterest in the past, that depress his spirit and suppress his opportunities, and that discourage the minute inspection of his materials and the mature fulfillment of his art.

This is cause enough for alarm, yet I think that there is an even larger factor, perhaps the generic one that affects not only the pianist but also every one of us, and that we can do something about—not *can*, but *must* do something about and immediately, for the entire intellectual life of our country has never been in greater jeopardy.

However divergent our individual interests, however opposite our opinions, we are all united in certain common objectives: we want our world to be happier and more secure; we want our nation to be strong. And those who care intensely for knowledge and beauty and human creativity further hope that our nation will be strong not merely in money and arms, but also in ideas and ideals.

Those who hope this and those who never give it a thought are both encircled, for no nation can be completely strong unless it properly values and utilizes its resources, all of its resources, and this must include its creative and interpretative thinkers and the finest work they can do.

A long, long time ago, Plato said that what is honored in a country will be cultivated there. If we apply this to our time and to our country, I think we shall find that the separation of State and Art in our land is significantly related to the plight of our artists and to the squandered estate of our cultural prestige throughout the world.

Many of us have followed the sad history of the various proposals and efforts by a few far-seeing citizens and legislative representatives to enlist Congressional interest in the arts apart from pious verbiage and emergency allocations motivated by crises.

At last pushed into action by competition, for which we owe totalitarianism some wry thanks, the government of the mightiest democracy in the world opened one eye to observe its opponents capitalizing on the age-old fact that artists can rush in where statesmen fear to tread. Eventually our lawmakers had to face the bitter truth that we were being outmaneuvered in our efforts to acquire esteem in all the countries that honor the arts and that gauge other countries by their cultural way of life. Finally we were forced to acknowledge that those whose approbation we were courting were accepting our overtures with outstretched palms, plugged-up ears, and uptilted noses.

Counteraction became imperative. Around 1954, and on a contingency basis, our government was induced to furnish financial aid to the American National Theatre and Academy. ANTA was facing a struggle in the brave effort to strengthen our cultural ties abroad by organizing tours for American companies and soloists. Now it was to be helped by national recognition and support. But the artist found a long string attached to the project that at first glance appeared so promising.

Only if individuals or groups were already booked overseas or were willing to book ("buy" is the more accurate word) tours on their own initiative were they eligible for assistance, which rarely amounted to more than a contribution toward their travel expenses.

The way it worked out proved that the arrangement was one whereby our artists willingly aided our government far more than it was willing to aid them. Many soloists and orchestras pitched in, nevertheless, and often at considerable personal sacrifice. Along with fellow performers in the allied arts, our musicians earned for us a new respect and many friends.

Their undeniable impact made the support of a permanent cultural program compulsory to our foreign policy. In 1956 the Eighty-Fourth Congress created a Federal Advisory Committee on the Arts, committing Uncle Sam to a permanent cultural program beyond our borders which covered practically every art, craft, and athletic activity in the land. The total appropriation for the whole caboodle was $2,225,000, less than half the cost of one DC-8 jet transport. Not a penny was appropriated for any cultural center or activity within our own country.

So did the legislature of the richest nation on earth demonstrate to the world the extent of its interest in its culture at home and in its cultural ambassadors abroad. Few of us even knew that such a bill existed, for American journalism shares with American legislature both the provincial view of art as an isolated phenomenon and a basic disbelief in its everyday value to our society.

That is how a revolutionary document, the International Cultural Exchange and Trade Fair Participation Act of 1956, entered the statute books almost unnoticed in the news columns of the nation's daily press.

Although the motive was non-cultural and the amount meager, the passage of the bill was nevertheless a landmark for a country with no ministry of the arts and no cultural bureau. It was a ray of hope. It opened a door, and we were all indebted to its chief sponsors and advocates: Senators Hubert Humphrey of Minnesota, Herbert H. Lehman of New York, and Alexander Wiley of Wisconsin; Representatives Walter H. Judd of Minnesota, James P. Richards of South Carolina, Frank Thompson and Harrison Williams of New Jersey, and John H. Udall of Arizona.

It was not their fault that our financial appropriation

was pathetically inadequate, shamed by the cultural programs of even the tiniest and poorest countries. The promotion of cultural pursuits in virtually every other civilized country derives from a basic philosophy rather than from a pragmatic policy. With them, the support of art and artists begins at home as a normal function of government. Our politicians might be told, as Ralph Waldo Emerson told the missionaries of his day: "Thy love afar, is spite at home." Abroad, art and artists are cherished as national possessions as well as instruments of communication and influence.

Our rusticity in these matters has been complacently explained away by "practical" men as a result of a youthful country's natural preoccupation with physical and material necessities. This argument was shown up painfully by our Canadian neighbors, who emerged from pioneer days more recently than we, and whose government early in 1957 proposed a fifty-million-dollar fund for the development of the arts, humanities, and social sciences within its own country. Its model was obviously not our brand of cultural patronage, but the Arts Council of Great Britain. This completely independent but state-subsidized assembly has long demonstrated what can be accomplished by an uncontrolled group with professional experience and intellectual integrity. Free from party politics, it has supported music, opera, theater, ballet, poetry, painting, and sculpture. It has furthered the status and standards of all its cultural expressions and representatives. It has restated in the most practical terms the principle that a nation's art is as important as its business or diplomacy, or even its sports. It has literally put its artists on the map, all over it, and enabled them to do their best in the assurance that they and their work are greatly valued and urgently needed.

American artists have never had such assurances. Before our officials awoke to the "advertising" potentialities of

artists, a consequential international art exhibit was announced in South America. It spurred the cultural mechanisms of every government except ours to round up its
best painters and their best canvases and pack them off
with every backing and blessing. A few American artists
pooled their own resources—a few pennies and many un-
sold canvases—and doggedly went down to form a self-
subsidized and self-appointed "U.S. tactical force." At the
gala opening, as the representatives of other governments
proudly and shrewdly guided their countrymen around,
it became obvious that our titular diplomatic "servant"
was conspicuously absent. "Where is he?" an American
painter inquired. "Where he always is," answered a native attaché, with a patronizing smile. "If it's the afternoon, he's playing golf. At night, it's gin rummy."

A year later, five well-known American musicians were
invited by the Federal Republic of West Germany to
make a good-will tour of the country. In reciprocation,
all the artists donated their services as soloists with the
Berlin Philharmonic Orchestra in a benefit concert, the
proceeds to go into a building fund for the orchestra's
new concert hall. The Germans packed the hall and
cheered the performances. The press glowed. The next
day the group was asked to a party and there met a number of American government officials stationed in Germany. Each and every one of them solemnly inquired who
the guests were, what they did, and what they were doing
in Berlin!

The American press was almost equally apathetic. Some
half-dozen of our better newspapers noted the fact that
the first musicians' group to participate in the exchange
program was leaving our shores for Germany. None noted
its inaugural significance in our musical history or initiated on-the-spot coverage of the artistic and promotional
results of the event.

Multiply such episodes of unconcern without stint, and

it is impossible not to be moved by the extent to which they have diminished the confidence and stature of our artists. This takes us back to our pianists and the psychological wounds inflicted upon their courage and their potency. In their faces and in their actions, in their words and in their music, we observe the dark shadows of rejection.

We cannot afford to waste this precious human material. Unless our artists are made to feel that their work is an organic work, that it matters to us whether it is utilized or squandered, the symbols of our civilization, its only symbols, will suffer mightily.

American artists and intellectuals are the natural enemies of American politicians. They are disliked and feared because they are the standing rebukes to governmental neglect, the living symbols of cultural immaturity and injustice.

Culture must be understood and cherished, fought for and maintained, just as liberty must be, and in an identical way. A few decent men who love it lead the way. Everyone else benefits by its privileges, the wise and the ignorant, the moral and the immoral alike. Its guardians must be constantly vigilant, however, for among us are callous men who resist it, and evil men who seek to profit from it by reducing its standards and misusing its practitioners in an iniquitous way. In any other field but art, the state would be screaming for their scalps.

All this directly explains the cultural climate that envelops our pianists. They are not only members of a hermetic profession that is largely a combine of maestros and merchants, but also citizens of an unenlightened and unconcerned state. No wonder that most of them lack security of mind, large perspective, and dominant personalities. How can we possibly expect such qualities from those who find their gifts dispensable, find themselves exploited, then suppressed, and eventually discarded? How can we expect anything but timidity and cynicism from those who are not given a sense of individual worth? What incentives have they to arm themselves when they have so little to battle for?

These are questions that concern us all, problems we cannot just take or leave, for they arise from much larger issues. And merely because the circumstances to supply ready solutions may not be present, we need not sink into a fatalistic conformity to things as they are.

We can inform ourselves and one another. We can talk together and think together. Especially we can feel together, for to feel intensely enough to act is to make ourselves and our cause so potent that neither can be safely ignored. To understand merely intellectually, to offer only lip service, is to continue on our own sweet ways in complacency. We can work within our organizations. We can rouse our colleges and universities from detached attitudes, for surely they are among the last cultural bulwarks that still proffer a reasonable measure of security and welcome to our intellectuals and idealists.

But we can do more. We can hit where it matters most. We can vote for or against. We can buy or not buy. It may be an impossible task to make uneducated or venal men understand anything they do not want to understand or seek to misappropriate. But politicians understand votes; newspapers understand circulation and advertising; managements and record companies understand red ink; and businessmen understand what can happen when an informed and aroused public compels its representatives to investigate the embezzling of our natural and national resources by private enterprise.

The fact that we may not have immediate remedies for the ills of our society does not mean that we are powerless. There is abundant power in honest purpose, far-reaching power in the hearts and ideals of dedicated people, whereas there is inherent weakness and frail faith in those dedicated only to the momentary and the mercenary. This applies no less to individuals than to nations and to the world.

For a long time now the world has been engaged in a conflict, a conflict between opposite beliefs, between opposed ideas as to the way life should be lived. We are awakening to the discovery that all the material resources in the world cannot enable us to emerge victorious from that struggle, for it is essentially a struggle for people's minds, for their co-operation, for their faith in the kind of life we articulate and exemplify.

The result of that struggle depends less on what we have than on what we are. And what we are is what we do. We can prate about equality and democracy until we are blue in the face, but it will avail us nothing if we practice and permit discrimination in our midst, whether it is racial, religious, or vocational.

And we could have grown purple urging legislation for cultural purposes without getting anywhere. Plenty of oratory was bellowed from Capitol Hill into the *Congressional Record* in lip service to the Importance of Culture. But nothing was done until our legislators were pushed by the realities that we were losing face throughout the world and that a bad cultural policy is bad business. That they understood; that spurred them into action which should have been taken years and years ago in the national interest. Culture was no longer a useless thing like spiritual force, but a tactical arm, a combat weapon. What do you know!

The time is now ripe for us to shed our swaddling clothes, ripe for a mature consideration of a Fine Arts Council of the United States. I know every argument against it: the possible abuse of power by government, the possible interference with individual freedom of choice and action, and so forth and so on. And every argument is in a class with the old contention that struggle is good for geniuses: let 'em starve.

Where there are men, there will be some abuse of power. What makes anybody conclude that such abuse is confined to government? We see it every day in private enterprise. Who can point to policies and practices more dictatorial, more political and self-perpetuating than those which govern the managements and boards of most of our orchestral institutions? And they are cultural institutions, or they are supposed to be.

Not all art and higher education dedicated to cultural advancement can or should be expected to pay for themselves and at the same time maintain the intellectual standards expected of them. In a real sense they do not even have the choice of making commercial successes or folding. They simply cannot be self-supporting today, if they ever were, and every attempt to cut deficits lessens their ability to fulfill their inherent obligations, renders them less able to hold unequivocal, long-term aims. They need backing—all kinds of backing—private, industrial, corporate, and Federal.

I think we are entirely ready for a long-range project whereby our government allocates an adequate sum of the tax-payer's money toward the support and encouragement of the arts—music, theater, ballet, literature, painting, and sculpture. We could well adopt the basic plan of the British Arts Council, which has shown conclusively that governmental patronage of the arts is a practical and achievable goal, and can remain apart from political partisanship and manipulation.

In our vast country an extended version of this plan would be necessary, or another plan might work out better. But let us work it out any way it can be worked. Let us once and for all get on with it. We can thrash out differences in detail and initiate corrections and additional safeguards later. A poorly administered Arts Council would certainly be unfortunate. None at all is barbaric. We must establish for ourselves a principle that every other civilized country has long recognized: that government has a proper and vested interest in promoting the arts.

This is our nation, whether we are pianists or businessmen, scientists or politicians or farmers. If we act together, it is within our ability to create a basis for its betterment, to combat whatever endangers the heritage of which we are now the custodians, and to call upon one another's good sense and efforts.

We dare not abdicate.

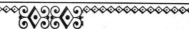

Episode

"Any fairly definite section separating the main themes, or interpolated into the development of a composition."
—DONALD FRANCIS TOVEY

Mainly Concerning the Pianist's Literature

Luckily for us, we have easy access to biographies of most great composers authentically handled with skill and insight by more than one writer. The techniques and philosophy of their styles have also been admirably described and analyzed by enlightened scholars.

Almost all my references to musical form, for example, are either recollections or interpretations of some spoken or written comments that derive from Tovey's unique analyses.

I shall therefore make no attempt to augment already existing and estimable material. The following commentaries are merely by way of setting down some reflections on certain composers and on certain aspects of their work, and of reminiscing about performances and recordings that pertain to them.

Mozart's "Clavierland"

NONE BUT the genius of geniuses could have survived
the mammoth representation that Mozart's bicentennial
generated. Everyone was playing his music. Everyone was
writing and talking about the miracle man whose artistic
mission was already fulfilled at an age when most men
are trying to decide what they should do in life.

Mozart survived. He lost not one whit of his unique
stature, which is more than we can say for most of his
interpreters. Perhaps his survival will help to convince
pianists especially that Mozart's textures are more akin
to indestructible steel than to the Dresden china they
make of them. What else could these textures be but indestructible, to have withstood the fallacious and popu-
larly adopted "Mozart style" of our day?

I have often wondered if it occurred to any of our busy
pianists to resolve that they would signify the eventful
year in service to the Mozart they profess to revere by a
more faithful study of his stated intentions and a more
authentic presentation of his music. Not a sign of it did
I hear, not a note. They were obviously too busy cashing
in on exactly what they had done about Mozart before,
and in the identical unenlightened way.

The world was busy about Mozart, too. Busier perhaps
than it had ever been since his own day. Oh, yes indeed.
The European musical world of the late eighteenth century recognized Mozart's genius as fully as those who exploited its fruits maltreated the man. Financially Mozart
was a failure, personally a misfit, and socially not much
better than a lackey. Artistically he stood alone. Even his
awe-inspiring contemporary Haydn acknowledged Mozart

to be the greatest of all composers. He was in constant demand, and had the ear of the mighty and the lowly.

Mozart regarded himself primarily as an operatic composer with a specialty in the satirical humor of comic opera. In this, he appears in retrospect as the sad prototype of the clown with the breaking heart. It may well be that he compensated for his bitter life struggle by transmuting his ordeals in the form of derisive laughter. Beneath the raillery and sparkling surface of his naughty mockery runs the poignant ebb and flow of tragedy and truth. In the language of high comedy, Mozart found the most dramatic expressions of gaiety and gravity. He speaks the same language in instrumental music, and in none more nearly perfectly than in his crowning creation, the piano concerto.

Whereas only a small percentage of Mozart's solo piano works are solid concert fare, the majority of his twenty-one concertos for one piano and orchestra on original material are masterpieces. It is necessary to label them so laboriously because Mozart wrote in addition seven early concertos based on compositions by others, as well as several concerto rondos and two-piano and three-piano concertos. The twenty-one remain his characteristic inspiration. No more significant set of works is to be found in musical history.

Their ripening took time and experience. Among the experimental concertos are three conversions of piano sonatas by Johann Christian Bach. They are adorable, but childish wonders, as we might expect from a ten-year-old genius, though Mozart performed them in later years. The first concerto on original material, K.175, shows a miraculous seventeen-year-old freeing himself from influences and launched on a phenomenal path. Thereafter, with the exception of the three-piano concerto written for lady amateurs, Mozart's work is so highly finished that it is often hard to distinguish what is important from what is unimportant. I am tempted to call the music I love important, that which does not thrill me unimportant. Frankly, I frequently yield to the temptation, but immediately remind myself that this is not criticism. I count myself lucky that the works I think important are the very works that have been taken to the heart of the public for almost two hundred years.

Actually, there are comparatively few pages within these treasures in which Mozart was not the creator of sublime music. But even in less inspired moments he was throughout the founder of a strikingly new and completely successful plan. In these varied forms—for no two are identical—Mozart discovered profound musical expression for that timeless human experience, the relation of the individual to the crowd. He solved it flawlessly, from sharp antithesis to harmonious compatibility, all with incomparably natural artistry.

It was Mozart, not Beethoven, who "liberated" the orchestra in collaborations of extraordinary prominence and independence. His innovations emerge so simply, so inevitably, that they seem to be conceptions that long existed and that Mozart merely uncovered. It is as though he blew from them the dust of the ages and lo!—there they lay in ordered perfection and infinite beauty. Gone are all the antagonisms between homophony and polyphony, between unequally balanced forces, tragedy and humor, animal spirits and spiritual ideals. Mozart's piano concertos represent the mature and reconciled formation of all the styles, textures, and designs he had encountered, adopted, and shaped throughout his earlier development. For me, the "pearls of highest price" are K.271, 414, 450, 453, 459, 466, 467, 488, 491, 503, 595, and 482, which I name last in order to relate that at its first performance, on December 23, 1785, the powerfully pathetic slow movement had to be repeated! Mozart was astounded, as we can be, at the cultivated taste of his Viennese public.

Although everything of significance in a man's music should be evident from the music itself, "should be ain't is," and we find pianists elbow-deep in Mozart's music showing a comprehensive inability to extract the most obvious facts from it. Such facts, nonetheless, are the stuff out of which profundities and subtleties arise. However, they are sometimes more strikingly revealed in historical terms.

Unless the reader is as lazy or as lacking in scholarship as too many of our performers, he already knows enough history and owns enough taste to sense that much of what he hears is not only imperfectly understood but also often in flat contradiction to every available fact. Available, that is, to anyone interested in ideas other than his own, and particularly in Mozart's. The Mozart family left a voluminous correspondence that provides detailed accounts of the practices of their time. If the reader has not encountered it, I urge his willingness to accept my word for easily ascertainable facts until he can himself attest to their validity.

Even a pianola knows that Mozart, from his glamorous infant-prodigy childhood to the shameful day of his burial in a pauper's grave, was a great keyboard virtuoso. But this meant something quite different from what it means now. An understanding of the vital differences might dispel some confusions that still exist.

Mozart's age was an age of extemporization. The practice continued long enough for Beethoven to say that no one could properly claim to be a virtuoso whose extemporizations could not qualify as written compositions. The skill was assumed in an era when concerts were principally display windows for composers who were expected to exhibit not only written works but also on-the-spot improvisations to show their imaginative power. When the youthful Beethoven went to Vienna, he was taken to Mozart, who reacted coolly to the boy's playing of some prepared pieces. Not until the prodigy improvised on themes inspired by the master he worshipped did Mozart say: "Keep your eyes on him; someday he will give the

world something to talk about." Later on we shall see
the pertinence of improvisation to the performance of
Mozart's piano concertos.

Despite every proof to the contrary, Mozart's piano
style is still believed by an appalling number of players
to be miniature. In his brief life span, Mozart witnessed
the decline of the harpsichord and the rise of the piano.
Before and during the transition period, the clavichord
was the common and inexpensive home instrument. By
the time Mozart had established his permanent residence
in Vienna in the early 1780's, the clavichord had all but
vanished from the mansions of the wealthy and sophisticated Viennese. Mozart certainly knew all three instruments at various times. But here the Mozart correspondence contributes to confusion by the constant use of the
word "clavier," obviously in its generic sense. In the thematic catalogue that Mozart kept during his last years, he
writes *"Klavier"* to designate keyboard works, but in his
manuscripts he never deviates from a lifelong habit of
writing *"cembalo"* or *"clavicembalo"* when he bothers to
indicate anything at all.

The mystery clears in his famous letter of 1777 in
which he vents all-out enthusiasm for the "pianoforte,"
and in our knowledge that shortly thereafter pianos were
usually available to him wherever he went. Nevertheless,
from Vienna in 1781 he again writes home: "This is the
best place in the world for my line of work. This *clavierland.*" He meant "pianoland," and he was ecstatic about
the Stein pianos he found, pianos substantially like the
instruments on which Beethoven and Chopin played.
Their sound was anything but a tinkle. Mozart's friends
used to ask him to make it "sound like an organ," and
he reveled in obliging them. There is every evidence that,
despite the difference in volume and sonority between
Mozart's pianos and our modern grands, the performance
of a Mozart concerto on the contemporary instrument is
far closer to Mozart's tonal experience than any perform-

ance on a harpsichord. The Dresden-china Mozart is a myth.

In the way that every great composer extended the technical resources of instruments, Mozart created piano parts for his concertos which are far more difficult than any that preceded them. His devilishly ingenious piano passages flow along so deftly and so effortlessly, however, that they set the most treacherous trap for the unwary. Woe to the pianist who relies only on his muscles to play them! Those passages are the most perilous in the entire literature because everything turns out slightly different from what it appears to be. Pity the poor pianist who discovers only through public disaster how much more difficult Mozart is for the brain than for the hand.

Most of Mozart's great concertos date from the Viennese period when he sought to leave the services of the miserable Archbishop of Salzburg, who saw Mozart as a genius in the pointed brim of the fool's cap. Mozart saw his opportunity in teaching and in offering subscription concerts to the public, in addition to private concerts. The programs for the public events indicate another great difference between his day and ours. Mozart found it possible to include symphonies and quartets and operatic arias, which were already public favorites, but what enticed the customers to pay the unusually fancy admission prices was the announcement of some *pièce de résistance*.

The most seductive come-on was a brand-new concerto or two in which the star could also display his prowess as an improviser. An enlightening report is found in *Cramer's Magazine* of March 22, 1783. "Today, the celebrated Chevalier Mozart gave a music academy for his own benefit at the National Theater in which pieces of his own composition, . . . already very popular, were performed. The academy was honored by the presence of an extraordinarily large audience and the two new concertos and other fantasies which Mr. Mozart played on the Forte

Piano were received with loudest approval. Our Monarch, who contrary to custom honored the whole academy with his presence, joined in the applause of the public so heartily that one can think of no similar example."

Mozart's piano solos were almost all entirely extemporaneous. In concertos it was primarily the cadenzas that furnished fullest opportunity for spontaneous inspiration. By all accounts, Mozart's were enormously exciting and impressive. Although no one can imagine what they sounded like, there can be little doubt that they were far more thrilling than all but a few of his written cadenzas. Obviously, even for Mozart the slow and complicated process of musical notation hampered the flood tide of the extemporary style.

This brings up the most hazardous aspect of performing Mozart piano concertos, for it was not only in the cadenzas that Mozart improvised. He left many pages in skeletal form, as in the coda of the middle movement of his piano concerto in A, K.488. He left many more such examples: the extreme case is the solo portion of the "Coronation" Concerto, K.537, which is nothing but a sketch throughout. Mozart notated the solo parts of his piano concertos as sketchily as he wrote the orchestral parts scrupulously. Manifestly, he ornamented his solos and otherwise gave them the breath of spontaneous life. This should surprise no one who has observed the word "*semplice*" found years later in Beethoven as a warning not to add embellishments. Still later we find the words "*senza ornamenti*" showing up even in Chopin!

The Mozart stylist understands that the autograph scores of Mozart's piano concertos (only four were published in his lifetime) are definitely not the authoritative record of what Mozart actually played. When his pupil Hummel edited eight of them, he left scarcely a bar of the piano writing untouched. We do not have to agree with one note of Hummel's versions, but we would be

obtuse not to reflect that Hummel knew a lot of things
that we do not, and that he corroborates the evidence
that Mozart left his scores incomplete.

Hummel, of course, wrote his own cadenzas. I know
from my own feeble and frustrating attempts what he
was up against. Certainly Hummel's are considerably better than some nineteenth- and twentieth-century cadenzas that sound like cavalcades of music from the composer's time onward, and are certainly more attractive
than Mozart's clichés, as for example the dull and per-
functory cadenza he tossed off for the first movement of
K.488. I do not pretend to have any pat solution. But the
problem is a real one, for we are indeed far from that
age in which instrumentalists and singers were judged no
less by their ability to embellish a score than by their
capacity to estimate and interpret what should be left
intact.

Our classical musicians have swung the pendulum so
violently as to boast of their precise adherence to the
text, no matter how demonstrably delusive it shows itself
to be. That is how far they have ventured to remain ignorant about their literature and all that has been made
available to them on its behalf. Untouched by criticism,
unprovoked by intellectual curiosity, they remain piously
unconscious of the outrageous disservice they render to
the masters of the age of extemporization.

The subtle art of improvisation is now practiced almost
entirely by our jazz musicians, in solo and simultaneous
extemporization. Naturally so, for improvisation is a stylistic element of jazz. And it was no less so in the music of
Mozart and his contemporaries and predecessors. But who
knows this? And who cares? Just a handful of musicians,
and most of them are harpsichordists.

Mozart's bicentennial found Wanda Landowska in her
seventy-eighth year. Her obeisance was a piano recording
of four sonatas, the A minor Rondo, the *"Ländler"* in
her own transcriptions, and some spoken observations on

Mozartean style. This unpretentious album stands as a monument of allegiance to Mozart. In authenticity and scholarship it dwarfs everything else I heard during the anniversary year, every huge gesture made on platform or disc which purported to pay homage to Mozart.

Mind you, I am as uncaptivated by Mme Landowska's instrumental approach to the piano as I am enamored of her musical erudition and her harpsichord mastery. But in view of what she has given us to hear and to think about, her way with the medium of her communication is relatively unimportant. We are moved by the lifetime devotion packed into these performances, by the broad vision and profound insight of a consecrated artist. We are convinced that *this* is the way Mozart should be played, with free ornamentation and elaborate embellishment—to emerge, anomalously, with regal dignity, grace, and simplicity.

It is devoutly to be hoped that Mozart will not have to await a tricentennial before our celebrated virtuosos grow literate and courageous enough to speak for him in his own language. A giant step in that direction will be the mere realization by performers that should they ever again flaunt their "conscientious obedience and literal fidelity" to the scores of Mozart and those before him, we shall instantly recognize them as sanctimonious frauds.

That, we can be sure, would be a worthy service and tribute to a sublime and monstrously maltreated spirit.

Beethoven's Five

"I have not studied enough," Beethoven said, long after his compositional power and mastery had been amply demonstrated. Every true artist has at times felt intellectually or technically inadequate to the demands of his imagination, but Beethoven was particularly assailed because he constantly was coming to grips with musical concepts and materials that compelled him to devise untrodden techniques. All his important works are marked by exciting solutions to problems that demanded a new departure or a new development.

We use the word "development" to mean the unfolding and expansion of an idea. In music, and especially in Beethoven's music, the word denotes an intensely dramatic form of action, and concerns mainly the first movements of works in sonata forms. Beethoven wrote over one hundred such works, and in his ceaseless search for structures that would support his tremendous emotional weight he achieved every conceivable variety of astonishing results. The organization of slow movements and rondo finales caused him few architectural difficulties. The first movement of the classical concerto, more specifically the opening orchestral tutti, was his stumbling-block.

Beethoven eventually solved the problem, and wonderfully, but the precise methods he devised and the startling discoveries he demonstrated in countless strokes of genius evidently escaped most musical theorists, to judge by current commentaries on the evolution of Beethoven's concerto forms. We are told, for example, that he turned his back on the classical forms of Haydn and Mozart. He did nothing of the sort. On the contrary, he attempted to discern the secrets of their methods and to multiply their resources. He discovered, but not immediately, what we also discover by proper observation—that the true classical concerto forms are not stereotyped molds but principles, and that their vitality depends not on structural formulas but on exciting innovations. That is why the critic is lost who relies on generalized doctrines to explain the unorthodox behavior of masterpieces—especially those by Beethoven, who found himself compelled to originate fresh methods for practically each successive work.

The basic problems that Beethoven faced in devising first movements within classical concerto principles embraced the age-old relation of the individual to the crowd —the problems Mozart solved with such maddening ease. The antithesis of that relationship opens every dramatic possibility from striking opposition, through compromise, to harmonious co-operation.

It is obvious that a solo instrument (the individual) has advantages of personal magnetism and mercurial mobility, but cannot vie with an orchestra (the crowd) in climactic force of volume. If an orchestra is allowed to swamp the solo or the solo is allowed to dominate the proceedings through deliberate repression of the orchestra, one or the other element will be sacrificed.

The classical solution was to capitalize on the disparity of these forces by permitting each to do what it was best able to do. The orchestra first "sets the stage" by stating the material importantly in a tutti calculated to arouse expectation; then the main character makes an impressive entry alone, and with counter-material. The dangers lie in creating an introduction so self-sufficient that it will fail to arouse enough suspense for the effective entrance of the solo instrument, or in creating an opening so insufficient that the orchestra becomes merely a subservient accompaniment, relinquishing its structural function. Perfect examples of the form avoid both dangers. They will further be found to vary the main material (stated by both orchestra and soloist) so that each succeeding entrance will be brought into fresh relationships and new perspectives.

Along the way, we may even meet brand-new themes. If we are eventually confronted with a solo cadenza followed by a reconciliatory climax, we are indeed in the presence of a true classical concerto. There are no more than two dozen successful examples in all musical literature. Most of them are by Mozart, and he composed them without effort.

Beethoven's first two piano concertos are sublime works, but they show in their symphonic discursiveness that he had not yet grasped Mozart's methods. The Triple Concerto, Beethoven's first structural success in this form, was heavily burdened by arid material. The Third Piano Concerto was the giant stride toward the marriage of inspiration and organization, perfectly united in the last two piano concertos and the glorious Violin Concerto.

The exciting potentialities the classical concerto offered a man of Beethoven's dramatic sensibilities drove his intellectual imagination to innovations that cannot be classified. The attempt to classify has soiled many an otherwise spotless musicological reputation. We should all welcome a dollar for every textbook that still maintains that with the Fourth Concerto, in which the piano states the opening five bars alone, and with the Fifth, in which a free improvisation precedes the orchestral tutti, Beethoven "abolished the traditional tutti."

We can trust the untutored music-lover more than the textbook-swallower to realize that immediately following the solo statements in both instances he is hearing life-sized tuttis. These two happen to be the most highly organized and gigantic of all Beethoven's piano-concerto openings, and have always furnished the dramatic excitement and satisfaction that their flawless designs were intended to provide. I have found that the layman, if permitted to remain uncorrupted by phony culture, always knows in his heart what is what.

It is no cause for surprise that a set of masterpieces providing soloists and conductors with the widest gamut of opportunities and rewarding the listener so richly have become sure-fire classics, constantly represented on the concert platform and on discs. Everyone has heard them hundreds of times, starting in the cradle. So have I, and as I pluck performances from memory I had better confine myself rigorously to mentioning those interpretations which seemed to me first-rate or not far from it.

I remember Beethoven's First Concerto exuberantly realized by Serkin in the vitality of the first movement, warm sentiment of the second, and exhilaration of the third. The winsome work also lingers in my memory as deliciously played and recorded by Ania Dorfmann with no small assistance from the meteoric Toscanini.

I have joyful recollection of the venerable Backhaus and the youthful Kapell both bringing spontaneous charm and crisp precision to their playing of the witty Second Concerto, although neither performed Rubinstein's unique service of enabling the corner movements to sound deeply lyrical without losing a jot of their humor, and making the middle movement sound profound but not solemn.

Impressed in my memory are outstanding interpretations of the Third Concerto from Ernest Hutcheson, Benno Moiseiwitsch, Rudolf Firkusny, and Emil Gilels; of the Fourth, nobly conceived, by Gieseking and Solomon; of the Fifth in a granitic concept by Backhaus, and with sweeping and perceptive grandeur by Serkin in collaboration with Eugene Ormandy at his best.

Have I forgotten Schnabel? On the contrary. I remember him too well not to isolate his achievements, for he was the only artist to play the whole set on a level that I have not encountered from any other pianist in a lifetime of listening.

Elsewhere I have discussed Schnabel's playing of the

Beethoven sonatas, so full of urgency and inspiration, though not always under complete technical control. The concertos revealed all the expected Schnabel characteristics of poetic vision, tonal beauty, and knowledgeable conviction. The unexpected plus was his greater mechanical command. This may have been in part owing to the fact that the concertos, difficult as they are, do not demand the degree of sustained virtuosity required in such sonatas as the *"Waldstein," "Appassionata,"* and the last five, particularly the *"Hammerklavier."* In all five concertos Schnabel was at his height in every way. His delicious grace and humor in the corner movements of the C major (published as No. 1, it actually followed No. 2) met their counterpart in the searching profundity and spaciousness he brought to the great E flat (nothing will induce me to call it the "Emperor").

Schnabel's mellow humanity in slow movements—as in the Third Concerto, where the solemn shock of E major transports us so far from the C minor tonality elsewhere —displayed two of his supreme awarenesses: that harmony, like melody, has emotional significance, and that perceptive ornamentation is a priceless ingredient of expressivity.

Apropos, all but devout disciples of the Urtext are likely to be puzzled by Schnabel's persistent pedaling throughout this movement, similar to his pedaling in the two recitatives of the first movement of the Sonata opus 31, no. 2, the six measures preceding the *più allegro* of the first movement of the Sonata opus 57, and in the rondo theme of the Sonata opus 53. The resultant harmonic blurrings are in literal obedience to Beethoven's original and uncanceled pedal signs. The subject has aroused heated controversy. It merits a lengthy essay, but perhaps we could take a moment here to discuss one aspect of it.

We need not consider Beethoven's deafness, which did not become acute until several years after most of these works were composed. We need not even consider the substantial differences between his piano and ours. But we ought to remember that Beethoven was the greatest pianist of his day. We can be certain that he used the pedals in gradation, as all great pianists do: not completely depressed to their full limit, but partially so when he wanted a cloudy color; and we can be sure that he was always ready to shake out any sounds that became too obtrusive by rapid and imperceptible vibrations of the right foot. This creates an effect quite different from the confusion that arises from jamming down the damper pedal of a modern grand to its fullest depth and holding it there, no matter who does it.

Schnabel's sustained achievements throughout the entire concerto set evidenced his profound scholarship and imagination. There is no need to deny that here and there he had pianistic lapses. But in music like this, flawless execution is immeasurably less relevant than emotional drama and intellectual depth. Schnabel had both. Happily, his recordings of the collection are with us for all to hear. I see few signs on the horizon that any pianist of our time could equal Schnabel's conceptional grandeur throughout the monumental five.

But in his own time—if we return for a moment to those who did not attempt them all—who remembers with me Rachmaninoff's performance of the First Concerto, Godowsky's of the Fourth, and Hofmann's of the Fifth? Whoever does will lament their unavailability on discs, as they will agree that such complete artistry, such ultimate mastery at the service of meaning and beauty, have all but vanished from this earth.

Chopin

CHOPIN, the philosopher of the beautiful, fashioned his iridescent harmonies and mysteriously woven lunar colors upon a black-and-white instrument. The classic master of romanticism stated his own artistic objectives in a letter to his confidante Delphine Potocka: "Bach," he wrote, "is like an astronomer who, with the help of ciphers, finds the most wonderful stars. . . . Beethoven embraced the universe with the power of his spirit. . . . I do not climb so high. A long time ago I decided that my universe will be the soul and heart of man. . . ." That's all, just the soul and heart of man.

In his greatest works (and Chopin produced proportionately the fewest negligible compositions of any great composer) he did indeed discern the heart of mankind and lure it into the soul of his music. And he also commented as a passionate visionary on the world in which he lived. Interpretations of his work may differ, but they must differ about the same world that provoked his emotions and materials.

Chopin's name was engraved upon history at a crucial time for Poland. Throughout the land rang the cry for liberty. Tadeusz Kosciuszko, who had fought heroically for independence in the American Revolution, was summoned home to lead his countrymen in their struggle. Among his volunteers was a foreigner, the Frenchman Nicholas Chopin.

Their cause went down to disastrous defeat, but Nicholas survived to unite with other idealistic and brave spirits who sought a new life for the crumbling country, a future founded upon the enduring values of education, science, and art.

This was the environment to which Frédéric, son of Nicholas, was born. It is little wonder the torch of patriotism burned so fiercely within him. Yet, it is not easy to decide whether Chopin, the most characteristically Polish of composers, created that nation's musical atmosphere or whether that atmosphere caused him to write as he did.

What we know without conjecture is that he became the most significant poet of the romantic school, that he was the supreme genius of the piano idiom, and that he composed numerous masterpieces of melodic beauty and originality, rhythmic subtlety and harmonic radiance that remain unique. No other composer possessing so strong a national identity ever produced an art of such universal scope.

Paradox always summons Chopin's image, no less than the piano. He was the "original" who was instantly comprehensible. The romantic movement claimed him for its own, but he remained aloof from its philosophic battles and polemical storms, detached from its literary influences, programmatic ideas, and descriptive titles. Above all, the great majority of his works reveals him as the poignant romantic whose structural precision was of classic caliber.

Chopin's expressivity emerged victorious even when it exceeded his capacity to solve all its artistic problems: it triumphed over every conflict between inspiration and technique, sometimes awkwardly as in the concertos and sonatas, flawlessly almost everywhere else. This is not to say that Chopin could not conquer large forms; the F minor Fantasie and F minor Ballade are perhaps his greatest works and, if one refrains from counting pages or analyzing titles, his largest organisms. Along with dozens of miniature masterpieces, these noble and profound works exemplify the essence of Chopin's art—boundless inspiration relentlessly disciplined by erudition, punctiliousness, and refinement. Elegance is the core of his creativity and the key to its interpretation.

Contrary to popular belief—a belief based on a far less astute observation of classical processes than Chopin's —his music shows a schematic severity more regular than one finds anywhere else except in his idol, Bach. His other idol, Mozart, demonstrates far wider variety in bar rhythms and phrase lengths. Most of Chopin's works reveal a rigid framework of four-bar and eight-bar rhythms. For small-form lyric music characterized by cross-rhythms, ornamentation, and tempo rubato, it was an admirably expedient plan. For its interpreters, it presents still another paradox as a stanch but fragile vehicle.

Consequently, few composers have suffered so from grotesque misrepresentation. Surrounded by commanding colleagues and devoted pupils (at least four of them notably gifted), Chopin wrote: "Unfortunately I shall have to reconcile myself to the thought that nobody will ever play my works to my liking as I had imagined them." He did rave about Liszt's playing of his bravura works, but in the next breath called him "a jackass in my Mazurkas." It is not too startling. One of Chopin's letters explains it fully: "Fétis amply praised me, saying that between my *piano* and *pianissimo* there are a hundred shades. At that Liszt put on a sour smile." Chopin's art is the triumph of nuance. Elegance and subtlety permeate his vast gamut of moods and means from lyric quietude to dauntless drama, from exquisite ornamentation to thunderous virtuosity.

Interpretative danger lurks in every bar of this music, for its dividing-lines are sharply drawn. The slightest exaggeration of its expressivity can become sentimentality; the tiniest excess of its heroism can become pomposity; one degree more or less can spell the difference between nobility and vulgarity, between individuality and mannerism. In matters of phrasing, touch, tone, pedaling, and dynamic relationships, it is treacherous terrain.

None of its phases, however, has set more traps for the unwary than "tempo rubato," vital to all music, indigenous to the romantic style. A statement attributed to Chopin provides another pitfall. Several of his pupils quoted him as saying that the left hand "must maintain strict time" while the right (meaning the melody) could "fluctuate freely." Did he really say something that specious? I, for one, am quite ready to believe it. Chopin's subtleties included a streak of irony which protected his hypersensitive nature. He suffered acutely from the effects of that dark day when "rubato" was discovered to mean "robbed," and when an incredible number of insensitive performers proceeded to confuse aesthetics with morality by ludicrous attempts to "restore" in exact rhythmic measure what they had previously "stolen." Chopin's precept, someone said, could easily have come from a man "robbed" of all patience. And robbed of all reason, too, by hearing his music contorted through constant alternations of retards and accelerations, distorted by attempts to gain eloquence at the expense of basic momentum.

From Chopin and his contemporaries we have sparse but cogent clues to his performance style. Freed of irony, he described rubato in the excellent metaphor that it is "like a tree whose trunk stands firm, while its branches and leaves yield to passing breezes." On another occasion he demonstrated to a pupil the ideal of rubato by blowing gently on a lit candle. The flame flickered for an instant, then shone brightly again. "That is *my* rubato," he said. Chopin then blew hard into the flame, extinguishing it. "That is *yours*," he said. He insisted on the use of the metronome.

Chopin never allowed students to play one hand before the other as a substitute for expressivity. He hated affectation and unnecessary motions of the arms or hands. He was merciless to those who sentimentalized his music. He demanded, at least from himself, singing legato; infinite variety of accentuation, color, touch, and tone; pedaling that provided a rich harmonic background but allowed for the purity of a vocal melodic line; phrasing within phrasing that punctuated broadly sustained cantilena; and expressive ornamentation that delicately adorned, but did not obscure, the cantabile.

There we have it: the fastidious art that relies upon precise balance, coherence, and refinement of unified detail. Yet, Chopin cautioned: "An artist should never lose sight of the thing as a whole. He who goes too much into details will find that the thread which holds the whole thing together will break, and instead of a necklace, single pearls will remain in his stupid hands." This statement sums up precisely the classical ideals of performance as set forth in countless eighteenth-century treatises.

In the precision and subtlety of Chopin's art, these ideals were revived and had to be relearned. Beethoven's playing, to judge from every written opinion of his contemporaries, was so incredibly free that were he to play for us today, he would be criticized for not knowing the Beethoven tradition. Chopin's precepts and the available accounts of his playing prove his adamant insistence upon the firm establishment of a presiding pace and the preservation of its rhythmic premise throughout the most refined deviations.

His specialties—the combination of an increasing volume and a decelerated pace, and of a diminishing volume and an accelerated pace—are evidently contrary to instinct. Few artists successfully refine and discipline their instincts to resist slowing down as they are getting softer and speeding up as they are growing louder.

Save for a few shining examples, contemporary performances and discs evidence the elusiveness of the romantic style: the difficulty of playing eloquently without sacrificing the fundamental pulsation, of sustaining quiet without vanishing below audibility, of fashioning lacy ornamentation that enhances, but does not obscure or confuse, melodic lines. It is equally uncommon to hear trills spinning in shimmering beauty from one dynamic level to another in one line unbroken by isolated after-notes; to hear long phrases sung with inner punctuation that does not become a hiatus, or a rhythm that can range from metronomic to rhapsodic without losing propulsion.

Instead of going into my usual flow of words depicting Chopin-playing past and present, I shall merely set the props for a guest critic. Here is one representative composition—Chopin's Andante Spianato and Grand Polonaise. Here are three of its recorded versions—by Hofmann, Rubinstein, and Horowitz. Now allow me to present Harold C. Schonberg, whose writings in *The New York Times* and elsewhere have established him as piano critic *par excellence*.

In his invigorating volume on chamber and solo-instrument music in *The Guide to Long-playing Records*, Schonberg says: "Rubinstein and Horowitz present magnificent performances. Hofmann's is transcendental. . . . It has a quality of aristocracy that no other pianist in my memory could bring to his music-making, and it has a degree of tonal and pianistic subtlety that disappeared when Hofmann retired. . . ."

It is easy to see why a Chopin performance that from first to last does not violate one of his precepts is a rarity. We may be comforted in the knowledge that this does not apply only to our generation. Hanslick, reviewing Clara Schumann in Chopin's Fantaisie-Impromptu, wrote: "Some may be surprised by her metronomic playing. In the middle section she maintains almost without exception, a strict uniformity of measure." The statement is packed with significance, chiefly in its implication that in those days, too, such pristine romanticism was news. It still is.

Toscanini once told me that he rarely attended recitals because the average soloist's "sick rhythmic sense" drove him frantic. "They do not use freedom to idealize rhythm, but to demolish it," he said. Toscanini's territory was the orchestra; Chopin's the piano. But rhythm was their common ground, and I'll bet they have a lot to talk about now.

Schumann

TIME WAS, and not so long ago, when young people in love quoted or wrote poems to each other. Nowadays, poetry appears to be written mainly by poets for poets. Once again we can observe a historic parallel in the descending course of romantic versifying and that of romantic music-making, for we have already noted that the poetic precision of romanticism is a blind spot for most of our twentieth-century virtuosos.

In the pianistic realm, Schumann's romanticism suffers a high mortality through the absence from the concert scene of Paderewski in the F sharp minor Sonata, Gabrilowitsch in the *Phantasiestücke,* Bauer in the *Kinderscenen,* Lhevinne in the Toccata, Hofmann in the Fantasy, *Kreisleriana,* Concerto, and *Etudes symphoniques,* and Rachmaninoff in the F sharp minor *Novelette* and *Carnaval.* Few indeed are the concert pianists of our day who bring to us any lingering enchantments of the magical era. One therefore clings to remembrances and seizes upon every possible example of the nearly lost art.

For many years now a few of us, haunted by unforgettable memories, have been insufferable observers to our companions at countless piano recitals, especially when the programs have contained certain compositions of the romantic repertoire that we had heard from exponents of the grand manner. Thrilling sounds linger with us which make most latter-day performances seem dim and dull.

At the moment, search my mind as I will, I can only cull entirely happy recent recollections of Novaës in the *Papillons,* of Serkin in the *Abegg Variations, Etudes*

symphoniques, and Concerto, of Dinu Lipatti's sensitive
and richly promising recording of the last, and of Rubinstein in the *Kreisleriana* and *Carnaval.* These performances spoke to me with poetic and rhythmic unity, with
tenderness and nobility, and they remain with me.

At one time I believed that, just as the romantic style
is alien to our unlyrical age, so was it the natural possession of all who dwelt in its vivid environment. I first
became distrustful of that notion upon reading the Hanslick review of Clara Schumann, quoted in my chapter
on Chopin. I was firmly shaken out of it a few years ago
after pouncing eagerly upon a set of recordings issued in
England by the Clara Schumann Society.

It represented, according to the accompanying bro-
chure, "authoritative renderings of Robert Schumann's
pianoforte works by Adelina de Lara, who is the last sur-
viving pupil of Clara Schumann to be actively engaged
as a pianist." It further declared, unequivocally: "Listen-
ers may notice certain differences in Adelina de Lara's interpretations. We are quite confident, however, in stating
that where such differences are apparent, Adelina de
Lara's interpretation may be taken as being the correct
one."

Before I got a chance to listen to the records, another
arrived presenting the late Carl Friedberg in Schumann's
Kinderscenen and the *Novelette* in D. The record sleeve
read: "Carl Friedberg was a friend and pupil of Clara
Schumann . . . and represents to us the last link with
the great musical era of romanticism."

Somewhat shaken to be innocently caught in a musical
conflict, I retreated to my hi-fi set and to Miss de Lara's
first record, which was a talk by the recording pianist on
"Clara Schumann and Her Teaching." I heard recollections and impressions of Clara Schumann's pedagogic ax-
ioms gleaned from Miss de Lara's six years of study with
the First Lady of the Piano. The aphorisms were most
familiar, and reminded me that musical wisdom, like phi-

losophy, has its own platitudes. They have become plati-
tudinous because they are valid and because every decent musician in every generation has practiced them,
affirmed them, and repeated them endlessly. We learned
of Clara Schumann telling her students what Papa Bach
surely heard from his mentors and told his pupils: "Be
truthful to the composer's meaning. Remember the importance of tone, rhythm, and phrasing. Speed is a men-
ace," and so on and so forth.

No one could quarrel with that. Nor with Miss de Lara's
statement that her teacher urged students to play the piano with the tonal variety of the different instruments of
the orchestra. But then we heard the gratuitous comment: "Schumann's keyboard music is extremely orchestral." This I consider a *non sequitur* as well as a gross
inaccuracy. Schumann suffered grievous ordeals as an orchestrator and conductor. Second only to Chopin, Schumann was the composer who equated music and the piano. His keyboard works outnumber the total of his other
instrumental compositions. In his songs, the pianist and
the vocalist are at least equal partners. Schumann did *not*
think orchestrally, not even in his symphonic works,
which live through the luxuriance of musical ideas and
despite their admittedly opaque scoring. His most successful instrumentation is to be found in the orchestral
collaborations of his works for a solo instrument with
orchestra. But no conductor could ever steal the show
from a soloist in a Schumann concerto.

A tradition is best revealed through an artistic result,
so I turned from the words to the music. Miss de Lara
made almost all of her discs at the venerable age (and
rpm speed) of seventy-eight. The liabilities that accrue to
executants in advanced years usually being those of impaired dexterity, I naturally did not expect much technical command. As for beauty of sound in recording quality, I expected nothing at all. However, I did hope for
some mature examples of expressivity and originality, of

tonal variety and fine phrasing. Imagine my astonishment to discover the playing of no less than the formidable "Paganini" section of the *Carnaval* as full of facility as the quiet sections were lacking in poetic insight, melodic flow, and shape.

Mr. Friedberg, on the other hand, posed himself no technical complexities in the Schumann works he elected to record. The wisdom of his choice was demonstrated by warm songfulness, sensitive delineation, and unforced energy remarkable in an artist past eighty.

In these records, even though they derive straight from the source's mouth, we have intentions rather than realizations to go by. But there is sufficient indication to leave us puzzled at the sweeping disparity in sheer artistic objectives from two pianists exposed to the identical authoritative influences. Is it, as Leopold Auer once said, that "there are no great teachers, only great pupils"? I beg to be excused from reaching any conclusion, but I could not withhold conjecturing that, to judge by Miss de Lara's playing and her own account of Clara Schumann's musical ideals, pupil and teacher must have lived through some rather stormy sessions.

Schumann's piano idiom discloses a profusion of lyric and declamatory phrases, expressive figuration, and rhythmic syncopation. His textures are primarily chordal and arpeggiated. He employs many octaves and practically no scales. As for polyphony, few can equal him, especially in the purity of his canonic technique.

His music requires for its fulfillment an uncommon grasp of its special characteristic. Large chunks of the piano works, such as the *Abegg Variations, Carnaval, Davidsbundlertänze, Kreisleriana,* and *Papillons,* are obfuscated by literary and personal allusions, while such others as the *Phantasiestücke* and *Kinderscenen* are saddled with titles appended after they had already been composed.

Schumann's human traits, as our psychiatrists would

tell us, were schizoid. His manifold personalities were not only written into his compositions, but were also given names and initials and significances that appeared in his essays and criticisms, and were even incorporated as members of the *Davidsbund,* the phantom society cre- ated in Schumann's prolific imagination. In Schumann's piano compositions all this led to copious literary sym- bolism that is sometimes as bewildering as Wagner's mythology and considerably less rewarding to all but Schumann's interpreters.*

Schumann's musical ways and technical means were arrestingly original. There is no mistaking his epigram- matic themes, his foursquare structures, his persistent rhythmic patterns, and his sequences. And there is no mistaking the power of his inventive genius in eluding most of their built-in pitfalls.

Schumann saved himself by the authenticity and breadth of his inspirations. But the material remains frag- ile. Just substitute slowing down for expressivity, crude biffs for puckish cross-accents, unbuttoned freedom for precise rhythm—and that way lies the destruction of Schumann's frangible materials. Take his long slurs lit- erally, and the melodic lines strangle to death. Use metri- cal accents for his sequential passages, and they sound endless; treat the shorter notes of his vigorous dotted- eighth and -sixteenth patterns as soggy triplets or airy grace notes, and you emasculate their essential feature.

What may befall Schumann's vital and noble music may perhaps be most easily illustrated if I state my reac- tions to a valuable recording I received some time ago. It is valuable for two reasons: because it provides perform- ances of some previously neglected but far from negli- gible Schumann works; and because it demonstrates how ephemeral Schumann's subject matter can be to a young

* The connotations of Schumann's literary and personal allusions in his piano works are comprehensively identified and analyzed in *The Literature of the Piano,* by Ernest Hutcheson.

pianist evidently considered by an important recording
company to be equipped beyond others for the assignment.
I refer to the disc of Schumann's Piano Concerto, *Konzertstück*, and the Introduction and Concert Allegro
played by Joerg Demus with the Vienna State Opera
Orchestra under Artur Rodzinski.

Demus starts out immediately in the opening solo passage of the Concerto by treating the vital dotted eighths
and sixteenths as a series of tired triplets. Hearing the
distortion of so organic an idea, one has immediate
grounds for suspecting a case of miscasting. Each revolution of the turntable corroborates the suspicion. Rhythmic flaccidity is substituted for evocation, overeffusion
for urgency. Melodic lines are mooned over and finally go
dead. Passionate sections sound labored. There is even
insufficient mechanical control in a piece that certainly
does not require a super-virtuoso equipment for performance with a reasonable degree of accuracy. Most
lacking, however, are lyrical simplicity and an explicit
sense of momentum.

In the *Konzertstück* and the Concert Allegro, the same
interpretative lacunae turn up. Almost nowhere can one
discern a fundamental pace not almost immediately denied by some deviation from it which utterly destroys
continuity and cohesion. The music emerges breathless in
the whipped-up places and torpid in the others. In Schumann's own "Rules and Maxims for Young Musicians"
there is much that could aid us to dramatize music without making it elephantine, much to show us the difference
between loudness and richness of utterance, and much
that could persuade us to be mindful of those beautiful
precision instruments of romanticism—direct exposition of
melodic lines, harmonic tension, and stringent rhythmic
pulsation.

Which reminds me. The orchestra's contribution to
the proceedings kept recalling to me Koussevitzky's im-

mortal comment at a Boston Symphony rehearsal: "Gentlemen, the ensemble is not together."

Regarding the works themselves, I see little point in defending them as flawless gems or in attacking those who believe them to be among Schumann's less-inspired works. Even in the scores in which Schumann's aberrations are apparent, his imagination was always equal to the invention of ardent material, regardless of his power to organize it.

Always he was an inspired dreamer. Always he had a foreboding intensity, and almost always, except for the first few blessed years with Clara, this fantasy-ridden genius was headed for shattering despair and a tragic fate. We owe him greater homage.

Liszt

OUR MUSICAL WORLD is rich in fallacies, great fallacies that remain ubiquitous and retain their stranglehold on truth because of the numbers and the prestige of the uncurious who accept and perpetuate them unquestioningly. Among their rich contributions to musical mythology, for instance, is the legend that a great Liszt interpretation is primarily a feat of virtuosity, whereas a great Brahms interpretation is entirely a triumph of musicianship.

The reverse is closer to the truth, though it is far from the whole truth, for nothing is more inartistic than the sacrifice of one element wholly for another. Where many elements are present, artistry begins when they are indissolubly blended. Liszt's indigenously pianistic compositions indeed require virtuosity, but of that high order which is entirely subordinate to supreme refinement and expressive power; otherwise his pensive music emerges inane, his dramatic music merely theatrical or with a sound not unlike that of a glass chandelier in vibration. Conversely, the thorny mechanics of Brahms's music require a technician of the first order to bring charm and lucidity to the graceful works, vitality and momentum to the large ones.

The irresponsible have led the unwary into another trap; the correct thing to say these days is that Liszt's actual contributions to music lay in his clever but unsubstantial ideas, which were turned to account by "really great men, you know," and in his wholehearted battles on behalf of others and their music. Don't believe a word of it.

Of course, all of us have the right, even the obligation,

to say what we like and what we do not like. But we should avoid regarding our reactions as Aesthetic Truth, particularly if we happen to be among those who can spot in a flash a vulgarity or a carelessness in a man's music without having the slightest ability to recognize its over-all magic. Liszt's music has its own unique magic, and the best of it is eminently the best of its kind. Its kind is ambrosial expressionism, and its finest achievements disclose opulent imagination, inexhaustible resource, and the ripest of experience.

Liszt's programmatic leanings encourage still another fallacy: that music seeking to describe things and events outside of itself is necessarily poorer music than absolute music. We need not become involved in the old argument. The use of appropriate titles, even in absolute music, has too venerable a history to be snobbishly despised. Liszt's illustrative compositions, like those of the English and French clavecinists, Berlioz, Schumann, and Richard Strauss, are neither strengthened nor weakened by their titles or stories.

Naturally, Liszt wrote program music; a man of his literary taste and general erudition would inevitably react to the stimulus of a poem or a picture. Besides, we ought have no difficulty in determining whether music is good or bad without reference to some "program" to which it does or does not adhere. Liszt demonstrated that he was able to tell some pretty exciting tales in non-program music. In any event, this element has small importance in the piano compositions when compared with Liszt's pre-eminence in discovering and extending the fullest possibilities of keyboard sonority and thematic device.

These virtues and Liszt's weaknesses, too, are nowhere more apparent than in his *magnum opus* for the piano, the B minor Sonata. Within its powerful, original, and ambivalent characteristics lies a musical portrait of the composer's life. We hear strong motives soon abandoned, inspirations that succumb to mechanical device, momentum that soon spends itself in sequence and repetition.

In his struggles for a larger musical time scale, Liszt was misled by a common and specious doctrine—that music is constructed by expanding fragments, that spaciousness and coherence are attainable by the transformation of melodies and figures through such arbitrary mechanisms as augmentation, diminution, and inversion. A melody or figure may certainly lend itself to all sorts of alterations that may or may not utilize conventional devices; but music will neither flow nor produce organic unity merely because it employs the appliances of thematic derivation.

Sir Donald Tovey, in a university lecture, once said: "The teaching of composition and the understanding of music would be greatly enhanced if a law were made forbidding the assertion that Beethoven's C minor Symphony is founded upon a figure of four notes. Melodies are not built out of figures. They are large musical objects that are divisible into figures." This is demonstrable in Beethoven, but not in Liszt, for his vision overran his structure; his aspirations exceeded his achievements.

In Liszt, artist and man were always closely allied. Both had dramatic ferocity and the sweet caress. Both assisted the cause of musicians and their music with a magnanimity unparalleled in musical history. Passion, intellectuality, grandeur, and tenderness—all and more belonged to the composer, transcriber, performer, conductor, teacher, writer, fighter, perpetual Don Juan, and itinerant son of the Church. Beneficence was his blessing and his cross. He gave too much: of himself, his art, and his possessions, and he wrote far too many compositions. Of his almost seven hundred works, only a handful remains in the standard concert repertoire, and practically all of these are to be found in the piano literature, and deservedly so.

Few, therefore, are the pianists who do not play some

Liszt. In this connection we are led to another commonly held fallacy: that piano techniques come a dime a dozen in our time, that easy virtuosity is the *plat du jour* of current concert menus. I have a private notion that this idea has been accepted because there is so little emotional intensity around, so little color and communication, that the average listener follows the average performer in his preoccupation with digital matters.

Actually, the kind of virtuosity that uses rather than abuses its function is as rare today as it ever was. To find it together with a burning temperament and a scholarly musicianship is to come upon genius. It may be a merciless norm for evaluation, but it seems inescapable that no less is required for the perfect realization of masterpieces. And those of Liszt present unique challenges to the pianist.

It follows that we are unlikely to experience more than a few occasions when all the grand qualities demanded by this music are present. I can list those I came upon in very short space. To my already-mentioned impressions of Levitzki's sensitivity and devilish daring in the E flat Concerto and Sixth Rhapsody add his unfeazed aristocracy in the difficult E major Polonaise.

As for the formidable *Etudes d'exécution transcendante,* I cannot think of them without applying the word transcendent to the monumental playing of those works by Busoni's pupil Egon Petri. His playing of both concertos and many of the transcriptions was likewise phenomenal. In no other literature did I find him so impressive.

Should the mention of Liszt's transcriptions cause some eyebrow-raising through inevitable association with such multicolored popcorn as the paraphrases on Verdi's *Rigoletto* and Rossini's *William Tell,* perhaps we should stop a moment to recall Liszt's artistic triumphs in the field of arrangement.

Liszt's arrangements of some hundred songs by Beethoven, Schubert, Schumann, Chopin, and Mendelssohn include unequaled examples of the art of transcription; whereas his treatment of instrumental works varies in quality, from the dreadful "derangements" of Bach's organ works to the consummate translations of Schubert's lyricism to Lisztian pianism in the luscious *Soirées de Vienne.*

Liszt's operatic fantasies were natural outgrowths of his gifts and the period in which they flourished. The art of extemporizing was still rife, operatic melodies were the rage, and showpieces aroused audiences to hysterical enthusiasm. Hence, those pyramids called pot-pourris. Most of them are quite absurd today, with the exception of two masterpieces—the arrangement of the *Liebestod* from Wagner's *Tristan und Isolde,* and the *Fantasy* based on Mozart's *Don Giovanni.*

Toward those of my readers who remember Hofmann's playing of the *Don Giovanni* I would feel apologetic were I to attempt a verbalization of the unforgettable vibrations that must live in their ears. Toward others, I had better not risk it.

The *Mephisto Waltz* brings William Kapell instantly to mind. The nobility of his expression and the sheer perfection of his workmanship live on in his recording of the work. He was twenty-two when he made it, and it would have been quite enough to place him securely among our century's pianistic geniuses.

Today few will deny that the flaming fury of Horowitz, his variety of touches and colors, his relentless rhythm and dramatic virtuosity nowhere find truer artistic expression than in the music of Liszt. Horowitz is equally the master of a miniature such as the *Valse Oubliée* and of the massive Sonata. Should anyone have any illusions about the fabulous virtuosity of today's striplings, just play Horowitz's recording of his own transcription of the *Rákóczy March.* It is a permanent cure, guaranteed.

Rubinstein makes Lisztian sounds that are quite different from Horowitz's, and completely irresistible in their own way. Chiefly, I recall Rubinstein's playing of the E flat Concerto and of the Tenth Rhapsody. Apart from his beautiful tone, colorful "orchestration," and sonorous sweep, Rubinstein's power of transition is perhaps his most individual gift. He can go from a boisterous mood to a tender one, from a furious tempo to a leisurely one, from bulky chords to lacy figuration, all with the most extraordinary ease and fluidity. No other music stands to gain so much from just these endowments.

And such performances as I have recalled show more persuasively than the cold text how inescapably Liszt's finest art belongs to musical evolution.

Brahms in D minor and B flat

OF THE many books and brochures concerning Brahms, none has been able to avoid mention of the sharply defined dualities of his character and his work. From the early days in his native Hamburg to the later years in his adopted Vienna, Brahms's ambivalence was revealed through behavioristic couplings of rude spitefulness and tender solicitude, stinginess and generosity, in being reserved and taciturn except when he was bubbling over and boyishly voluble. To all marital inquiries he had a stock paradoxical answer: "Alas, I am still unmarried. Thank God!"

Psychological investigations have enabled our generation to understand that conflicts within ourselves are a normal and integral part of life. Brahms, the musician as well as the man, has been pictured, even by esteemed biographers, as the uncompromising pure-beef Hamburger constantly in conflict with the savory *wiener Schnitzel* that was his other self. Ample evidence, however, in the organizational power and scrupulous consistency of Brahms's work shows him as one who squarely faced his artistic conflicts, sought their solutions, and resolved them to gain that freedom and strength which come only from enlightened evaluation and conscious decision.

The basic problem Brahms faced was that of the musician whose artistic force caused Schumann to hail him as "the new musical Messiah," while Brahms at the same time felt "the shadow of the great Beethoven" constantly behind him. Ironically, it was Brahms who followed in the shadow, not only of Beethoven but also of Bach,

Schubert, Schumann, and still others, and was destined to be another of those Revolutionists without the "R." Brahms assimilated, as Bach did before him, all that was to be learned from predecessors and contemporaries. He deliberately fought one of the hardest of artistic battles—turning into a highly personal account the structural and thematic influences of his affinities. He was completely victorious, achieved an astounding individuality, and was never more convincingly original than precisely in those moments when his material was most derivative.

His two piano concertos rank among the greatest ever written. Some of their most distinguished interpreters consider them unequaled. As with every art form Brahms approached, he was fully aware of the responsibilities involved, and both these works cost him mighty strivings and struggles through long years.

Everyone knows that the First Concerto, in D minor, was originally conceived as a symphony. But it is also unquestioningly accepted that Brahms's self-criticism told him that the work was "not adequate as a symphony," and that he therefore next attempted to convert it into a "sonata for two pianos" before it took its present shape.

Brahms did indeed begin to sketch the work as a symphony, but the rest of its history seems to me a compounded error. Brahms planned the composition as a symphony because his principal themes are obviously symphonic. The theory that Brahms, after wrestling with his material, felt himself or his ideas "inadequate to a symphony" appears implausible. What is a symphony? Architecturally it is a sonata for orchestra, just as a concerto is a sonata for one or more solo instruments with orchestra. Names are insignificant. Brahms's concertos possess symphonic scope and content, and not only was their creator adequate to a symphonic task, but he also understood clearly what most annotators do not—that a classical concerto poses bulkier problems than a classical symphony.

At any rate, it would be perfectly natural for a composer of Brahms's cautious workmanship while in the
throes of creative trial to set down his ideas in a convenient two-piano form to be scored later. What happened then, and it could well have been aided by the
medium of his "shorthand sketch," was that piano figurations and sonorities began to intrude themselves irresistibly upon the project. The inevitable result was a piano concerto.

It is significant that a quarter of a century later Brahms
took no detours in mapping out his Second Piano Concerto. I do not share the opinion that greater maturity enabled him to take the direct route to its final form, for the
First Concerto discloses a composer whose genius was
completely liberated from all immaturities. The answer
would seem to lie in the fact that the First Concerto was
virtually an abstract inspiration in search of the right
medium and frame. The Second was born with an unmistakable physiognomy—a classical piano concerto containing an added movement and an orchestral partnership of unique dimension.

How I managed to miss performances of the Brahms
concertos in the old days I do not know, but I suspect
that the interpretations of such masterpieces from such
masters as were around would have vitally affected my
basis of comparative opinion. In more recent years, I
think I have heard more satisfactory performances of
these tremendous pieces than of any other set of works I
know. This puzzled me for quite a time, especially in
view of their difficulty. I have finally come up with a few
conjectures.

In the first place, they are anything but showpieces, so
that they are unlikely to attract any but substantial musicians. Everything in them is music; everything reflects
the force and ardor and serene spaciousness of their creator. Their vast power and organization are enough to
make any serious-minded artist demand from himself the

minimum task of devoting to their re-creation a measure
of that inexorable self-criticism and artistic responsibility
which Brahms lavished upon their creation.

According to Grove's *Dictionary*, in Ebenezer Prout's
fatal definition of a concerto as "an instrumental composition designed to show the skill of an executant," Brahms
wrote no piano concertos at all; nor, if one pursues such
a notion further, did he write a violin concerto or one for
violin and violoncello. That, at any rate, is what his contemporaries meant when they informed Brahms that
what he produced was not concertos but symphonies,
with all but inaudible obbligato parts for solo instruments.
Even the brilliant, loyal Hanslick was trapped into par-
roting the absurdity. It gives us an idea of how much
more Brahms knew about the antecedents of his concerto style than the scholars who surrounded him, none
of whom appears to have grasped the salient organic
principles of the art form that stimulated Mozart, Beethoven, and Brahms to their greatest powers.

Today we are wiser after the fact. Not alone because
of twentieth-century theorists, but also because so many
pianists and conductors have found in these "ineffective"
concertos a sufficiently rewarding quality and quantity of
music to justify their slaving over them and performing
them on every possible occasion. Well they might, if they
are eventually able to pass its formidable test, for only
then can the Brahms concertos be said to represent interpretative opportunities. Otherwise they are suicidal.

Now the reader will understand better my surprise at
the number of splendid performances I have heard. I
do not say that every element of the Brahms concertos
was accomplished by every artist to the same degree at
every point. That would be impossible, for each artist has
an induplicable set of capacities that he and he alone
possesses. But, by and large, hearing them has been a
privilege on an extraordinary number of occasions.

Of those no longer with us, I heard only Gabrilowitsch

in both concertos, and to both he brought the utmost in devotion and inspiration, if not in exactitude and power. In our time, Backhaus, Curzon, Rubinstein, Serkin, and Solomon have all in their own ways given me grateful remembrances of how the First Concerto can and should be made to sound. The pleasure of hearing them was at least doubled by the eloquent collaborations of conductors Boehm, Van Beinum, Reiner, Szell, and Kubelik.

Coming to the Second Concerto, I must first mention a heroic performance by Horowitz and Toscanini which, for excitement and precision, was one of the greatest thrills of my concert-going life. From the standpoint of ensemble, it was an incredible display of mutually held ideals. As a demonstration of sheer control of electric temperaments, it was fabulous. After the introduction, Horowitz plunged elbow-deep into the first solo sections with a feverish intensity and a pristine accuracy that brought despair to every pianist present who had ever wrestled with this blood-sweat-and-tears concerto. For many years I was certain that Brahms had written many passages here with tongue in cheek, as a sadistic challenge to interpreters to solve the insoluble. But that was before I heard Horowitz that night.

Hearing the incomparable Toscanini's lucid balances and blendings, his masterly scrupulousness in every phrase, no one could have guessed that Brahms's concerto-scoring was for so long a stumbling-block for conductors who found it "coarse-grained and thick." On this occasion Brahms's polyphony had the transparency of Bach's, his figuration the buoyancy of Mendelssohn's, and his instrumentation the impeccable economy of Mozart's. Toscanini's rhythmic genius for non-metrical accentuation, for shaping phrases so that they delineate melodic lines, not bar lines, and his harmonic and textural sensitivity further illumined Brahms as an unerring orchestrator and tonal colorist of crystalline clarity.

Others of my grateful recollections are a grand performance by Serkin and Ormandy which was a model of co-operative responsibility on the highest artistic plane, and one by Rubinstein with Alfred Wallenstein as his collaborator.

History relates that in Vienna, when the intrepid young Ella Pancera played this work under Hans Richter, Brahms did not hesitate to tell her: "It is decidedly not for little girls." Decidedly, it is not; not even for "big girls," as too many of our keyboard amazons have persisted in demonstrating irrefutably on too many occasions.

Schnabel is reputed to have played both concertos with unique perceptivity and fire. We know this from his old recordings, just as we know from the same source that the unwieldy technical problems cost him at least as many strivings and struggles as they cost Gabrilowitsch. Backhaus was the pianist who easily managed the unmanageable in both works. I am now talking of pianism, not of the passion or the lyricism that made the interpretations of Gabrilowitsch, Schnabel, Serkin, and Rubinstein stirring experiences.

Tchaikovsky's Human Documents

PERHAPS THE most emotional aspect of criticism is the fear of emotion. The failure to weigh human values and human responses has produced some of the most short-sighted criticism in the whole passionate history of music. Academicism does itself no good by seizing upon works that have become popular through their emotional appeal and scorning them categorically as tinsel.

In my student days I met my share of those practitioners of music who periodically take temperatures of compositional affinities to find symptoms of Tchaikovsky fever. I was well on my way to becoming a guilt-ridden hypochondriac when I came upon Beethoven's words written on his Mass in D: "Written from the heart; may it go to the heart." As I read it, a melody suddenly ran through my head: it was the second subject of the final movement of Tchaikovsky's *"Pathétique"* Symphony. Then and there I resolved to rediscover Tchaikovsky for myself, to get away from those who generalize their antipathies into artistic laws, and to cease being the kind of clever idiot who pokes holes in a man's work without the smallest ability to differentiate between honest emotion and sham.

Since then I have met battalions of music-lovers who confess a love for Tchaikovsky's greatest works with the abject humility and helplessness with which they would confess to alcoholism. Is it because he wrote some inferior music? So did others, but who judges Beethoven by his Romance in G? Is it our taut twentieth century's rejection of the intuitive for the intellectual? That cannot be, either, for the public adores Tchaikovsky's masterpieces, and artists love to play them.

No. Early in this century the musical intelligentsia fell prey to the New Doctrine. Within it were many warring factions, many tangled cults and schools, but all of them were united in the common determination to engage one specific enemy in mortal combat. Crying "tolerance for modernism," they waged a hysterical and utterly intolerant attack on romanticism.

That war has been over for a long time now. Even, or perhaps one should say especially, the atonalists proclaimed romantic ideals, aspirations to depict the subjective feelings of humanity. But somehow the absurdities of anti-romanticism persisted. People have been taught to regard their communion with Tchaikovsky as musical immaturity. They have been sold a false criterion. It arises in blind hostility to some simple touchstone; it rejects the expressive content in a work of art; and, above all else, it betrays an insecure musical culture.

Certainly we retain the right to love or hate anything we choose, but it is irresponsible to appraise anything as great because we love it or to call it bad because we hate it. The value of a work of art lies in many matters on many levels, none of them isolated from the others. A flaw in much that passes for criticism is a pouncing upon one quality and ignoring all others. No profound insight is required to discover Tchaikovsky's lapses. No more insight than it takes to discover the lapses of those arbiters of musical fashion who show themselves incapable of differentiating communicative music from bad music. When we are scolded for reacting favorably to a work or for not reacting favorably to another that orthodoxy insists ought to inspire us because it is marvelously made, we can legitimately maintain that it is quite useless for us to be told how we ought to react when we do not.

We must be careful to acknowledge our responses as

subjective feelings and not ask that they be given the weight of objective facts. We must also not claim to be music-lovers unless we try constantly to extend the range of our tastes in every direction and are prepared to find those tastes varying in degrees of enthusiasm from time to time. In turn we may ask others not to tell us that a quality that moves us is a defect, for that is as far from the truth as the Philistine convictions that a fugue is an intellectual exercise or that chamber music is "thin."

Tchaikovsky had the divine fire, and nothing short of ignorance can question his compositional mastery. In his last three symphonies, the overtures *Romeo and Juliet* and *Francesca da Rimini*, the *Sleeping Beauty* and *Swan Lake* ballets, the Third String Quartet, and many other works, his dramatic and touching spirit speaks to humanity of elemental matters. Their frailties are as nothing compared with their emotional force, melodic power, and originality.

In the light of such intense and lovable aspects of Tchaikovsky's art, pedantry descends to an unrealistic level when it repudiates him. It denies one of art's primary missions: to reveal the inner life of the emotions. That, incidentally, is one way in which the ascetic schools of contemporary music have estranged themselves more and more from concert-goers, the concert-goers for whom romanticism still glows with a lovely light wherever it appears: in Bach or Mozart, Beethoven or Brahms, Tchaikovsky, Prokofiev, or Stravinsky.

Tchaikovsky's piano masterpiece is the Concerto in B flat minor. It is not necessary to contend that this is a flawless work, nor would I claim that it represents a perfect concerto plan. But it does represent Tchaikovsky's plan, and that somehow seems quite sufficient. On occasion I have grown as tired of it as I have of other concertos that fully represent a perfect concerto plan. After a while, when I hear a stirring interpretation, I love it again, and so have cause to be grateful that distinguished artists and the public persistently succumb to its inspiration. It may be that some pianists choose the work because they think it assures success, not because they recognize its qualities. The fact is never concealable. The public's enthusiasm is owing to reasons that musicologists are likely to overlook in the maze of technical concerns. A piece of music that brings comfort to an unhappy heart, order to meaningless experience, and the courage that makes us feel life worth living—this music has been written by a man who has something vital to say and knows how to say it.

When Emil Gilels made his New York debut in the Tchaikovsky concerto, an eminent critic rued the choice. Personally, I was glad, for many years had passed since I had heard a completely gratifying interpretation of the embattled war-horse. As a pianist I know how much musicianship is needed to play its melodic lines with simplicity and restraint, how much virtuosity is required to handle the bravura passages with ease and lucidity, and how much architectural sense is needed to unify its dramatic scheme. Besides, I shall never cease to respect its history.

Hans von Bülow was the musician who played its *première* (Boston, 1875) and who called it "original, noble, mature, powerful, and distinguished." Yet no pianist ever had a more enviable intellectual standing. Liszt once said of him: "Bülow is a schoolmaster, but of aristocratic rank." An artist of extraordinary perceptivity, Bülow was essentially a conservative rescued from pedantry by close association with Liszt and Wagner. On one tour here Bülow played from memory the complete piano-solo works of Beethoven on sixteen consecutive evenings. He regarded the sonatas, which he edited, as the New Testament (the Old Testament, of course, being Bach's *Well-Tempered Clavier*). If there was ever an artist untainted by suggestions of shallowness, it was the scholarly pianist who launched Tchaikovsky's First Concerto on its fabulous course.

Later in its now venerable history, Horowitz, Solomon, Curzon, and Gilels chose it for their debuts in New York. Others too, possibly, whom I have not tracked down. Do I hear someone say that musicians select it because it is "sure-fire"? Maybe from an audience point of view, but not from where an artist sits.

The challenges posed by this Palladium of pianism are so formidable that in my opinion at this moment not one wholly satisfying recording of it is available. Having made the statement, I owe the reader some detailed reactions to at least a few of the most representative versions.

The disc made by Gilels with the Chicago Symphony under Fritz Reiner is among the finest in sheer sound and balance. A rich broad opening promises a spacious concept. This is almost instantly negated by losses in tension and dynamics just before the embellished restatement where piano and orchestra exchange their materials. The first solo is splendidly handled until the treacherous descending passage where the pianist's left hand leaves his right hand to carry on alone. Then comes the tricky *allegro con spirito* section. Its effect lies in its rhythmic originality, a pattern of the first two notes of an incomplete triplet. Every pianist I have heard except Solomon distorts its primary feature by treating the second note as a main note. Each time, the orchestral answer promptly and properly contradicts the error by stressing the first note. Each time, the soloist answers in stubborn rejection of the correction. It grows quite ludicrous, and it sounds just as absurd in Russian. In the second movement Gilels is only occasionally convincing. The opening is tenderly sung, but sectionalized, and is soon blurred by Gilels's customary dependence upon the pedal, even in the *sempre staccato* section. The *prestissimo* episode initiates a struggle, and discloses less than first-class technical precision. The last movement displays the most ardor and conviction, but, despite its finer sense of proportion and propulsion, this too is remote from a definitive and creative interpretation.

Other versions heard or reheard show almost all their interpreters in characteristic vein. Horowitz unfurls his demonic rhythmic drive and virtuosic brilliance. Toscanini's orchestral collaboration presents superbly luxuriant moments in the lyrical themes, assertively sparkling and didactic effects elsewhere. The total conception is fervent, supercharged, and thrilling. Yet it illustrates the truth that interpretation has its saturation points of speed, dynamics, and excitement, beyond which more speed, more dynamics, and more excitement yield only diminishing returns that cannot produce a durable artistic experience.

Rubinstein approaches the work expansively, expressively, and dramatically. Sometimes Mitropoulos seems not to agree with his soloist's thesis, with resultant antithesis rather than synthesis, especially in the last movement. Generally, however, they endow the work with vibrant meaning and show us what a really fine piece it is. That is the interpreter's highest service. Although one cannot help responding warmly to the eloquence and sweep of the performance, one is also aware of the soloist's undeniable lapses from technical exactitude, too many and too injurious to the total effect.

Shura Cherkassky reveals the gamut of his remarkable pianistic gifts in one of the most fascinating interpretations. One immediately recognizes the unique influence of Cherkassky's master, Josef Hofmann, behind this mercurial and sophisticated performance. Cherkassky has profited by Hofmann's imagination to produce a rare variety of colors and textures in a finely planned design. Technically, he is in masterful command. Musically, he does wonderful things and disturbing things. Ideas as subtle as Hofmann's can be dangerous. The slightest deviation can become distortion, and Cherkassky too frequently indulges in tortured exaggerations. Nevertheless, his performance proves him the possessor of provocative and invigorating qualities.

Solomon, in addition to being the one pianist faithful to Tchaikovsky's rhythmic inspiration in the first movement, provides an expressive, sensitive, and urbane reading. But this sumptuous and heroic work is not quite his piece. Solomon's essential style is exquisite, easy, and radiant. Here he seems somewhat overpowered, not only by the roulades and cadenzas but also by the orchestra under Dobrowen, which often swamps his subtle and lucid pianism.

Alexander Uninsky contributes a gleaming and gracious performance, with able co-operation from Willem van Otterloo except in the *molto più mosso* of the finale. Uninsky's fine wrists and fingers provide absolute technical clarity and honesty. The over-all impression is of refinement, fluidity, and charm rather than of dramatic action or insight.

Gina Bachauer essays the work under the sympathetic baton of her husband, Alec Sherman. Mme Bachauer's gifts seem to me quite miscast in this concerto. Melodically, the work emerges with little color or phraseology. Technically, almost every figuration or chordal passage is so marred by excessive speed and pedal that it is hard to figure out exactly what is going on. Only in the opening of the second movement does the soloist show poise, expressivity, and conviction; everywhere else she sounds thoroughly uncomfortable.

Obviously, this concerto imposes burdensome responsibilities on its interpreters. Nevertheless, the splendor and force of the music rarely fail to stir our blood and move our hearts. Fashions vary from time to time, and few are the compositions or styles that have entirely escaped attack on grounds that differ according to the aesthetic ideals of the day.

Difficult as it may be to elude those who would convince us that our response to Tchaikovsky's concerto is evidence of our low taste, there is comfort in the likelihood that it is going to be around for quite a while. I think that it has a future.

The Rachmaninoff Concertos

RACHMANINOFF's First Concerto was written in his eighteenth year. Although its youthful foundations are somewhat overweighted by the superstructure of later revisions, its content already shows the thematic breadth and dramatic contrasts essential to large designs. The Second Concerto, a full-blown masterpiece, served as a source of inspiration for the Third Concerto, of such difficulty and dimension that its creator said: "I composed it for elephants"—elephants, one assumes, with the mobility of whippets and the grace of gazelles. Annotators have easily found enough similarities in the Third Concerto to justify calling it a complicated rewrite of the Second. It is less easy to find annotators who have discovered the vital ways in which the differences outweigh the resemblances.

The Fourth Concerto is something else again: here the creativeness and coherence of its two inspired predecessors are replaced by weary echoes and fragmentary construction. The *Rhapsody on a Theme by Paganini,* on the other hand, is a resourcefully organized and elegant piece, containing strokes of genius and many beautiful variations wrought by a composer who understood the real nature of his thematic material.

In my chapter concerning interpretation I referred to the recorded album of Rachmaninoff's works for piano and orchestra in the composer's own performances with the Philadelphia Orchestra led by Leopold Stokowski and Eugene Ormandy. Those who have compared the recordings with the published pages must already have found incontestable proof that from an interpretative point of view a score is but a set of general directions; that even metronome marks are variables, no less subject to fine adjustment than loose designations such as *andante* and *moderato* or dynamic indications such as *mf* or *mp*. Each problem of tempo, balance, and nuance provides an artist of the skill of Rachmaninoff with an infinite number of solutions and possibilities.

Confronted with documents, not discs, it seems finicky to linger on any but their sublimest aspects. Yet it must be said that Rachmaninoff himself did not completely subscribe to every note in these recordings. To forestall a mass suicide among the pianists who read this, it must be remembered that Rachmaninoff's standards were merciless and incorruptible to the very end. He was contemptuous of uncritical worship.

His descents from Olympus were, however, rare. Here they occur mainly in the first movement of the Second Concerto, where one observes uncharacteristic sentimentalities and surprisingly frequent cessation of motion. It is only fair to recall that this performance was Rachmaninoff's first recording in the large forms, made on old 78's. The departures from his usual classic proportions may in part be owing to a desire to ease the shock of rude interruption by shading off in volume or tempo, or both, toward the end of each record side. Also in this movement, as in some of the headiest complexities of the Third Concerto and the *Rhapsody,* his control and ease fall short of the pianistic perfection attained from beginning to end in both the First and Fourth concertos. Beyond that, Rachmaninoff's blend of power and refinement, of lucidity and reckless daring, of stability and spontaneity, remains a beacon light.

It is paradoxical that in compositions of such intense personal lyricism Rachmaninoff is the pianist who demonstrates most forcibly that objectivity and straightforwardness are the direct routes to the most eloquent projection of his music. Perhaps the best example is the simplicity in his statement of the famed lyric theme of the Second Concerto, ordinarily the most agonized-over tune in the whole concerto literature. His "orchestrated" chords, with each finger a different instrument, or with all of the fingers together an exquisitely unified choir, are shaded from the heedless heroism of the introduction and the cadenza of the First Concerto to the solemn tenderness preceding the *alla breve* in the finale of the Third Concerto.

Rachmaninoff's playing illustrates the organic quality of his figuration, as we hear in the swirling waves of nuance which accompany and outline the Second Concerto's opening theme, or in the delicious tracery just before the above-mentioned solemn chords of the Third Concerto: the melodic and harmonic contours (also wonderfully illustrated in the fifteenth variation of the *Rhapsody*) always remain visible beneath the passages. The architectural character of his rhythm is marvelously shown in the exposition of the finale of the Fourth Concerto. His *rubato* is dictated no less by the emotional adventure of thematic lines than by harmonic intensification and structural compression or expansion.

When Rachmaninoff returns to the "norm," to the premise from which he departs, he moves with a relentless pace. Note the *vivace* section immediately following the solo's announcement of the First Concerto's principal theme, one of countless examples of his extraordinary ability to re-establish a basic tempo before liberty becomes license, before pulsation goes limp or dead. We can also note here that Rachmaninoff's iron rhythm is not reserved for metrical marches: it can also be maintained in filigree of gossamer texture and iridescent coloration. Add to this a rich tone that sings throughout a full dynamic range, a great variety of touches, pedaling that produces another wealth of color and sonority. We behold an art equal to the fullest transmission of musical thought and discourse.

It was not Rachmaninoff's privilege, nor has it been

ours, to hear that caliber of artistry brought to the interpretation of his piano-and-orchestra works more than a few times, by a few artists. I am sure that this accounted for his extreme bitterness and frequent complaints that Hofmann, the pianistic god to whom Rachmaninoff dedicated his Third Concerto, never played a note of it.

Rachmaninoff particularly admired Horowitz's interpretation of that work, Moiseiwitsch's reading of his *Rhapsody,* and a performance of the same work in the early thirties by Gitta Gradova with the New York Philharmonic under Barbirolli. Rachmaninoff was always wreathed in smiles at the recollection of these performances. He wrapped himself in stony silence at the mention of all others.

I shall be less recessive, for I am tired of hearing the inaccurate clichés that the works we are discussing are "sure-fire" and that no pianist can fail to make a success with them. While it is true that they have so endeared themselves to our concert public that they are almost always greeted with storms of applause, they have the power of X rays to expose the artistic anatomy.

A performance of the Third Concerto, for example, disclosed more about Emil Gilels than was apparent from his playing of any other work during his appearance here. It stamped him as a sensitive and serious artist who lacks musical sophistication, melodic directness, and technical daring. Especially in music like this, as Rachmaninoff and Horowitz have shown, nothing is more exciting than risk: if one wins, one triumphs completely; if not, the gamble was taken, the thrilling gesture made. None but the stoutest heart and the stanchest equipment can carry it off.

But, as we know, still more is required to bring searching realization to one or all of these formidable works. In thinking back on all the performances and recordings I have heard of one or more of these compositions (which sheer politeness deters me from listing) I can assure the pianists involved that these works were no help to them in obscuring their aesthetic cavities.

Sure-fire they are not. Victorious they can be, but only in the hands of a first-class pianist and a first-class musician. For lesser artists they are quicksand.

George Gershwin—Paradox in Blue

THE DURABILITY of the *Rhapsody in Blue,* the Concerto in F, and *An American in Paris* must be puzzling to those who never quite certified George Gershwin. Internationally, and for decades now, these works, despite their obvious organizational defects, have exerted magnetic power to pull unprecedented throngs into concert halls. But it takes a naïveté equal to Gershwin's aesthetics to attribute his prestige merely to the banal taste or imperfect culture of his vast audience. It fails to explain why—suddenly, in Gershwin—form and matter, means and ends, are not quite the inseparables we thought they were. It seems evident that in Gershwin's large-form works the slight accident of genius has clearly outweighed every theoretical and technical issue. Otherwise, there seems to me no sound explanation for the phenomenal and abiding impact of his music.

In the small song form Gershwin is the complete master. In his inimitable musical-comedy and film scores his music holds long scenes together admirably. Here, we remember, he worked with the aid of expert collaborators —notably his brother Ira, a genius in his own right. *Porgy and Bess* is a throbbing masterpiece, for all its unorthodoxies. It is in the instrumental works that Gershwin's ideas are framed within formulas, hampered from taking full flight with the freedom that stems only from solid knowledge and inexorable discipline.

Gershwin's achievements are far beyond the possibilities of unaided technical processes. He had inspiration, the indestructible element in art. A work without it, no matter how perfectly constructed, cannot live. Inspiration

may inhabit a march or a mass; it may pervade a pot-
boiler or a masterpiece; it still remains the magic to which
the great heart of the public is as susceptible as is that of
the most exacting expert. Gershwin's concert works contain the unanswerable potency of emotional communication to the man on the street, whether he walks in Hongkong, Moscow, or New York. And that is all Gershwin
ever wanted.

He spoke of it from the days of his obscurity, from the
days of our first meeting. At the time we both lived in
Harlem, just a few blocks away from each other. I was a
sober sixteen, he an exuberant twenty-one. The age difference was dissolved by mutual interests: girls, tennis, and,
mainly, music. George was then a song-plugger for Rem-
ick, and the owner of a few small songs and many big
ideas. The things that made him so special to me were his
confidence, force, and love for music; his incredible ease,
joyous spontaneity, and originality at the piano. He was
the only pianist I ever heard who could make a piano
laugh, really laugh. Above all, George brought me the
fresh and forbidden fruits of a jazz world that my parents and teachers had carefully taught me to resist and
reject.

We soon got into a fight. My nose was stuck to the musical grindstone. George was having a love-affair with music; no regular piano practice, no slaving away at theory,
harmony, counterpoint, orchestration, or form. One day
in 1919, on the corner of Lenox Avenue and 113th Street,
he confided more of his big ideas. "George," I said, "don't
you think it would be a good idea to take some lessons
from Goldmark? Nobody can do what you want to do
without basic training."

He stood still and glared at me. "You're just the kind of
person who is keeping me from doing my great work," he
shouted, and stamped off, leaving me standing there. We
didn't speak for almost a year. Meanwhile, the musical-
comedy career that eventually won a Pulitzer Prize was

already launched with *La La Lucille*, and Gershwin's "Swanee" blared from every phonograph and player piano.

We patched up our quarrel and resumed a friendship that continued through the twenties. Those times, those days! How often I think of them. The nerves of our postwar generation were stretched like taut wires. Spiritually, we wavered between old ideals that we could neither trust nor recapture and the chilling spaces of an uncertain destiny. Exhausted by emotion and suspense, we sought security and escape from deep feelings. We used our energies to run and forget: remembering was too painful. We exercised like mad. And we worked hard, although I can't quite recall how or when. More vividly I remember our dizzy social lives. The parties, the yachts, the speakeasies, the gorgeous women and amusing men, and everyone so plush, everyone so busy. We never had time to look at the sky or the task at hand. Nevertheless, music was somehow the focal point of all our interests and activities, and George was the central figure of every gathering.

The music of an epoch is never an isolated phenomenon. The classics are always the classics. But serious contemporary music had become the province of cliques. Repudiation was their banner. Repudiation of romantic ideals, of impressionism, and of expressionism, too. Interior vision and all the richness of subjective emotions were out. The death of sentiment was proclaimed, the path cleared for a "scientific" art whose exponents wrote for themselves and one another, entirely estranged from the public. Popular music, apart from the best tunes of such men as Kern and Berlin, consisted of oom-pah rhythms, infantile harmonizations, melodic molasses, and verbal inanities. In Gershwin's hands it became svelte, chic, and sophisticated.

There was then an iron curtain between "bad music" and "good music." In 1924 Gershwin demolished it with his *Rhapsody in Blue*. It was the passport to immortality

with which he linked the concert and popular worlds of
music. The *Rhapsody* became his era's anthem, and
George became the musical man-of-the-hour. He had
everything it takes to make a popular success. Typical of
his age and era, he spoke directly to his fellow men. The
language he spoke was an eclectic one: black-face humor,
Russian sentimentality, Jewish sorrow, Broadway pep, and
French *ooh-la-la*. In short, typically American. It made our
worlds one world.

Many celebrated musicians and critics got on the
Gershwin bandwagon, enchanted no less by the freshness,
vitality, and radiance of the man's personality than by
those same qualities in his music. For every musician who
found the *Rhapsody* disorganized, blatant, and derivative, there were a dozen others earnestly urging the virtually untutored Gershwin to write works of symphonic
scope. He needed no great persuasion. Few would need it
who basked in such idolatry, who could read of their
work what Harry Osgood wrote of the *Rhapsody:* "a
more important contribution to music than Stravinsky's
'Le Sacre.'" The comment was typical of that Babylonian
era in which every conservatory suckling was writing elephantine orchestral works without any sense of sin or responsibility. But men like Gershwin shake all pious and
pedantic concepts. Within two years of completing his
Concerto in F he was to see no less a genius than Ravel
write a piano concerto irresistibly influenced by his own.

Looking back, it occurs to me that Gershwin's explosive
rejection of formal study may have been a piece of wisdom. He may have known then that he could not submit
to the discipline of training in harmony and counterpoint
without a serious loss of inspiration. In this he would show
a very rare capacity: the insight through which exceptional people know their strengths and limitations. Gershwin was searching for his true identity and for instantane-
ous communication with the widest possible audience. To
criticize his works for not being "weighty" is like criticiz-

ing an ice-cream soda for not being hot. I think that Gershwin always knew that what transcends erudition can never be attained without erudition.

Gershwin's entire career makes a paradox of the doctrine that there is no mercy in art. In the case of other composers, it is demonstrable that the technique of their dullest works is not equal to that of their most inspired. Gershwin managed miraculously to keep his creative virtues separated from his technical defects. It is easy to see that his works for piano and orchestra are especially diffuse and constricted. It is easy to see that his greatest ideas remained undeveloped, repeated in sequence, vitiated in rigid recapitulations, or blown up in afflated grandiosity. What is less easy to see is the precise reason for the inevitable triumph finally achieved through a series of loosely connected epigrams. For even the most scintillating epigrams cannot produce a large-form musical architecture any more than they can produce a play or novel. Exhilarating, ingenuous, and piquant as is *An American in Paris*, it remains an undeveloped collection of sectional ideas, a delightful set of highly colored picture-postcards of a Paris seen by an amorous, quite superficial, and tipsy tourist. Yet—drat this Gershwin— the felicitous rhythms, the lovely tunes, and the humorous embroidery are a heady mixture. And no one else has felt or written quite that way. Perhaps that resolves some of the paradox.

Gershwin's pianistic ability was heredity itself, a form of habit so utterly natural that any conscious interference with it at his stage of the game would have been a great mistake. I recall that early in the thirties he was scheduled to play his *Rhapsody* and Concerto at the Lewisohn Stadium. We hadn't met for several years. He came up one summer afternoon, sat down at the piano, and began to practice Czerny studies. I could not recognize his playing, could not find his former unique approach to the keyboard. Stopping him, I asked if he had ever heard of the unfortunate centipede who lay perspiring in a ditch, paralyzed because a malicious snail innocently had asked him which leg he put down first. "George," I said, "you don't have to play the Beethoven concertos. Just 'Do Do Do What You Done Done Done Before, Baby,' and let your subconscious do it. Now you sound throttled."

"You know," he said after a minute of thoughtful silence, "you're right. Now I know what's been happening to my playing."

I am now wondering whether it already had happened when he recorded the *Rhapsody* with Whiteman, reissued by Victor in 1951. When I heard it, it just about broke my heart. Gone are the youthful ease, the rhythmic bite, the sensitive songfulness. George sounds constrained and bored. I much prefer to think that he was just bored: that, despite his reputation for egocentricity, his famed enthusiasm for his own music was *not* inexhaustible. Whiteman's orchestra sounds equally full of ennui. The piece itself was so cut to ribbons as to sound like a *Listener's Digest* version.

Pianists have found it essential to have either the *Rhapsody* or the Concerto or both in their repertoires. Both or either have made up many an orchestral deficit. Most of the American pianists who perform these works are, in varying degrees, products of a contemporary school of pianism which is far more brilliant than imaginative. Their extraordinary adroitness is matched by their rigidity, their emotional modesty. Here it is singularly damaging, for no music needs more "give," more flow and breadth, than compositions of an episodic and rhapsodic nature. Such music also needs that improvisational freedom within a basic rhythmic impetus which is so lacking in our current crop of skillful young artists. Theirs is a stop-go rubato, ruinous to Chopin, fatal to Gershwin. It seems paradoxical that such essentially American pieces are not their pieces, not even their kind of pieces. But really they are not.

To be specific, the crux of Gershwin's style is rhythmic romanticism. This means that his music demands elements that have long been scarce on the concert platform: melodic effulgence, harmonic intensity, and nonmetrical pulsation. Equally, because long-line continuity does not permeate the pieces themselves, an architectural perspective is needed to unify Gershwin's sectionalized structures. That kind of perspective is far more common to composers than to performers, and Gershwin had it to a tremendous degree. When he was in the mood, his playing was hypnotic, and could no more be described than imitated. It is nowhere faithfully available on records. But ask those who heard him in the living-room. They will tell you that Gershwin's playing compelled one to take his works for what they were. One never gave thought to what they were not.

Among current Gershwin interpreters, Oscar Levant and Morton Gould are closest to realization of the composer's specific sentiments. Their performances and recordings display authentic affinity, perspective, and conviction. They know what these pieces are all about, and their understanding comes through despite their limitations as executants. Levant has the knack and the drive, but not the discipline either technical or rhythmical. Gould has the musicianship and precision, but not the virtuosic sweep or declamatory suavity. Nevertheless, they reveal Gershwin's panorama, its humor and its compassion.

When all is said and done, Gershwin remains a vital creator. His is a spontaneous spirit. Its precious substance is inspiration. His style is improvisation, with all its merits and demerits. He speaks an eclectic language, yet expresses everything his way and directly to his fellow men. His work is significant to history because it carries the musical expression of his environment with such force and accuracy as to explain itself to future, as well as to foreign, audiences. Vital works always carry such evidence, no matter how much they may lack the divine completeness of perfect masterpieces.

What composers of concert music can be said to have contributed as directly to everyday American life as our popular song-writers, novelists, and playwrights? None but Gershwin. That fact may finally loom as his greatest contribution.

. . . and Others

IN AN orchestral age such as ours, the contemporary composer's faith and hope and the bulk of his creative energy are bound to be channeled into symphonic music. The public taste for musical theater, films, and ballet provides further incentives for composers to contribute orchestral music, from which effective concert pieces can also be derived.

There is nothing wrong with any of that. But it has left us with a group of creators whose most serious and striking efforts are only occasionally directed toward solo literatures. The curtailed production has created a major problem for pianists aware of a responsibility to contemporary creativity and seeking works of value and communicability. There are not many such pianists, which is not unconnected with the fact that there is not much piano music of importance and potency now being written. But we are far from bereft.

My own introduction to modern piano music began around 1918 when an eager, gaunt young Russian with reddish-blond hair, wide blue eyes, and flapping ears was brought to our home. We had hardly enough time to learn that his name was Serge Prokofiev before he ran to the piano without being asked and immediately sat down, mumbling something in Russian. I caught the words "my preludes," and I remember being enticed by his strange music and greatly excited by his vital playing. He played for an hour, going from one piece to another without stopping, superbly indifferent to our reactions. But when he stopped, our enthusiasm seemed to please him greatly. It brought a flushed smile and another hour of his fanciful

music. Sitting motionless, "like patience on a monument,"
he made the instrument speak with tremendous intensity
and lyric power.

After he played he talked, and with equal power. Molding each phrase with huge hands, he grew terribly tense
as he confided that he wanted to create "an entirely new
music." This he did not quite do, but he did create his
own music, and some of it is easily among the finest music
of our time. And some of it is easily disturbing, too, for it
shows how environment can adversely affect human emotion and thought, even when they reside in so undeniable
a musical genius as Prokofiev.

Like many another creator who was a formidable pianist, Prokofiev brought the gamut of his compositional
characteristics to the music written for his own instrument. His own interpretations of his works were deeply
impressive. Some are documented on discs, and they are
wonderfully galvanic. But quite a few of them have won
performances of a caliber several notches above his own
pianistic art, for their streamlined brilliance, angular
mockery, melodic urbanity, cunning and artfulness in
harmonization and modulation are completely native to
the temperament of most contemporary artists.

Uppermost in my mind are Horowitz's readings of the
Seventh Sonata and the Toccata, which nobody, but nobody, plays with such leonine rhythm and prodigal color.
The perfectly fused Third Sonata was first fully revealed
to me in a masterly interpretation by Seymour Lipkin, who
perceived exactly the irony and charm of this virile work.
Gary Graffman too, in his performances and recording of
the same sonata as well as the Second, is above any but
the most appreciative comment. Especially because these
two sonatas, in my estimation, are the only wholly successful organisms among the nine published piano sonatas
that were spaced throughout forty years of Prokofiev's
creative activity. The Second and Third alone disclose
Prokofiev's primary and contrasting qualities merged in

units of faultless proportion. Romantic and realistic, lyrical and percussive, sensitive and bitingly satirical, all at the same time or in fascinating juxtaposition, they show Prokofiev's undistorted originality in reconciling the age-old struggles between matter and manner, instinct and culture.

The rest are amazing works, nevertheless, full of marvelous and awful things. In the Fourth Sonata, even when a rhythmic idea monopolizes Prokofiev or roguish laughter seizes him or violent harmonization beats against the barriers of his essential romanticism, he still remains faithful in his fashion to his spiritual traditions. From then on, we see a musician trying to find expression for the discord and instability of his epoch and of his own afflicted soul, an instinctive poet in revolt against rude actuality, a master craftsman who rarely fails to achieve some striking effect even when he wavers. The last sonata tells the whole story. It is an expiation in which Prokofiev can no longer conceal his unregenerate romanticism. But it derives from a finally diluted imagination. It is like a drink that has been too long neglected, that once held strong spirits and is now a little pool of melted ice.

The opportunity to hear all of these works was provided by Yury Boukoff, the Bulgarian pianist, who recorded the entire collection for the first time in 1957, fifty years after the incubation of the First Sonata. Boukoff is an excellently schooled and meticulously honest performer. Although he has not yet transformed his skill into intense musical values, his playing of the Fourth Sonata strikes me as undeviating in finish and devotion.

I shall not forget Dimitri Mitropoulos's monolithic force in the dual role of conductor and pianist in Prokofiev's Third Concerto, nor a reading of the same concerto by William Kapell altogether memorable for its melodic declamation as well as its wholesome violence. This same work and the Second Sonata interpreted by Emil Gilels, both on disc and both coached with the composer, reveal in Gilels the kind of rhythmic momentum, bravura, and musicianship which have been found nowhere else in his playing. These performances finally substantiate the reputation he enjoys.

Prokofiev's Second Concerto found an ideal interpreter in Jorge Bolet. He plays it in performances and on disc with a relentless continuity that never becomes brutal, with loving care and wily understanding of its expressive content. He owns it completely.

The First Concerto and the *Visions fugitives* are admirable works that I have not yet heard admirably played except by their creator. I wish, before some irate pianist among my readers does me in, that he would first please play them for me in a way to sweeten my pen and gladden my old age.

Although Béla Bartók wrote no symphonies, he wrote plenty for orchestra, and I cannot think of any other form or medium to which he did not contribute something significant. Always there is the master craftsman at work, always the engaging spectacle of an uncompromising mind and spirit and human being.

It is undoubtedly the elemental force, the austerity, and sometimes even the savagery of his rhythms and harmonies which have stamped Bartók as a "primitive." Certainly these traits are strongly revealed in his piano music, for Bartók had a vertical view of the piano as a primarily percussive instrument. Not that he did not know and occasionally exploit the full lyrical possibilities of the instrument, for he was a superb concert pianist who emerged from the Rubinstein Competition in 1905 second only to Wilhelm Backhaus.

Virtually the full range of Bartók's compositional personality is found in the *Mikrokosmos*, that remarkable collection of 153 progressive studies. They show him to be a fearless experimenter, but one who never scorned the natural in a conscious effort to be "original." His famed and untiring investigations into the genesis of Magyar folk music typed him unmercifully and set unjustified limits to his creative significance.

Although the major part of the *Mikrokosmos* comprises elementary teaching material that does not provide concert repertoire, most of it aims higher than supplying a method for acquiring instrumental facility. Actually, it constitutes a highly original introduction to contemporary idioms in general and Bartók's idiom in particular. The set takes the student from four-bar sketches in unison which take twenty seconds, through colorful little folk songs and dances, to five-page pieces of polytonal and polyrhythmic intricacies. Apart from the five-finger exercises, most of them have vitality and interest despite their essential economy of range and sonority. Some are beautiful in a strange way; others are harsh enough to make one writhe, but they are all Bartók.

So are the Second Concerto, the Sonata 1926, and the *Allegro barbaro*. I mention these works and the *Mikrokosmos* especially because I have learned to appreciate them more than Bartók's other piano works, for which edification I tender special thanks to two of the composer's friends, advocates, and compatriots, Andor Foldes and Gyorgy Sandor.

Speaking of matters Hungarian, Ernst von Dohnanyi comes to mind; yet the music of his that I admire most would make one think he was anything but Hungarian. The C minor Piano Quintet is a beauty, but a Brahmsian beauty, and no addition to solo literature. His F minor Capriccio is, however, and it is one of the most effective little piano pieces around. There remains the *Variations on a Nursery Song* for piano and orchestra, and it is here that pianists have a first-class work in a cosmopolitan idiom.

Karol Szymanowski was also a cosmopolite, but a genuine genius, too. Perhaps this explains why his evolutionary blend of romanticism and impressionism, like that of the short-lived Charles T. Griffes, was marked for brutal assassination by the youthful revolutionaries. My startled discovery of the beauty and profundity of Szymanowski's ideas and the coherence and fascination of his musical individuality and piano writing I owe to Artur Rubinstein, who played privately for me dozens of his countryman's piano works that made my head spin. No matter what Rubinstein demonstrated, whether preludes, studies, variations, or sonatas, Szymanowski emerged as an authentic poet and master craftsman of unbelievable originality. I was stunned. It seemed to me that pianists could ill afford to neglect such gems. I then studied the music. I became exasperated. I now ask pianists—where, except in the most significant music of a Chopin or a Debussy or a Prokofiev, can one find piano music of superior vision and power? In few works, is the answer, and they grow fewer and fewer in an age whose outstanding creators are justifiably tempted to do their best work for those who want them and will do them justice.

Igor Stravinsky illustrates the situation graphically. The towering creative figure of the twentieth century has aroused plenty of acid argument except on one indisputable point: his genius. Almost everything Stravinsky has written shows imagination, vitality, and mastery that few composers at few times have been able to bestow on their work. And what are the glaring exceptions? The piano works: two empty concertos, two dehydrated sonatas (one for solo piano, the other for two pianos), and some minor, tongue-in-cheek pieces that are neither very funny nor to be taken very seriously. Greatness is found among the piano works only in the Concerto for Two Solo Pianos (authoritatively recorded by Gold and Fizdale) and in the piano transcription of a masterpiece, *Petrouchka*—by the real, the one and only, Stravinsky.

The pattern is continued by Paul Hindemith. This bold musician and feverish contrapuntalist has contributed powerfully, abundantly, and even beautifully to operatic, symphonic, and chamber-music literatures. But his Piano Concerto remains an unsuccessful experiment, his 1922 *Suite* as discordant and manipulated a piece of self-conscious modernism as one could find anywhere; and his *Ludus Tonalis* emerges as a remarkable example of consummate polyphonic ingenuity and of the inability of erudition to bring inspiration to construction. In his numerous piano works Hindemith's human spirit rarely shows except in his Sonata for two pianos and in his Second and Third sonatas for solo piano. I discovered this from a study of the music, not from any of the infrequent performances I have had an opportunity to hear.

Whether or not the atonal innovations of Arnold Schoenberg will furnish the key to a musical Utopia, I leave to the historians. As for me, I know the scrupulous veracity and fanatical dedication of the man. I know the early Straussian and Wagnerian works that drove him to invent the twelve-tone technique in order to free himself from the adhesive past. I also know most of the music that followed from him and his upholders.

Nothing has excited me less than the periodically "new concepts" of tonal relations or rigid systems of harmony, except possibly the God-forsaken sounds that have derived from them. Not until theory demonstrates itself in music that erupts from within, driven by emotional power and imaginative organizational ideas, am I roused to reaction and action. Music that is forced from without by external manipulation does not persuade me that it possesses within it the key to musical salvation.

Theory is the servant, not the master, of art. It can only serve, not lead, creativity. From the first note of the first rehearsal of Alban Berg's *Wozzeck*, I knew that I was in the presence of a dramatic masterpiece by a genius whose communicative power overwhelmed his language and style.

In contrast—for Berg's contribution to piano music is nil—we turn first to Schoenberg's twelve-tone-row syntax in his piano works, opera 11, 19, and 23. After repeated hearings and study, they represent nothing to me but constructions that demonstrate a theory. They elicit nothing so much as tedium.

Not tedium exactly, but disquiet has accompanied my many efforts to digest the Piano Concerto and *George Washington Piano Variations* by Ernst Křenek. They were written for pianist Miriam Molin, who kindly enabled me to study them conscientiously. Of all Schoenberg's disciples, Mr. Křenek has composed the most piano music. I find little in these works that is individual, pianistic, or evocative.

Aaron Copland reflects our time in the qualitative and quantitative contrast between his piano works and his others. The Piano Variations, Piano Sonata, and Piano Concerto undeniably show genuine force and craftsmanship. But these jagged and quite inaccessible works contain more midnight oil than the warm red blood that a wide public drank eagerly in Copland's two-piano suite made from his ballet score *Billy the Kid*.

I would like to digress for a moment from the man's music to the man. We have been friends for years; we have worked together at the American Composers Alliance and at ASCAP; we were fellow members of the faculty at Tanglewood in the Koussevitzky days. During many of those years I loathed most of his music, and he knew it. Toward my own conservative brain children he did not even give the time of day. We were friends, nevertheless, and we battled constantly, over modernism, over tendencies and idioms and ideologies. Now I can honestly say that I have never encountered among creative musicians a more modest, more objective, or sharper

mind than his. I am sure that without any nagging from
colleagues who felt as I did about Copland's responsibility
to himself and to the musical public, his steady journey
toward simplicity and communicability was inevitable
and essentially self-motivated. He learned through his
deep needs to impart and to convince.

Samuel Barber's *Excursions* strike me as thoroughly en-
joyable and firm contributions to contemporary piano literature. His Piano Sonata is very effective, but somewhat
contrived. Pianistically it was contrived for Horowitz,
who introduced it in 1950, and who then and there
should have secured a performance copyright, for every
other performance I have heard of this work has been inadequate.

Norman Dello Joio's Third Sonata seems to me his best
piano work, for it incorporates most concisely and expressively the sensitive qualities evident in his best orchestral
works. It is an interweaving of reflective and rhythmically sparkling elements. It is often played, and it wears
well. My appreciation of its value came from devotional
study and performances of the work by Constance Keene.

Another Third Sonata, by Harold Shapero, impressed
me deeply by its inner life, variety, and coherence. My enthusiasm must include Seymour Lipkin, who played the
splendid work to the hilt and lavished upon it not one
whit less superlative pianism than he brought to the old
masters in his 1956 Town Hall recital.

There is naturally a great deal of musical fruit that no
one person can possibly pick up within one lifetime. I am
certain that there are composers whose accomplishments
warrant serious attention, but whose music I have not had
the opportunity to hear. What I have been able to harvest
from contemporary fields has inevitably led me either to
hope that the creator would produce more for pianists to
gather or to pray that he would not.

Among the active composers of the Americas, in addition to Barber, Dello Joio, and Shapero, quite a few others have demonstrated exceptional ability to write expressively and appropriately for piano. Judging from few, but telling, examples, Paul Creston, Leonard Bernstein, Carlos Chávez, Albert Ginastera, Camargo Guarnieri, Roy Harris, Ulysses Kay, Douglas Moore, Walter Piston, and Virgil Thomson should all be stimulated to write more keyboard music.

These composers, as well as some non-piano composers such as Quincy Porter and Randall Thompson, have all kept remarkably free from "isms" and grandiosity. They have never been captured by any clique. They have not set out to write The Great American anything. Yet in their works there are unlabored and refreshing originalities absent from many an agonized and ambitious project published complete with philosophy and/or theoretic salestalk.

I always try, but it is not always easy, to divorce what a composer says about his music from the music itself. Charles Ives's words have always fascinated me. I cannot say the same for his music. His Second and Third symphonies are undeniably and strongly original works. But originality is an element, not the whole, of a work of art. The greater its force, the greater its wastefulness unless it is accompanied by other elements. In Ives I find phrases of homespun charm, sections of compelling power. I cannot find, among the large-form works I have heard, one that does not finally strike me as sprawling, savagely complex, or just cussedly eccentric. When a work like the *Concord Sonata* for piano is finished, so am I. Even in the expert hands of John Kirkpatrick it suggested to me a basic disequilibrium, an expression of a composer at war within himself.

Which, by contrast, brings to mind the unaffected expressivity and direct clarity of the full-fledged American romantic, Edward MacDowell. The piano was his first love, and he composed for it a large literature that has lost its savor for concert artists and audiences of our time. No one is at fault. Not MacDowell, who could not help the fact that his stylistic gift was not of the first order; not we, for preferring the very music that was the genesis of his ideas and his methods.

MacDowell's Irish-Scotch ancestry, his German and French schooling, his equal susceptibility to Celtic and Norse legends and to American Indian themes and Negro rhythms, are characteristic of the *mélange* peculiar to nineteenth-century American culture. In the large forms— in his two piano concertos and four sonatas—MacDowell's harmonic speech is not novel. His thematic material is rarely significant, and when he develops it, he is back in the world of Schumann and Liszt. His rhythmic ideas are often overworked, his structural methods are too improvisational and sequential to sustain extended development. Nevertheless, and despite their faults, these works are the works of a great man. They are the products of a noble heart and a beautiful mind. Their individuality is owing to MacDowell's culture and to the simplicity and elegance of his feelings.

Impeccable craftsmanship, originality, and fine piano writing are to be found in the shorter works. Who has not at one time played one of those colorful little landscapes from the *New England Idyls, Woodland Sketches, From Uncle Remus, Sea Pieces,* or the Studies? Whoever has, and does not carry with him the haunting sounds, has little heart and less musical taste. Having heard composers sneer at MacDowell's "sugared sentimentality"—composers who had found a haven at the MacDowell Colony at Peterboro—I think that our cynical age could use a sharper remembrance of the humanity and integrity of this creative shrine's namesake.

Now let us move east again and try to find out why it is that most of the finest Spanish music has been written by

Frenchmen and Slavs, what exceptions there are, and what proportion has been allocated to piano writing.

Spain is rich in natural musical resources, in colorful folk tunes, popular rhythms, and characteristic harmonies. Its musical *patois* has a strong and unmistakable individuality. Individuality is a good thing, but in art it is possible to have too much of a good thing, especially when individuality is so laden with fixed conventions and mannerisms that it leads to provincialism rather than to universality.

Debussy, Ravel, and Rimsky-Korsakov brought their European vines and planted them in Spanish soil to produce a vigorous wine of unique *pétillance*. Only in the *Bolero* was Ravel's creativity blighted by Spanish clichés. The process of Isaac Albéniz, and later of Manuel de Falla, was to graft French cuttings upon their indigenous Spanish roots.

Had Albéniz lived in our time, we probably would not have found his crowning achievement to be a set of twelve piano pieces. But there, in *Ibéria,* is the best he had to give, the authentic music of a genuine nationalist liberated in Paris and assisted by Vincent d'Indy, Fauré, and Dukas. Other works, such as the six pieces of *España,* are rhythmically and melodically ingratiating, but they are far from great pieces. They only sound great when Rubinstein plays them.

The works of Falla that have taken firm root in the piano repertoire are his *Nights in the Gardens of Spain* and his own transcriptions of the "Ritual Fire-Dance" and the "Dance of Terror" from his exquisite ballet, *El Amor Brujo.* Again, Rubinstein is inescapably linked with their fame.

And it was Rubinstein who provided the opportunity for a Lusitano-American genius to flower. Villa-Lobos responded pianistically with *Rudepôema,* dedicated to his benefactor, two sets of charming pieces called *Baby's Dolls* and the *Infernal Dance,* and a few others less well known. He nods to the pianist in the fifth, eleventh, and thirteenth of his strikingly original *Chôros,* and in the third of the superb *Bachianas Brasileiras,* but the total is a meager handout from a composer who owes so much to a pianist, who indeed at one time was himself a pianist and married one.

It would seem that I am being ungracious and ungrateful to complain about creative artists who have already endured so much for the sake of their art and who have contributed so much of beauty and importance to our civilization. But, really, I am not grumbling. I am registering regret rather than complaint that the piano has not activated more of their power and poetry.

The relevance of my regret is again plain in the case of Jean Sibelius. His is a great accomplishment and a great name. His unique symphonies and tone poems have invariably been described as elemental. They are, just as surely as his piano pieces are elementary.

Ernest Bloch, who has also been established as a master of classic dimension, has likewise not contributed significantly to the solo piano repertoire. In his magnificent *Concerto grosso,* Piano Quintet, instrumental sonatas, and suites, he shows not only his passionate fervor and striking originality but also that he knows how to write for the piano. Every work that employs the piano shows how powerfully Bloch can write for our instrument until we come to the piano solos: the *Poems of the Sea, Sketches in Sepia, Enfantines,* and *In the Night.* From a composer of Bloch's grandeur, these are not grand works.

From *Les Six* our literature has gained only a little. At one time Francis Poulenc enjoyed considerable popularity, especially his *Mouvements perpetuels, Pastourelle,* and *Toccata.* Effective they are, but wearing thinner every day.

Darius Milhaud is a brilliant stylist in almost every

idiom and medium, and there are few this prodigious and prolific composer has not tried. That Milhaud knows exactly what the piano can do is masterfully demonstrated in his sparkling and durable two-piano suite, *Scaramouche.*

I have often wondered why his numerous solo piano works were difficult to obtain and to find on concert programs. One set that is neither might be a clue, if it is typical of the works I do not know. I once heard Zadel Skolovsky play both books of Milhaud's *Saudades do Brasil.* He represented them so faithfully that the composer, who was present, turned in his seat to express his appreciation of the interpretation to Ross Parmenter, who was reviewing for *The New York Times.* Individually, the *Saudades* are charming miniatures. Heard together, even when so authoritatively presented, their repetitive dance rhythms and coquettish tunes soon sounded trivial and tautological.

The influences of Poulenc and Milhaud are felt in the charming *Concertino* for piano and orchestra by Jean Françaix, whose elegant and witty piano writing provided every reason to expect that maturity would bring a significant development to his Gallic gifts. So far, nothing has come to my attention which has much weight or import.

There is not any more of consequence to find in the self-conscious wrong-note humor of the piano preludes and polkas by Dimitri Shostakovich. Even less rewarding are his arid preludes and fugues. When Gilels introduced them here, his dedicated readings revealed them mercilessly as sophomoric products of the naïve beliefs that polyphony and its devices evidence deep scholarship and that technique can be separated from aesthetics. From a composer who had it in him to produce one of the greatest first symphonies ever written and to create the profoundly inspired Fifth Symphony, Shostakovich's piano output is a keen disappointment.

From Nicolai Miaskovsky, the founding father of the Soviet symphonic school, nothing for piano has found its way into the repertoire. I heard one of his sonatas, and it seemed to me a discouraging sample. His pupil, Aram Khatchaturian, hit the jackpot with his brilliant piano concerto. Introduced here by Maro Ajemian, it was brought to vogue by the scintillating performances and recording of William Kapell. Once it has been heard, that is that. But it has splash and effectiveness, like the piano Toccata and *Gayne* ballet, which, added to its exoticism and vitality, produce audience success. I distrust its staying-power, however, for it is even more destitute of intellectual and spiritual depth than either the Grieg or any of the Anton Rubinstein concertos.

Dimitri Kabalevsky, though immensely indebted to Prokofiev, seems to me easily next to him in accomplishment as the most expressive and resourceful piano writer of the Soviet group. I have heard only one of his piano concertos, and that only once: the Third, written in 1952 and introduced to New York five years later by Walter Hautzig with the American Chamber Orchestra conducted by Robert Scholz. Despite a rigidly uncommunicative presentation of the piano part, the work came through as a masterful piece of workmanship and musical distinction.

What I know well and for a long time are Kabalevsky's sonatas, sonatinas, preludes, and pieces for children. They are all charming and perfectly straightforward works, beautifully conceived for the piano, and entirely spontaneous and ingratiating. The fact that they are without much inventive distinction may have more to do with the artistic credo of the Central Committee of the Communist Party than with his own creative limitations. If this is not the fact, we can only hope that he will take on some intellectual weight. Then, I think, we could look forward to more meaningful and original music from a man who knows the piano inside out. This was instantly apparent many years ago when Horowitz introduced the Third Sonata here. Since then I am mainly indebted to the distaff side—to convincing performances of the Preludes from Nadia Reisenberg, of the Second Sonata from Jeannette Haien, and of the Third Sonata and First Sonatina from Constance Keene—for my conviction that Kabalevsky has significant potentialities as yet incompletely fulfilled.

Before we leave the subject of piano music, I would like to describe some of the compositional infirmities of Abram Chasins. Of his Twenty-Four Preludes for Piano, he was unwise to publish more than a third of them. In his First Piano Concerto, the first and third movements are adroitly organized, but disclose thematic material that the audience could have hummed with a fair degree of accuracy on its way to the *première* in 1929. The second movement is all right, and the composer should someday incorporate it into a stronger work. The Second Concerto is better, but it contains too many perishable elements. The composer finally showed excellent musical judgment by declining all charitable offers to publish or record these works, and by deciding against further composition until he can find something of his own to say and enough time to devote to it.

Narrative is his best piano work, and he finds a certain comedy in the emergence of the cute, synthetic *Chinese Pieces* as public favorites—widely played, taught, recorded, and transcribed for just about everything but piccolo and drum. Composers are least fond of such works, possibly for the same reasons that parents feel most tenderly toward their less successful children.

Most of the two-piano works and transcriptions are quite effective, very busy, and immensely difficult. The composer was dreaming of duo-pianists with the musicianship and instrumental mastery of Rosina and Josef Lhevinne, of Vera Brodsky and Harold Triggs, who played them superlatively—and of Beryl Rubinstein and Arthur

Loesser, whose playing, individually and together, was memorably brilliant and beautiful.

Beryl Rubinstein, incidentally, wrote some lovely piano works in the *genre* of French impressionism. Arthur Loesser has contributed a historic monument to musical literature in his book, *Men, Women and Pianos*. And that fine book reminds me that I had better get back to my main subject.

Recapitulation and Coda

Recapitulation and Coda

I BEGAN this book in a haze of inspired remembrances of unparalleled pianistic standards, unique to a former era. This led me to seek and describe every vestige of comparable greatness or of another kind of greatness in our time. As I came to the younger people, I betrayed my exasperation that so many have succumbed so easily to the *ad hoc* behavior of a mechanized and materialistic society, that so many are as out of tune with basic artistic values as they are with a large proportion of the masterpieces they elect to play. I have attempted to present and explain their numerous problems. Now we have found that another of their currently insoluble problems is the comparative paucity of the music they feel and love and play best.

But there is nothing new about that. Every artist is most in accord with his own world, and only a small percentage of the art in any field emerges from any one period. When we count our artistic blessings, we are likely to compress history, to forget the interspaces of creativity, the distance between golden ages. In this way, impatience with one's age is natural. It belonged to every epoch before our own.

Who in 1550 could have predicted the Elizabethan era? Who could have predicted that a drunken musical hack would father a Beethoven? No one, and the fact is enough to remove any sense of hopelessness about the future, no matter what the present may indicate.

I am therefore glad that I have written about not only the pianistic joys of my life, but also the causes of my discontents. Somehow, pouring it out bolsters my innate faith that "what thou lovest well, remains." My inextinguishable love for music and for all who find in its mystical power the real meaning of life assures me that, unless humanity pulverizes itself, there will always be music in men's lives. Some poor music that may thrive for a time, some great music that may take a day longer than it should to be properly estimated, some artists to play it like angels or butchers, audiences to feed upon it, and critics who will immortalize themselves by their big, fat mistakes.

There will be periods of disturbing transition such as ours, periods in which one aspect of human activity is in the doldrums while another is enjoying affluence. And there will always be those who live for art, and those who live from it. And among those who live from it, many who live by the sword.

But the artist is not helpless. Not unless he lowers his standards in complete surrender, not unless we remain passive while the world hacks away, compelling all but the superman to succumb. There is nothing new about this, either. Civilization's loftiest aims have always been in crisis, and it is no cause for wonder that today they are in greater crisis than ever.

I therefore do not hold with the prophets of doom or inevitability. I hold optimistic convictions about the future, convictions that my own evidence may not seem to warrant, but that persist nevertheless. Although often shaken and swerved, they still persist because we humans all start afresh, we come into the world at the beginning of a new time.

Think of it, ours could be the greatest civilization of all and in every way. Not as it is, but one we are somehow going to build, or help to build. It is a dream waiting to be materialized, a concept of peace and productivity and human dignity in terms of men proud and free to contribute what they have uniquely to contribute, even

to search for abiding values. It is a view of mechanization
and prosperity not as all-consuming objectives, but as in-
strumentalities for ever higher standards of living and
working. It is also a faith in the final worth of humanity.
After all, what we revere of former civilizations is the
enduring values they held, the edifices they retained, constructed, and transmitted to us.

And if our contemporary artists and intellectuals are
helped to greater security and dedication, if they will
honor and study and preserve old traditions while they
build new ones, they will be on their way to incalculable achievements.

This is all possible, even if things have to get worse
before they can get better. We all await a great change.
When that day will dawn, we cannot know. But we
can all act as though it were within our grasp, and cherish every heartening sign of its appearance.

As I write this, the morning papers report that Senators
Jacob K. Javits of New York and Joseph Clark of Pennsylvania are co-sponsoring a bill for the creation of a
United States Art Foundation. Advocating his bill before a professional group, Senator Javits said: "I feel
this is an extremely important move on behalf of all the
performing arts and is absolutely essential to their continued life." None of the proposals along these lines introduced in Congress has progressed beyond lip service
since President Eisenhower recommended establishment
of an advisory arts commission during his first term. Perhaps this one will.

One notices more and more meetings of personalities
in the arts as panelists urging government participation
in a domestic arts program, offering suggestions that range
from the removal of Federal taxes on tickets to the establishment of a Secretary of the Fine Arts in the Cabinet.
Definitely, awareness is in the air. Without it, nothing
happens. With it, anything can happen. And only the in-

dividual can make it happen; only the individual can dream dreams and motivate events. He is all there is, and the actuality is all the more heartening.

Just the other day I was walking out of Radio City, and there, outside that citadel of modernism, was a peanut-vendor. On top of his little stand was a radio, and from it poured the celestial strains of Mozart's C minor Piano Concerto, K.491. It was the first movement, the one that caused Beethoven to exclaim helplessly to a friend: "Ah, such things as this will never occur to the likes of *us.*"

But they did. Not the same things, but things quite as miraculous in their way. The process never ceases for very long. Just give us a little time. Say, fifty or a hundred years. And then, *they* will be speaking of pianists. . . .

Closing Phrases:
In Lieu of a Discography

DEAR READER:

I had originally hoped, at the end of our journey, to add a discography here, ending with a final half-joking comment: "Now try and get 'em."

Since then, so many of my friends have related so many trying adventures in their quests for almost all but the newest discs that I have finally decided to skip the matter entirely.

Today's record is tomorrow's collector's item. The attempt to stay abreast of our machine age is a losing game, and I often winced as I urged the purchase of certain recordings. But I plunged ahead, hoping that you or your companions might already own them or could get them, or that you might come upon them on the radio.

And there is the concert hall, where many artists we have met will still be heard for a very long time, I trust. The music itself will always be there unless a mad civilization without love and without the need to create and maintain beauty destroys it, and along with it the Taj Mahal, the Louvre, the Lincoln Memorial, and itself. Perish the thought and all who hold it. Somehow we will find a way out.

Meanwhile, keep your piano tuned and your fingers agile. Doing it ourselves is another kind of joy, enabling us at all times to hear the most fascinating of artists.

Faithfully yours,

June 1957

Abram Chasins

Index

Abram Chasins was born in New York on August 17, 1903. He took his basic academic training at the Ethical Culture School, his basic musical training at the Juilliard Foundation and the Curtis Institute. From 1926 to 1946 he was active as a concert pianist, touring the United States and Europe. He is the composer of more than one hundred published compositions, mostly for piano. Mr. Chasins has been on the teaching staff of the Curtis Institute and the Berkshire Music Center, and from 1932 to 1938 was a pioneer in the field of broadcast lecture-recitals, playing over both CBS and NBC. He is at present Music Director of radio station WQXR and director of the annual musical-education projects sponsored jointly by that station and The New York Times. *Mr. Chasins is married to the concert pianist Constance Keene and lives in New York.*

A NOTE ON THE TYPE

The text of this book is set in Caledonia, a Linotype face designed by W. A. Dwiggins (1880-1956), who was responsible for so much that is good in contemporary book design. Though much of his early work was in advertising and he was the author of the standard volume Layout in Advertising, *Mr. Dwiggins later devoted his prolific talents to book typography and type design, and worked with great distinction in both fields. In addition to his designs for Caledonia, he created the Metro, Electra, and Eldorado series of type faces, as well as a number of experimental cuttings that have never been issued commercially.*

Caledonia belongs to the family of printing types called "modern face" by printers—a term used to mark the change in style of typeletters that occurred at the end of the eighteenth century. It is best evidenced in the letter shapes designed by Baskerville, Martin, Bodoni, and the Didots.

The book was composed, printed, and bound by H. Wolff, New York. The paper was made by P. H. Glatfelter Company, Spring Grove, Pennsylvania.